The Book of FIRSTS

The Book of

FIRSTS

Reader's Digest

A READER'S DIGEST BOOK

This edition published by The Reader's Digest Association
by arrangement with Cassell Illustrated

FOR READER'S DIGEST

Project Editor: Robert Ronald
Project Designer: George McKeon
Executive Editor, Trade Publishing: Dolores York
Senior Design Director: Michele Laseau
Director, Trade Publishing: Christopher T. Reggio
Vice President & Publisher, Trade Publishing: Harold Clarke

Printed in China

1 3 5 7 9 10 8 6 4 2

Library of Congress Cataloging-in-Publication Data
Harrison, Ian, 1965-
The book of firsts : the fascinating stories behind the world's
greatest achievements, discoveries, and breakthroughs/compiled
by Ian Harrison.
    p. cm.
Includes index.

ISBN 0-7621-0474-0
1. Civilization, Modern—History—Anecdotes. 2. World records—
History—Anecdotes. 3. Discoveries in geography—History–
Anecdotes. 4. Discoveries in science—History—Anecdotes.
5. Inventions—History—Anecdotes.
I. Title.
CB358.H38 2003   909.08–dc21   2003046934

Address any comments about *The Book of Firsts* to:
    The Reader's Digest Association, Inc.
    Adult Trade Publishing
    Reader's Digest Road
    Pleasantville, NY 10570-7000

For Reader's Digest products and information, visit our websites:
    www.rd.com (in the United States)
    www.readersdigest.ca (in Canada)

Contents

Foreword

STEVE FOSSETT ON BEING FIRST

When I first agreed to write this foreword I began to look at just what we mean by a "first." A real "first" is a discovery, an invention, a new trail or path, a new method, a new concept. To me, this is the highest challenge—to do something no-one has ever done before. The benefits can be immensely practical, inspirational, or entirely transitory. Like life. Achieving a "first" is more than winning a race. Winning a race means you are fastest on the day—and this indeed can be very satisfying. Yet there will always be another day. Records, as they say, are made to be broken.

But being first is forever—you can only be first once.

Of course, from every "first" leads a new series of unopened doors—to new, as yet unimagined challenges. Perhaps also to fame, maybe even to riches. It certainly leads to better self-knowledge and to a special sense of satisfaction. I cannot speak to every category covered in this book, but I do have a particular interest in speed sailing, aviation, and endurance sports—including mountaineering, my first sport. Two timely examples of important "firsts" come to mind: 100 years ago this year (17 December, 1903) Orville and Wilbur Wright made the first controlled, sustainable, powered flights by a heavier-than-air craft. Their achievement led to a 20th-century revolution in transportation and communication, dramatic changes in peace and in war, the creation of new industries, and an explosion in economic growth—all changing the nature of our world. And, of course, this revolution was punctuated and driven forward by a whole new series of aeronautical firsts— from Blériot's 1909 first crossing of the English Channel to Lindbergh's 1927 first solo non-stop transatlantic flight from New York to Paris, from Yeager's 1947 first supersonic flight to Armstrong's first step on the surface of the moon in 1969. These all fired the imaginations of both their contemporaries and of future generations of adventurers, scientists, inventors, and entrepreneurs.

Fifty years ago this year (29 May, 1953) Edmund Hillary and Tenzing Norgay stood together on the summit of Mount Everest—the first men to successfully ascend the highest mountain on Earth. Unlike that of Wilbur and Orville,

Steve Fossett is one of the world's greatest adventurers, setting numerous world 'firsts' and world records in ballooning, sailing, in gliding, and powered aircraft.

His 2002 first solo balloon flight around the world aboard *Bud Light Spirit of Freedom* is a milestone in aviation history, achieved on his sixth attempt. Steve has also flown faster than anyone by manned balloon: during his 2002 around-the-world flight, he covered 5,127 kilometers (3,186 miles) in one 24-hour period and hit a top speed of 320km/h (200mph).

Between 1994 and 2003, in addition to the first solo around-the-world flight, Steve achieved the first balloon crossing of the continents of Asia, Africa, Europe, and South America, and the first ever balloon crossings of the South Atlantic, South Pacific, and Indian oceans, as well as the first solo balloon flight across the Pacific.

Hillary and Tenzing's achievement led to no great industrial or technological revolution, but in its own way this less material "first" was no less influential—once again demonstrating man's stubborn natural inclination to explore, to discover, and to challenge and conquer the highest goals. It inspired a new generation of adventurers—not just the great mountaineers who followed (including Reinhold Messner, who made the first solo ascent of Everest in 1980) but other committed explorers of the limits of human endurance.

I am often asked, "Where are the new 'firsts' still to be achieved?" Just about everywhere. To those who say all the "firsts" have been accomplished, I respond: "Okay, most of the 'great routes' have been conquered. But look beyond the known—go out and find new and interesting challenges, new routes, explore your own limits."

And do not be afraid of failure. In every failure there is both a step toward success and a step on the journey of knowledge. Some of the great polar explorers of the past century whom I admire most—Shackleton and Nansen, to name two—never actually achieved the "firsts" they sought. Yet they demonstrated something exceptional: that you can accomplish great feats for their own sake. Through organization, preparation, and leadership they lost neither spirit nor crew members on their journeys. The journey became the victory.

Steve Fossett – Beaver Creek, Colorado

Chapter One

Human Endeavor

The first official land speed record was set at 39.24 mph (63.15 km/h) in 1898 using an electric car. The internal combustion engine took the record in 1902, then in 1997, almost a century after the first record, Andy Green broke the sound barrier in the jet-powered car *Thrust SSC*.

Human Endeavor

LAND SPEED RECORDS

TIMELINE

1898 Count Gaston de Chasseloup-Laubat (France) sets the first official record at 39.24 mph (63.15 km/h) in a Jentaud electric car

1899 Camille Jenatzy (Belgium) becomes the first person to travel faster than 100 km/h (62 mph) and the first to travel faster than 1 mile per minute

1902 William K. Vanderbilt Jr. (U.S.A) sets a record of 76.08 mph (122.43 km/h), the first time the record has been held by a gasoline-driven car

1904 Louis Rigolly (France) becomes the first person to travel faster than 100 mph (160 km/h) at 103.55 mph (166.64 km/h)

1963 Craig Breedlove (U.S.A.) reaches 407.45 mph (655.70 km/h) in his jet-powered *Spirit of America* but the FIA does not recognize the record because there is no category for jet cars

1970 Driving *Blue Flame*, Gary Gabelich (U.S.A.) becomes the first person to travel faster than 1,000 km/h (621 mph) on land

1997 Andy Green (England) sets a new record of 763.035 mph (1,227.952 km/h), becoming the first person to travel faster than the speed of sound on land

n 1983 Richard Noble (Scotland) broke the land speed record in his car *Thrust 2*, but that didn't satisfy him—14 years later he was back, trying to break more than his own record; this time his goal was the sound barrier. Noble employed RAF pilot Andy Green to drive the jet-powered car, whose name, *Thrust SSC* (Super Sonic Car), was a measure of their confidence.

Noble's refusal to be content with simply holding the record was part of the ethos of the land speed record. In 1899 Camille Jenatzy (Belgium) had become the first person to travel faster than 100 km/h (62 mph), in an electric car called *La Jamais Contente*—"The Never Satisfied." It was the sixth land speed record; the first five had been held alternately by Jenatzy and Count Gaston de Chasseloup-Laubat (France) since the Count had set the first official land speed record on December 18, 1898, also in an electric car.

In 1902 William K. Vanderbilt Jr. (U.S.A.) set the first land speed record to be held by the internal combustion engine. Jet cars were first officially recognized in 1964 when the first official jet record was set at 413.02 mph (664.96 km/h), after which the sound barrier became a realistic target.

Above The electric car, *La Jamais Contente*
Right Andy Green with *Thrust SSC*, the first supersonic car, which broke the land speed record and sound barrier in the Nevada Desert in 1997

On October 15, 1997, 50 years and a day after U.S. test pilot Chuck Yeager had become the first human being to travel faster than the speed of sound, *Thrust SSC* reached 763.035 mph (1,227.952 km/h). Even without the official readout, the sonic boom was enough to confirm that it had broken the sound barrier. Craig Breedlove (U.S.A) is planning to beat Noble and Green's record, but for Green being the first to break the sound barrier is all-important. "Does it matter if Craig Breedlove beats us? Even if he took all his friends to the top of Everest and had a massive dinner party, when he gets there he'll still find the Union flag flying there at the top, because we were there first."

DID YOU KNOW?

● The speed of sound varies with temperature and altitude, and in breaking the sound barrier on land Andy Green traveled nearly 100 mph (160 km/h) faster than test pilot Chuck Yeager's 670 mph (1,077 km/h) when he became the first human to break the sound barrier in flight

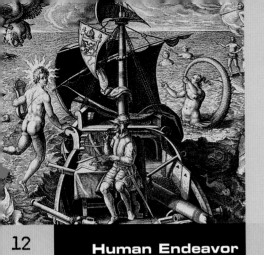

Ferdinand Magellan's expedition of 1519–22 provided the first conclusive proof that the earth is spherical, but Magellan was killed during the voyage, leaving captain Juan Sebastian del Cano and 17 surviving seamen to become the first men to circumnavigate the globe in a single voyage.

ROUND-THE-WORLD JOURNEYS

Magellan was a Portuguese navigator who believed he could discover a westward passage to the Indonesian Molucca Islands. The king of Portugal refused to support Magellan's proposed voyage so Magellan approached the king of Spain, who had a claim to the Moluccas; thus it was a Spanish expedition with a Portuguese leader that set sail on September 20, 1519.

Magellan's fleet of five ships sailed across the Atlantic Ocean to South America and then southwards along the coast, eventually discovering the Strait of Magellan, which enabled the expedition to continue westwards into an ocean Magellan named the Pacific. Ninety-eight days later the fleet reached the Philippines, where Magellan was killed in a battle between rival Filipino groups. After his death it was decided that the remaining crew would return in two ships. One made a failed attempt at an eastward passage and the other, *Vittoria*, continued westwards under the command of Juan Sebastian del Cano (or Elcano), finally returning to Spain on September 6, 1522 with just 17 survivors, having made the first round-the-world voyage.

Nearly four centuries later, in 1898, Canadian-born U.S. mariner Joshua Slocum made the first solo circumnavigation, which he completed in his sloop *Spray*; he supported himself by lecturing along the way, making the trip arguably the first round-the-world lecture tour. The remaining round-the-world challenge under sail was a nonstop solo circumnavigation, a feat achieved by English yachtsman Robin Knox-Johnston in his ketch *Suhaili* in 312 days between June 14, 1968 and April 22, 1969.

In 1933 American aviator Wiley Post completed the first solo circumnavigation by air, flying his Lockheed Vega monoplane *Winnie Mae* around the world in 7 days, 18 hrs 49 mins between July 15–22. The first

1519–22 Juan Sebastian del Cano and his crew (Spain), the survivors of Magellan's expedition, become the first people to circumnavigate the globe	**1577–80** Francis Drake and his crew become the first from England to circumnavigate the globe	**1847** HMS *Driver* arrives at Spithead, England, becoming the first steamship to circumnavigate the globe	**1898** Mariner Joshua Slocum (U.S.A.) completes the first solo circumnavigation of the globe	**1933** Aviator Wiley Post (U.S.A.) makes the first solo round-the-world flight	**1960** Nuclear submarine *Triton* (U.S.A.) completes the first submerged circumnavigation

▌TIMELINE

nonstop circumnavigation by balloon came in 1999 when Bertrand Piccard (Switzerland) and Brian Jones (U.K.) made the journey in *Breitling Orbiter 3*. The first *solo* nonstop circumnavigation by balloon was achieved in July 2002, when Steve Fossett (U.S.A.) took *Bud Light Spirit of Freedom* round the world in just 13 days—more than six times faster than the heroes of Jules Verne's novel (*Around the World in 80 Days*, 1873).

Opposite Magellan leading the first round-the-world expedition; etching by Johannes Stradanus (1605)
Below Steve Fossett in *Bud Light Spirit of Freedom*, flying above Ceduna, Australia, on his way around the world and into the history books (July 3, 2002)

| **1967** Francis Chichester completes the first English solo circumnavigation, in *Gipsy Moth IV* | **1969** Robin Knox-Johnston (England) completes the first solo nonstop circumnavigation by boat | **1978** Naomi James (New Zealand) becomes the first woman to sail round the world single-handed, and is later made a Dame for her feat | **1979–82** Sir Ranulph Fiennes's (England) Trans-Globe expedition traces the Greenwich Meridian around the earth, crossing both poles in the process | **1999** Brian Jones (England) and Bertrand Piccard (Switzerland) complete the first nonstop circumnavigation by balloon, taking *Breitling Orbiter 3* round the world in 15 days, 10 hrs 24 mins | **2002** Adventurer Steve Fossett (U.S.A.) completes the first solo nonstop circumnavigation by balloon |

Modern Europeans discovered the Americas by accident and named it serendipitously after a merchant-traveler, but Australia, named before it was found, was discovered only after a long search for *Terra Australis Incognita*, the "Unknown Southern Land."

NEW WORLDS

DID YOU KNOW?

• When Christopher Columbus discovered the New World he thought he had reached the Indies, so he called the native people Indians. When his mistake was realized, the place became known as the West Indies

• Tradition has it that the Americas are named after Amerigo Vespucci, an Italian-born naturalized Spaniard said to have coined the phrase "New World." In 1507, having read a distorted account of Vespucci's travels, German cartographer Martin Waldseemüller used the Latinized version of Vespucci's first name on a map of the recently discovered continent and the name stuck. A new theory, however, claims the continent is named after Welshman Richard Amerike, who liaised between John Cabot and England's King Henry VII

• Australia is the only country that is also a continent. In area it is the sixth largest country in the world but the smallest continent

Top "See the Lands of the Vikings," poster (Ben Blessum, 1937)
Right Cigarette card commemorating John Cabot's 1497 voyage to Newfoundland

When Italian explorer Christopher Columbus discovered America he was actually looking for Asia. His revolutionary assertion that the Indies (comprising India, China, the East Indies and Japan) could be reached by sailing westwards was later proved correct by Magellan, but what Columbus did not realize was that an entire continent lay in his path.

Columbus secured the support of Queen Isabella of Spain, and left Palos, Spain, on August 3, 1492. On October 12 he sighted what he thought was the Indies and went ashore on what is now known to be one of the Bahamas, his shore party becoming the first modern Europeans to set foot in the Americas. Columbus made three more voyages during the next 12 years, exploring more islands as well as the coast of mainland South America.

In the meantime, Italian navigator John Cabot, sailing under letters patent from King Henry VII of England, became the first European to set foot on the North American mainland since the Vikings. Cabot landed at Newfoundland on June 24, 1497 to claim North America for England.

FRANKLYN'S CIGARETTES

CABOT SAILING FROM BRISTOL.

c.40–50,000 b.c.	c.15,000 b.c.	c.a.d. 1000	1492 & 1493 Explorer	1497 Navigator	1498 Columbus
Aboriginal immigration to Australia from India, Sri Lanka and southeast Asia	First evidence of human beings in North America	Vikings believed to have explored the east coast of North America	Christopher Columbus (Italy) becomes the first European to discover the New World (Bahamas, Cuba, Jamaica, Puerto Rico, Hispaniola)	John Cabot (Giovanni Caboto, Italy) becomes the first modern European to discover the North American mainland	becomes the first European to discover the South American mainland

TIMELINE

In 1606 Spaniard Luis Vaez de Torres sailed through the Torres Strait and became the first European to sight mainland Australia, though he thought it was simply another island rather than the elusive southern continent. Later the same year the shore party of Dutch navigator Willem Jansz became the first Europeans to land in Australia, although Jansz thought he had landed in New Guinea.

Other Dutch navigators subsequently explored the north, west and south coasts of Australia but reported that the land was arid and the people poor. In 1770 English Captain James Cook became the first European to explore the more fertile east coast, and laid claim to New South Wales for Britain. Englishman Matthew Flinders circumnavigated the continent from 1801–03, proving that it was *Terra Australis*, which soon became known as Australia.

Christopher Columbus approaches native Americans on the island of Hispaniola (Haiti)

| **1512–13** Juan Ponce de Léon (Spain) becomes the first European to discover Florida | **1565** The Spanish settlement of St. Augustine (Florida) becomes the first permanent European settlement in North America | **1606** Explorer Willem Jansz (Holland) becomes the first European known to have set foot in Australia | **1642** Explorer Abel Janszoon Tasman (Holland) becomes the first European to discover Van Dieman's Land, renamed Tasmania in 1855, and New Zealand | **1770** Captain James Cook (England) becomes the first European to explore Australia's east coast, and claims New South Wales for Britain | **1788** Sydney is founded as a British penal colony |

The races to the North and South poles were two very different stories, one a heroic tale of bravery and self-sacrifice, the other a sorry catalog of dishonesty and racial bigotry. The quest to be first to the ends of the earth exposed aspects of human behavior that were poles apart.

POLAR EXPLORATION

Above Scott's ship, HMS *Discovery*, in the Antarctic
Below Cartoon depicting Peary and Cook disputing which of them was first to the North Pole; the artist has incorrectly shown penguins in the northern hemisphere

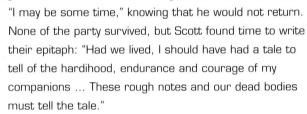

"Great God! This is an awful place." English explorer Captain Robert Falcon Scott had good reason to be unimpressed by the South Pole because when he arrived there on January 17, 1912 he found a Norwegian flag left on December 14, 1911 by Roald Amundsen, with a note asking Scott to report Amundsen's triumph to the king of Norway.

Disappointment dogged every step of the return for Scott's party, a journey legendary for the selflessness of Captain Oates, whose frostbitten feet were hindering progress. Oates left the tent during a blizzard with the words, "I may be some time," knowing that he would not return. None of the party survived, but Scott found time to write their epitaph: "Had we lived, I should have had a tale to tell of the hardihood, endurance and courage of my companions ... These rough notes and our dead bodies must tell the tale."

The conquest of the North Pole is more famous for the row over who got there first than for any bravery or courage. Americans Robert Peary and Matthew Henson claimed to have reached the pole with four Inuit guides on April 6, 1909, but on their return they found that Dr. Frederick Cook was claiming to have reached the pole a year earlier. Cook's claim was discredited and the National Geographic Society (NGS) acclaimed Peary as the discoverer of the North Pole, but Henson, a black American, was ignored until a petition to the US president led to his official recognition on April 6, 1988—ironically, the same year that an NGS-commissioned investigation concluded that Peary and Henson had, in fact, been up to 96 km (60 miles) away from the pole.

In 1989 another NGS-sponsored investigation concluded that they had been only 8 km (6 miles) away and had, after all, discovered the pole. However, this left a team led by Ralph Plaisted (U.S.A.) with a very strong claim to have been the first to reach the pole overland (in 1968), and Cook still has his supporters. With three claimants, the controversy continues—but the fact remains that the first humans to stand at the North Pole were probably Inuit.

DID YOU KNOW?

• Not only was Frederick Albert Cook's claim to have been the first to the North Pole discredited but so was his claim to have been the first to reach the summit of Mount McKinley in Alaska. Cook was later imprisoned for mail fraud, although he was pardoned shortly before his death

• Since the North Magnetic Pole was discovered at 80° N. in 1831 it has moved more than 10 degrees. Its average annual migration is 10 to 40 km (6 to 25 miles) to the north/northwest

• The youngest person to visit both poles is English schoolboy Robert Schumann, who was 10 and 11 when he visited the North and then the South Poles in 1992 and 1993

Amundsen pictured in 1925, 14 years after leading the first expedition to reach the South Pole

TIMELINE

1908 Explorer Frederick Albert Cook (U.S.A) claims to have reached the North Pole on April 21, but the claim is not upheld

1909 Robert E. Peary and Matthew A. Henson (both U.S.A.) claim to have reached the North Pole with four Inuit. The claim has since been discredited and re-substantiated

1911 Explorer Roald Amundsen (Norway) and four teammates become the first people to reach the South Pole

1912 R.F. Scott and four teammates become the first Britons to reach the South Pole

1926 Richard E. Byrd and Floyd Bennett (both U.S.A.) make the first flight over the North Pole (recently disputed). Roald Amundsen (Norway), Umberto Nobile (Italy) and Lincoln Ellsworth (U.S.A.) make the first flight over the North Pole in an airship (the *Norge*)

1929 Byrd and pilot Bernt Balchen (U.S.A–Norway) make the first flight over the South Pole

1957–58 Geologist Vivian Fuchs (England) makes the first overland crossing of Antarctica

1958 The first submarine passes under the North Pole, USS *Nautilus*

1977 Atomic icebreaker *Arktika* (U.S.S.R.) becomes the first ship to reach the North Pole

1978 The first person reaches the North Pole solo, Naomi Uemura (Japan)

1986 The first woman reaches the North Pole on foot, Ann Bancroft (U.S.A.)

1989–90 Will Steger (U.S.A.) leads the first expedition to cross Antarctica without motorized vehicles

1993 JANUARY 7, Erling Kagge (Norway) becomes the first person to reach the South Pole solo on foot. FEBRUARY 7, Sir Ranulph Fiennes and Dr. Michael Stroud (both England) complete the first unaided crossing of Antarctica on foot

Mount Everest has provided the ultimate challenge for climbers since 1852, when a survey showed it to be the highest point on the surface of the earth. But it wasn't until 101 years later, at 11:30 a.m. on May 29, 1953, that human beings stood on top of the world for the first time.

MOUNT EVEREST

" I looked at Tenzing and in spite of the balaclava, goggles and oxygen mask all encrusted with long icicles that concealed his face there was no disguising his infectious grin as he looked all around him." So wrote New Zealander Edmund Hillary of the moment when he and Nepalese Sherpa Tenzing Norgay became the first men to stand on the world's highest peak, 8,848 m (29,028 ft) above sea level. Newspapers reported the height they had climbed as being 29,002 ft, a measurement set by a British survey of the mid-19th century; the present official height was established by an Indian government survey of 1954, the year after this historic climb.

Hillary and Norgay spent 15 glorious minutes on the roof of the world, and each left a token of thanks at the summit: Norgay buried sweets and biscuits as an offering to the gods of the mountain, while Hillary left a crucifix. It was a quarter of an hour that was the culmination of months of meticulous planning and the combined efforts of a team of 10 climbers and 5 Sherpas. Three days earlier an unsuccessful attempt on the summit had been made by two other members of the expedition, but Hillary and Norgay returned, triumphant, to describe "a symmetrical, beautiful snow cone summit" very different from the bleak rocky ridge seen from below. Just over a week later, on June 7, Hillary and expedition leader English Colonel John Hunt were knighted for their achievement, and Norgay was awarded the George Cross.

News of the expedition's success reached Britain on June 1, the eve of Queen Elizabeth II's coronation, and the following day displaced details of the Queen's coronation dress to the back page of the *News Chronicle*, whose headline read: "The Crowning Glory: Everest is Climbed."

DID YOU KNOW?

● Edmund Hillary was a professional apiarist (beekeeper). He reached the South Pole in 1958 and the North Pole in 1985. In 1990 his son Peter reached the summit of Everest

● More than 1,000 climbers have reached the summit of Everest and nearly 200 have died in the attempt

● Although Everest is the world's highest mountain it is not the world's tallest—at

10,204 m, (33,477 ft) the Hawaiian volcano Mauna Kea, meaning "white mountain," is 1,356 m (4,450 ft) taller than Everest, but more than half of Mauna Kea is underwater and it rises only 4,205 m (13,795 ft) above sea level

● The pronunciation Ever-rest is technically incorrect because the mountain is named after Sir George Everest (Surveyor-General of India from 1830–43), who pronounced his name Eve-rest

Hillary and Norgay about to leave the South Col to establish Camp IX below the South Summit

The moon race began in earnest on April 12, 1961 when U.S.S.R. cosmonaut Yuri Gagarin made the first successful manned space flight. Just over eight years later the United States won the race by making the first manned moon landing, on July 20, 1969.

Human Endeavor
SPACE EXPLORATION

DID YOU KNOW?

• The first space burial was launched from the Canary Islands in 1997. Dr. Timothy Leary and Gene Roddenberry, the creator of *Star Trek*, were among 20 people whose ashes were sent into space and will orbit the earth until the rocket burns up on re-entry to the atmosphere, due some time in 2003

• The first television commercial to be filmed in space was for Tnuva Milk, and showed cosmonaut Vasily Tsibliyev drinking the milk aboard the space station *Mir*

Probably the most famous words spoken by any human being during the 20th century were those of Neil Armstrong when he stepped onto the surface of the moon: "That's one small step for a man, one giant leap for mankind." With these words the United States claimed the ultimate prize in a race that until then had been led by the U.S.S.R. with the first man-made satellite, the first dog in space, the first man in space, the first woman in space, the first man-made object on the moon and the first spacewalk.

In 1957 the Soviets had launched *Sputnik I*, the first man-made satellite, and a month later launched *Sputnik II*, which carried the first dog into space. Laika (nicknamed "Muttnik" by the American press) later became the first dog to die in space when it was fed a meal of poisoned meat by the automatic feeder on board. *Sputnik* II later burned up on re-entry to the atmosphere in April 1958. There is some uncertainty about the first man in space: in 1957 cosmonaut Alexis Ledovsky (U.S.S.R.) allegedly made the first manned space flight and in doing so became the first human space fatality; however, it is not known whether his craft cleared earth's gravity and was lost in space, or burned up in re-entry. What is certain is that the first successful manned space flight took place on April 12, 1961, when Yuri Gagarin became the first man to orbit the earth.

The first moon landing was such a significant event that it was watched on television by a fifth of the world's population, yet by the beginning of the following century shuttle flights were commonplace and space tourism was a reality. In 1990 TBS Television (Japan) paid for TV journalist Toyohiro Akiyama to become the first paying passenger in space, traveling with the crew of the

1957 OCTOBER, *Sputnik I* (U.S.S.R.) is launched as the first man-made satellite. NOVEMBER, Laika becomes the first dog in space, dying shortly after

1957 Alexis Ledovsky (U.S.S.R.) allegedly makes the first manned space flight, but in doing so becomes the first space fatality

1958 JANUARY, *Explorer* is launched as the first U.S. satellite

1959 AUGUST, satellite *Discoverer VI* (U.S.A.) takes the first television pictures of the earth from space. SEPTEMBER, *Luna II* (U.S.S.R.), launched two days earlier, becomes the first space craft to reach the moon

1961 APRIL, making the first successful manned space flight, Yuri Gagarin (U.S.S.R.) becomes the first person to orbit the earth. MAY, Alan B. Shepard (U.S.A.) becomes the first American in space, reaching a height of 186 km (115 miles) in *Freedom VII*

TIMELINE

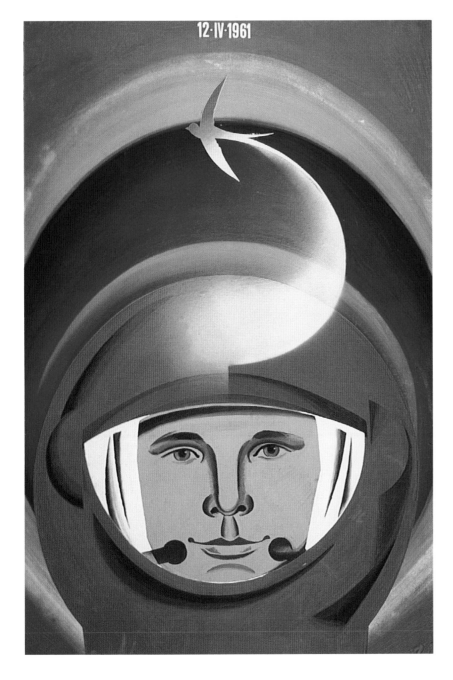

Above Soviet cosmonaut Valentina Tereshkova, the first woman in space. Tereshkova piloted the *Vostok 6* spacecraft, launched on June 16, 1963. The flight lasted 70.8 hours and orbited the earth 48 times

Left Soviet poster commemorating the first successful manned space flight, made by Yuri Gagarin on April 12, 1961

Opposite top A plywood jigsaw puzzle commemorating the first men on the moon

| **1962** John Glenn becomes the first American to orbit the earth | **1963** Valentina Tereshkova (U.S.S.R.) becomes the first woman in space | **1965** MARCH, Aleksey Leonov (U.S.S.R.) makes the first space walk. JUNE, Edmund White (U.S.A.) makes the first American space walk | **1969** JULY 20, Neil Armstrong and Buzz Aldrin (both U.S.A.) become the first people to land on the moon. JULY 21, Armstrong is the first person to walk on the moon | **1971** APRIL, *Salyut I* (U.S.S.R.) is launched as the first space station. MAY, space probe *Mars 3* (U.S.S.R.) orbits Mars and releases a capsule that makes the first soft landing on the planet | **1979** The European Space Agency, comprising 10 member countries, launches the first European rocket, *Ariane* |

Soviet *Soyuz TM II*. Just over a decade later 60-year-old Dennis Tito (U.S.A.) became the first private space tourist when he paid a reported $22 million for a trip to the International Space Station with the Russians, and by the following year the price of such an exotic holiday had gone down: Mark Shuttleworth (South Africa) paid a mere $20 million for his trip to the space station, an interconnected group of Russian and American capsules that he described as looking "like a line of caravans stuck together." Despite his surname, Shuttleworth, who made his fortune in computer software, said he would not have wanted to travel in the shuttle even if NASA had allowed it: "I wanted to do it in a rocket. There's a huge retro element that appeals to me and I wanted to be part of a Sixties-style space experience."

DID YOU KNOW?

● In 2002 space tourist Mark Shuttleworth told British newspaper *The Observer* that, "There's this tradition—set by Yuri Gagarin—that we have to take a leak on the rear right wheel of the bus that takes us to the rocket."

● The first watch to be worn on the moon was an Omega Speedmaster chronograph worn by Neil Armstrong in 1969

● *Apollo XI* astronaut Michael Collins was born in Rome, Italy, making him (philosophically, at least) the first Italian in space

Right The first space tourist, Dennis Tito, on his return to earth
Opposite *Mir* Space Station in orbit

1983 JUNE, Sally Ride becomes the first American woman in space. AUGUST, Guion S. Bluford (U.S.A.) becomes the first African–American in space. NOVEMBER, Ulf Merbold (W. Germany) becomes the first German in space	**1984** Marc Garneau becomes the first Canadian in space. JULY 17, female cosmonaut Svetlana Savitskaya (Soviet Union) becomes the first woman to make a space walk	**1987** Space probe *Pioneer 10* (U.S.A.), launched in 1972, becomes the first man-made object to leave the solar system	**1990** TV journalist Toyohiro Akiyama (Japan) becomes the first paying passenger in space, paid for by TBS Television	**2001** Businessman Dennis Tito (U.S.A) becomes the first private space tourist, paying a reported $22 million to visit the International Space Station

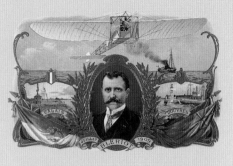

The Book of Firsts

In the early days of aviation, ocean crossings caught the imagination of both the public and the pioneers of flight, due both to the sheer challenge and the vast prizes being offered by the newspapers of the time. As a result, names such as Blériot, Lindbergh and Earhart are still familiar today.

24 | **Human Endeavor**

OCEAN FLIGHTS

DID YOU KNOW?

● Later in the same year that he made his Atlantic crossing, John Alcock was killed in an airplane accident in France

● When airship R-34 made its Atlantic crossing in 1919 a crew member had to parachute to the ground on arrival in New York in order to help anchor the airship

***NOT* THE FIRST...**

● Hubert Latham (England–France) attempted a cross-Channel flight on July 19, 1909, but ditched in the water after 11 km (7 miles). Latham was due to make a second attempt the following week but was beaten to it by Louis Blériot

Above Louis Blériot, the first man to make a powered flight across the English Channel
Right Amelia Earhart, the first woman to fly solo across the Atlantic Ocean

On July 25, 1909 French aviator Louis Blériot became the first person to fly across the English Channel, and in so doing won a prize of £1,000 being offered by British newspaper the *Daily Mail*. Blériot made his historic crossing in a small 24-horsepower monoplane. He did not carry a compass and it is said that a French journalist guided him to a safe landing place near Dover by waving the French tricolor as Blériot crossed the British coastline.

Just 10 years after Blériot's 49.8 km (30 mile) flight, English pilot John W. Alcock and navigator Arthur Whitten Brown (born in Scotland of American parents) traveled more than 60 times farther at 3 times the speed to make the first nonstop transatlantic flight—and the prize offered by the *Daily Mail* had increased tenfold to £10,000. Alcock and Brown took off from Newfoundland, Canada, on June 14, 1919 in a Vickers-Vimy biplane, and crash-landed in a bog near Clifden, Ireland, 16 hrs 27 mins later, having flown 3,057 km (1,400 miles) to claim the prize. Both men were knighted soon afterwards, but Alcock, a test pilot for Vickers Aircraft, was less than enthusiastic about his achievement, describing the flight through appalling weather as "a terrible journey."

The remaining transatlantic goal was a solo flight and this was achieved by American aviator Charles Lindbergh, who for his feat was awarded a $25,000 prize, the Distinguished Flying Cross and the Congressional Medal of Honor. Lindbergh took off from New York on May 20, 1927 and flew 5,792 km (3,600 miles) to Paris in 33 hrs 39 mins in his Ryan monoplane *Spirit of St. Louis*. On May 21, 1932 American Amelia Earhart landed in Londonderry, Northern Ireland to become the first woman to fly the Atlantic solo.

The first nonstop transpacific flight was made in 1931 by Americans Hugh Herndon and Clyde Pangborn, flying from Japan to the United States from October 3–5.

Above Racing cyclist Bryan Allen pedaling *Gossamer Albatross*, the first man-powered aircraft to cross the English Channel

Below Cover of *The Boy's Story of Lindbergh, The Lone Eagle*, a biography of the first aviator to make a solo nonstop transatlantic flight

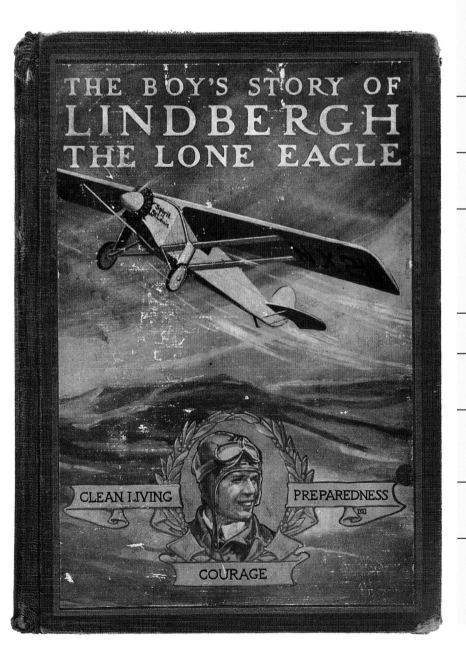

THE BOY'S STORY OF LINDBERGH THE LONE EAGLE

CLEAN LIVING   PREPAREDNESS

COURAGE

1785 The first aerial crossing of the English Channel is made by Jean-Pierre Blanchard (France) and Dr. John Jeffries (U.S.A.), in a hydrogen balloon

1909 Louis Blériot (France) makes the first powered flight across the English Channel

1912 Harriet Quimby (U.S.A) becomes the first woman to fly across the English Channel

1919 MAY, navy pilots Read and Stone (both U.S.A) make the first transatlantic flight, in three main stages (Newfoundland–Azores–Lisbon). JUNE, Alcock and Brown (both England) make the first nonstop transatlantic flight, also making the first successful delivery of transatlantic air mail. JULY, British airship R-34 makes the first Atlantic crossing by airship, and carries the first transatlantic aerial stowaway

1927 Charles Lindbergh (U.S.A.) makes the first solo nonstop transatlantic flight

1928 Charles Kingsford-Smith and Charles Ulm (both Australia) make the first transpacific flight

1931 JUNE, Lissaint Beardmore (Canada) makes the first cross-Channel flight by glider. OCTOBER, Hugh Herndon and Clyde Pangborn (both U.S.A.) make the first nonstop transpacific flight

1932 Amelia Earhart (U.S.A.) becomes the first woman to fly the Atlantic solo

1939 Pan American Airways inaugurates the first transatlantic airline service

1978 Ben Abruzzo, Maxie Anderson and Larry Newman (all U.S.A.) make the first Atlantic crossing by balloon (137 hrs in *Double Eagle II*)

1979 Bryan Allen (U.S.A.) makes the first cross-Channel flight in a man-powered aircraft

1981 Ben Abruzzo, Ron Clark and Larry Newman (all U.S.A.) and Rocky Aoki (Japan) make the first transpacific crossing by balloon, in *Double Eagle V*

Since Captain Matthew Webb became the first person to swim the English Channel in 1875 swimmers and relay teams of many nationalities have been lining up to emulate his feat, although it was not to be repeated until 48 years later, in 1923.

Human Endeavor

CHANNEL SWIMS

Above Captain Matthew Webb matches
Below Gertrude Ederle is covered in grease for insulation prior to becoming the first woman to swim the English Channel

Annette Kellerman, film star, swimmer and pioneer of three firsts, pictured in 1920

The English Channel, linking the Atlantic Ocean with the North Sea and separating England from mainland Europe, is the world's busiest shipping lane. But despite the traffic and the treacherous currents, swimmers still brave the waters to meet a challenge first achieved by Englishman Matthew Webb. On August 24, 1875 the 27-year-old merchant navy captain, covered in a layer of porpoise grease for insulation against the cold water, stepped into the sea close to Admiralty Pier in Dover. He swam continuously until, 21 hrs 45 mins later, he emerged from the water at Cap Gris Nez in France, and became the first person to swim the English Channel.

By the time New Yorker Gertrude Ederle became the first woman to swim the Channel on August 6, 1926, 51 years later, only four men had repeated Webb's feat. "People said women couldn't swim the Channel, but I proved they could," she said afterwards. Where all the men had used breaststroke, Ederle swam front crawl, completing her swim 2 hrs quicker than the previous record time. On Ederle's return to a tickertape welcome in the United States, New York Mayor James J. Walker confused the Channel with a river by enthusiastically comparing her achievement with Caesar's crossing of the Rubicon.

DID YOU KNOW?

● Matthew Webb drowned in 1883 attempting to swim the Niagara rapids

● The earliest Australian attempt to swim the Channel was made in 1907 by Annette Kellerman, a swimmer and film star who was also the first woman to wear a one-piece bathing suit (1910) and the first woman to appear naked on screen (in *Daughter of the Gods*, 1915)

● The first wristwatch to be worn for a cross-Channel swim was a Rolex Oyster given to secretary Mercedes Gleitz on October 7, 1927 by Hans Wilsdorf, the founder of the Rolex company. Wilsdorf wanted to demonstrate that the world's first waterpoof watch (developed in 1926) really was waterproof—it was

● In 1925, the year before becoming the first woman to swim the Channel, swimmer Gertrude Ederle, on her first attempt, was pulled from the water just seven miles from her goal. In 1924 she had won three swimming medals at the 1924 Paris Olympics

● The French name for the Channel, *la manche*, means "the sleeve" and derives from the shape of the Channel

TIMELINE

1875 Matthew Webb (England) becomes the first person to swim the Channel

1926 Gertrude Ederle (U.S.A.) becomes the first woman to swim the Channel

1927 Mercedes Gleitz becomes the first Englishwoman to swim the Channel

1950 The first cross-Channel swimming race is won by Lt. Abdel Rehim (Egypt)

1961 Swimmer Antonio Albertondo (Argentina) makes the first nonstop double crossing of the Channel

1965 Linda McGill becomes the first Australian to swim the Channel

1970 Kevin Murphy becomes the first British swimmer to make a nonstop double crossing of the Channel

1981 Jon Erikson (U.S.A.) becomes the first person to swim the channel three times without stopping (England–France, France–England, England–France)

1987 Philip Rush (New Zealand) breaks several world records on a three-way swim, including the fastest England–France–England, 16 hrs 10 mins; the fastest France–England–France, 20 hrs 26 mins; the fastest three-way swim, 28 hrs 21 mins

1988 Richard Davey (England) sets a new record for the fastest France–England swim, 8 hrs 5 mins

1994 Chad Hundeby (U.S.A.) sets a new record for the fastest England–France swim, 7 hrs 17 mins

1996 A relay-team of six 13- and 14-year-old swimmers from Bombay, India, becomes the youngest relay team to swim the Channel

NIAGARA FALLS

Niagara Falls once enjoyed the contradictory nicknames of honeymoon capital of the world and suicide capital of the world. Among the first to confront Niagara with the intention of survival rather than suicide were Charles Blondin, Captain Matthew Webb and Annie Edson Taylor.

Above Jean Albert Lussier goes over Niagara Falls in a steel and rubber sphere fitted with oxygen cylinders

Below The secrets of the barrel in which Annie Edson Taylor became the first person to go over Niagara Falls and survive

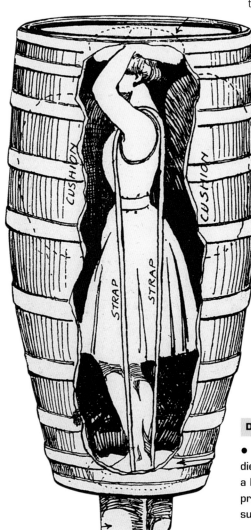

The first person to cross the Niagara River on a tightrope was Frenchman Jean François Gravelet, better known as Charles Blondin, in 1859, an achievement described by the *New York Times* as: "The greatest feat of the Nineteenth Century." Paintings depicted Blondin crossing directly above the Horseshoe Falls, but in fact his Manila rope, just 75 mm (3 in.) thick, spanned the gorge a mile downstream of the Falls themselves. Blondin subsequently made the crossing blindfolded, performed handstands and somersaults on the rope, pushed a wheelbarrow across, and twice made the crossing while carrying his manager, Harry Colcord, on his back. Blondin even cooked an omelette midway across and lowered it on a rope to passengers on the tourist boat *Maid of the Mist*, who were watching from the river below.

In 1875 Captain Matthew Webb became the first person to swim the English Channel, after which he began to look for ever greater challenges. Eight years later he stepped into the Niagara River in an attempt to become the first to swim the rapids downstream of the Falls. Although he had calculated the effort he thought would be required, he found himself inexorably drawn toward the vortex of the whirlpool at the center of the rapids, where he was dragged beneath the water to his death.

Many other people lost their lives trying to go over the Falls, but in October 1901 Annie Edson Taylor had herself sealed in a padded barrel and became the first person to survive the plunge. Afterwards she advised that no-one else should try what she had done—whether this was genuine concern for people's well-being or an attempt to prevent others from undermining her fame is not clear, but it was another decade before anyone repeated her feat, this time in a purpose-built steel barrel. Annie Taylor told the press she was 43 years of age, but it was later discovered that she was actually 63 when she performed her historic stunt.

DID YOU KNOW?

● In 1901 Maud Willard (U.S.A.) died while taking her dog with her in a barrel through the rapids—the dog pressed its nose against the air vent, suffocating its hapless owner

1859 Charles Blondin (France) makes the first crossing of the Niagara River on a tightrope

1883 Captain Matthew Webb (England) drowns while attempting to become the first person to swim the rapids downstream of Niagara Falls

1901 Annie Edson Taylor (U.S.A.) becomes the first person to go over Niagara Falls and survive (in a wooden barrel)

1911 Bobby Leach (England) becomes the first man to go over Niagara Falls and survive (in a steel barrel)

1928 Jean Albert Lussier (Canada) becomes the first person to go over Niagara Falls in a steel and rubber sphere

1989 Peter deBernardi and Jeffrey Petkovitch become the first people to go over Niagara Falls together (in a metal container)

▎TIMELINE

Charles Blondin gives his manager a piggyback ride across the gorge of the Niagara River

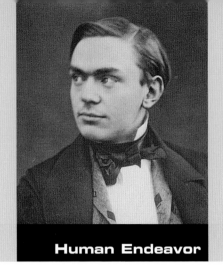

Swedish chemist Alfred Nobel left U.S. $5,000,000 in his will to finance prizes in Physics, Chemistry, Physiology or Medicine, Literature and Peace. The prizes were first awarded in 1901, and the Bank of Sweden inaugurated a new Nobel Prize for Economics in 1969.

Human Endeavor

NOBEL PRIZES

In 1866 Alfred Nobel invented a form of nitroglycerine that could be handled safely. He called it dynamite. In 1875 he went on to invent gelignite. These explosives were used in engineering applications such as railway construction and quarrying but they also had an obvious military application. As a committed pacifist, Nobel hoped that his explosives would provide such a deterrent to war that they would bring peace to mankind. His inventions did not bring peace, but they did bring him a massive fortune, which he used in his will to endow the annual Nobel Prizes, awarded to those who have "conferred the greatest benefit on mankind" in five categories including Peace.

Nobel died on December 10, 1896. The first Nobel prizes were awarded on December 10, 1901, and have been awarded annually ever since on the anniversary of his death. Each award consists of a gold medal, a diploma bearing a citation and a sum of money, the amount depending on the income of the foundation. The first prizes were awarded as follows:

Peace Jean Henri Dunant (Switzerland, founder of the International Red Cross) and Fredric Passy (France, founder of the French Society of the Friends of Peace)

Literature poet Sully Prudhomme (France)

Physics Wilhelm Konrad von Roentgen (Germany) for the discovery of X-rays

Physiology or **Medicine** Emil von Behring (Germany) for research in serum therapy

Chemistry Jacobus Henricus van't Hoff (Netherlands) for formulating the laws of chemical dynamics

In 1903 Marie Curie became the first woman to win a Nobel Prize, sharing the prize for Physics with her husband, Pierre Curie, and Antoine Henri Becquerel for Becquerel's work in radioactivity that led to the Curie's discovery

of polonium and radium (the former named after Marie's native Poland). In 1911 Marie won the prize for Chemistry, becoming the first person to win two Nobel prizes. She died in 1934 of leukemia, almost certainly brought on by her long-term exposure to radiation. That same year, the Curie daughter Irène made the world's first artificial radioisotope with her husband Frédéric Joliot, for which they were jointly awarded the 1935 Nobel Prize for Chemistry. Irène died in 1956, from leukemia.

Opposite top Alfred Nobel (1833–1896) photographed in 1863
Opposite below Cartridge packed with dynamite, fuse attached, made at the Nobel Explosives Co., Ltd, Ayrshire, Scotland. *The Illustrated London News* (April 26, 1884)
Above Medal issued to commemorate the centenary of Marie Curie's birth (1967)

DID YOU KNOW?

● The radioactive chemical element nobelium is indirectly named after Alfred Nobel, taking its name from the Nobel Institute in Stockholm where it was first produced

● Jean-Paul Sartre (France) turned down the 1964 Nobel Prize for Literature because he said it would compromise his integrity as an author

● Nobel laureate Dorothy Mary Crowfoot Hodgkin was the first Royal Society Wolfson Research Professor at Oxford, a Fellow of Somerville College, Oxford, a Fellow of the Royal Society and, later, Chancellor of Bristol University, a winner of the Lenin Peace Prize, the first female Fellow of the Australian Academy of Science and the first woman since Florence Nightingale to be awarded

the Order of Merit. The *Daily Mail* headline when she won the prize for Chemistry in 1964 was: "British wife wins Nobel Prize"

● One of Dorothy Mary Crowfoot Hodgkin's students of X-ray crystallography was one Margaret Roberts. Roberts married Denis Thatcher in 1951 and became Britain's first female prime minister in 1979

THE BEST OF THE REST...

Atlantic crossings

The first person to sail across the Atlantic solo was Alfred Johnson (Denmark), who landed in Wales on August 11, 1876 after a 46-day voyage in his 20 foot boat *Centennial*. The first person to row across the Atlantic solo was John Fairfax (U.K.), who landed in Florida on July 19, 1969—just 8 days before Irishman Tom McClean landed in County Mayo, Ireland, to complete the first west–east solo row and the first complete mainland-to-mainland row. Fairfax had left Las Palmas in the Canary Islands on January 20 while McClean completed his voyage in less than half the time, leaving St. John's, Newfoundland, on May 17

The sound barrier

The first human to break the sound barrier was test pilot Chuck Yeager (U.S.A.), on October 14, 1947 in a Bell X-1 rocket plane.
The first woman to break the sound barrier was Jacqueline Cochran (U.S.A.) in 1953, piloting an F-86 Saber

Chuck Yeager

Transcontinental flight

In 1930, the year after receiving her pilot's license, aviatrix Amy Johnson (England) became the first woman to fly solo from England to Australia, winning a prize of £10,000 from British newspaper the *Daily Mail* in the process. On February 22, 1920 the first transcontinental mail service flight arrived in New York from San Francisco. The trip took 33 hrs, 20 mins. Also in 1930, Charles Lindbergh and Anne Morrow set a transcontinental speed record when they flew from Los Angeles to New York in 14 hours, 45 mins

Transpacific raft

In 1947 anthropologist Thor Heyerdahl (Norway) and five companions were the first people of the modern age to sail across the Pacific Ocean, taking 101 days to make the crossing from Peru to Tuamotu Island on their balsawood raft *Kon Tiki*

Transatlantic sailboard

Stéphane Peyron (France) made the first transatlantic crossing by sailboard in 1987, taking 47 days, between June 10 and July 27, to travel from La Rochelle in France to New York

West to East swim

The first person to swim from the United States to Russia was Lynne Cox (U.S.A.), crossing the Bering Strait from Alaska to Siberia in 2 hrs 12 mins on August 7, 1987

Transatlantic walk

In 1988 Remy Bricka (France) became the first person to "walk" across the Atlantic Ocean. He left the Canary Islands on April 2, 1988 and "walked" 5,634 km (3,500 miles) on two 4.2 m (14 ft.) floating polyester skis, arriving in Trinidad on May 31

Mountaineering

Reinhold Messner (Italy) was the first person to conquer the world's highest mountains—Everest, K2 and Kanchenjunga

Chapter Two

Food & Drink

The first sandwich is usually said to have been eaten by English nobleman the 4th Earl of Sandwich, who liked its convenience. In May 1928 the sandwich became even more convenient when the world's first presliced loaf of bread went on sale in Battle Creek, Michigan.

Food & Drink

SANDWICHES AND SLICED BREAD

DID YOU KNOW?

● The islands of Hawaii were named the Sandwich Islands by Captain James Cook in honor of the First Lord of the Admiralty—the same Earl of Sandwich who gave his name to the universal snack

● When Otto Frederick Rohwedder asked bakers in 1928 whether they thought sliced bread was a good idea they pointed out that it would go stale very quickly, so what he actually patented was a machine for slicing *and wrapping* bread

● The club sandwich, made with three slices of bread and two decks of filling, is thought to be named after the double-decker club cars that came into use on American railways at the end of the 19th century

The first written record of the word sandwich appears in historian Edward Gibbon's journal for November 1762, but the idea had been around for quite a while before that—some 1,762 years earlier the Romans were enjoying a similar snack, which they called *offula*. The 18th-century version was named after John Montagu, the 4th Earl of Sandwich, a politician often accused of corruption and ineptitude, a notorious gambler and a member of a semisecret society known variously as the Knights of St. Francis of Wycombe, the Hellfire Club and the Mad Monks of Medmenham. It was Montagu's exploits at the gambling table that made his name recognized internationally. It is said that he regularly spent the entire day gambling, calling for meat to be brought to him between two slices of bread so he could continue playing while he ate.

The sandwich soon became popular in Britain but not in continental Europe until the 19th century.

Sliced bread became a reality after 16 years of determined effort by American jeweler Otto Frederick Rohwedder, and proved so popular that within five years of its introduction it was being bought by an estimated 80% of the American population. In 1915, three years after starting work on his first bread-slicing machine, Rohwedder was told that he had only a year to live. Two years later he was still alive but a fire meant that his tools and his prototype bread-slicer were...well, toast. Still defying his doctor's prediction, Rohwedder completed his machine in January 1928, and five months later the first loaf of presliced bread went on sale.

| **c.1750s** The 4th Earl of Sandwich (England) popularizes a snack of meat between two slices of bread | **1762** Edward Gibbon's journal provides the first written record of the word sandwich | **1893** Crompton & Co. (Britain) produces the first electric toaster, which only toasts one side at a time | **1926** McGraw Electric (U.S.A.) produces the first pop-up toaster, patented in 1919 by Charles Strite | **1928** Jeweler Otto Frederick Rohwedder (U.S.A.) produces a machine that slices and wraps bread. In May, a bakery in Battle Creek, Michigan uses Rohwedder's machine to produce the first wrapped, presliced loaf | **1930** Wrapped, presliced bread goes on sale in England for the first time |

TIMELINE

Opposite The Raadvad hand-operated bread slicer
Right Colored x-ray of a 1960s' electric pop-up toaster, showing the heating elements and spring mechanism
Below The submarine sandwich, or sub, was so named for obvious reasons

Food & Drink

Fast food means big business, with hamburgers and pizzas leading the way. But these two European dishes did not get the fast food treatment until after Richard and Maurice McDonald opened the world's first fast food restaurant in San Bernadino, California, in 1948.

FAST FOOD

- The world's first pizza margherita was made in 1889 by baker Raphael Esposito (Italy) in honor of a visit to Naples by King Umberto and Queen Margherita. The topping consisted of tomatoes, mozzarella and basil, representing the red, white and green of the Italian flag

- Film star Marlene Dietrich once announced that her favorite meal was hot dogs and champagne

- In 1961 James Monaghan gave his half of what is now Domino's Pizza, the largest pizza delivery company in the world, to his brother, Thomas, in return for a used Volkswagen Beetle

- British burger chain Wimpy is named after J. Wellington Wimpy, the burger-eating character in the cartoon *Popeye*

Above Hot dog stand, New York City
Opposite McDonald's, Tokyo, Japan, which in 1981 had the world's largest volume of sales of fast food

The hamburger sandwich was first officially recorded at the St. Louis World's Fair in 1904; hot dogs were popularized at the same fair, and the first pizzeria in the United States opened in New York the following year. The stage was being set for the advent of fast food, but it was to be nearly half a century before the McDonald brothers introduced their Speedee Service System, marking the beginning of the fast food phenomenon that has since spread from North America across the world.

North American car culture had given rise to a huge number of drive-in restaurants, particularly in California, and the McDonald brothers joined the bandwagon in 1937 with a drive-in hot dog restaurant in Pasadena. Soon afterwards they moved to San Bernadino and in 1940 they opened the McDonald Brothers Burger Bar Drive-In. Then, in 1948, they decided to try something new: they simplified the menu so that there was nothing that required a knife, spoon or fork; they replaced all the crockery and glassware with disposable cups, plates and bags; they dispensed with waitresses, bus boys and carhops, leaving customers to come to the counter to order and collect their food; and, most importantly (so far as the concept of fast food is concerned), they divided the food preparation tasks into a production line. McDonald's had become a food factory.

They called it the Speedee Service System, and the result was so successful that a host of other fast food restaurants soon followed: Keith G. Kramer flew to California, ate at McDonald's, then flew home to Florida where he founded Burger King (as Insta-Burger-King) in 1953 with his father-in-law, Matthew Burns, and Dave Thomas founded Wendy's Old-Fashioned Hamburger Restaurant in Columbus, Ohio, in 1969. George Clark, cofounder of Burger Queen, said later that: "Our food was exactly the same as McDonald's. If I had looked at McDonald's and saw someone flipping hamburgers while he was hanging by his feet, I would have copied it."

1904 The hamburger is first officially recorded, at the St. Louis World's Fair (properly the Louisiana Purchase Exposition). The hot dog and the ice-cream cone also establish national popularity

1922 Roy Allen and Frank Wright form A&W in Sacramento, California

1937 Richard and Maurice McDonald (U.S.A.) open their first eatery, a drive-in hot dog restaurant in Pasadena, California

1948 The McDonald brothers open the world's first fast food restaurant, a hamburger bar in San Bernadino, California

1952 The first Kentucky Fried Chicken franchise opens, near Salt Lake City, Utah (the recipe had been formulated in Corbin, Kentucky, by Harland D. Sanders, a.k.a. Colonel Sanders)

TIMELINE

1953 Keith G. Kramer and Matthew Burns (both U.S.A.) open the first Insta-Burger-King (Burger King), in Florida

1958 The first Pizza Hut restaurant opens, in Wichita, Kansas

1960 Thomas and James Monaghan (U.S.A.) buy DomiNick's pizza shop in Ypsilanti, Michigan. Thomas renames it Domino's in 1965

1962 Glenn Bell (U.S.A.) opens the first Taco Bell restaurant, in Downey, California, having previously sold the chains Taco Tias and El Taco

1964 The first Tim Hortons —selling coffee and donuts—is opened in Hamilton, Ontario, by former NHLer Tim Horton

1969 Dave Thomas (U.S.A.) opens the first Wendy's Old-Fashioned Hamburgers restaurant, in Columbus, Ohio

Soft drinks (so named to distinguish them from hard liquor) developed from two strands: the aeration of water, first achieved by Englishman William Brownrigg in 1741, and the mixing of flavored syrups with carbonated water, first tried in the United States at the beginning of the 19th century.

CARBONATED DRINKS

Opposite Color lithograph by Bernard Villemot used for advertising Orangina (1965)

Below Jacob's Pharmacy, Atlanta, Georgia, the birthplace of Coco-Cola

William Brownrigg (England) created the first artificial mineral water in 1741, but despite this, and small-scale commercial production by Thomas Henry (England) during the 1770s, the father of the soft drinks industry is usually held to be German-Swiss jeweler Jacob Schweppe, the first large-scale commercial producer of aerated waters (from 1783). But it was Townsend Speakman (U.S.A.) who took the vital step toward soft drinks as we know them today, by producing the first *flavored* carbonated drink in 1807.

During the 19th century American pharmacists were trying to improve on the natural curative properties of mineral waters by adding ingredients that included birch bark, dandelions, ginger, sarsaparilla, lemon, coca and kola. The most famous of these drinks was Coca-Cola, formulated by pharmacist Dr. John Styth Pemberton and first sold on May 8, 1886 at Jacobs' Pharmacy in Atlanta, Georgia. Soft drinks were usually served from the soda fountain at the local pharmacy, but shop-based trade was a limited market

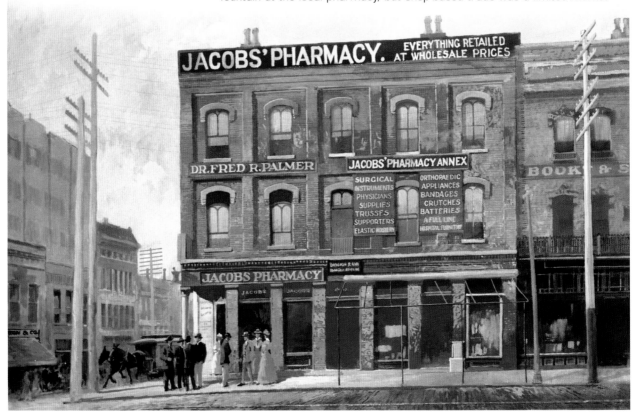

TIMELINE

1741 William Brownrigg (England) creates the first artificial mineral water

1783 German-born naturalized Swiss jeweler Jacob Schweppe commences the first large-scale commercial production of aerated waters

1807 Townsend Speakman (U.S.A.) manufactures the first fruit-flavored carbonated drink (pop or soda-pop)

1813 Charles Plinth (England) invents the first soda siphon, known as the Regency Portable Fountain

1833 First written reference to aerated lemonade

1875 The swing stopper is first used for soft drinks bottles. It is patented by William Painter (U.S.A.) (see 1891)

1885 Dr Pepper, named after Dr. Charles Pepper, is launched in Waco, Texas

1886 Pharmacist Dr. John Styth Pemberton (U.S.A.) formulates Coca-Cola, which is first sold on May 8

1891 The crown cork (crown cap) is invented by William Painter (U.S.A.) and produced by the Crown Cork & Seal Co. of Baltimore, Maryland, in 1892

1898 Caleb Bradham (U.S.A) changes the name of Brad's Drink to Pepsi-Cola. Dr. Louis Perrier (France) buys land including the French spring whose water will eventually bear his name

1903 St. John Harmsworth (Ireland) leases and later buys Dr. Perrier's mineral water spring, closes down the spa and begins commercial production of bottled Perrier water

1916 Coca-Cola first appears in the distinctive contour bottle

1936 Pharmacist Dr. Trigo (Spain) introduces a drink called Naranjina at the Marseilles Fair, France. Léon Beton (France, based in Algeria) is so impressed that he buys the rights and renames the drink Orangina

1952 The first diet soft drink is introduced—No-Cal Ginger Ale, manufactured by Kirsch Beverages (U.S.A.)

and it wasn't until the advent of bottling that the soft drinks industry really took off. Keeping aerated drinks in the bottle was a problem, and more than 1,500 types of cork and bottle-stopper were patented before William Painter (U.S.A.) made a huge breakthrough with the crown cork (crown cap) in 1891, paving the way for carbonated drinks to be sold in shops and transported to the home.

DID YOU KNOW?

● Cola (or kola) is the name of an African evergreen tree that produces cola nuts, used for medicines and flavoring soft drinks

● Coca-Cola's 1915 design brief for what is known as the contour bottle stated that it should be recognizable in the dark, and even if broken

● Pharmacist and chemist John J. McLaughlin perfected the formula for Canada Dry Pale Ginger Ale in Toronto, Ontario, in 1904. During Prohibition use of Canada Dry Ginger

Ale as a mixer skyrocketed. Canada Dry introduced tonic water and Collins mix in the 1930s

● The design of the Perrier bottle was based on the Indian clubs that St. John Harmsworth used for exercise

● A 1950s' Schweppes advertising campaign included the publication of the "Schweppeshire Post" available at a cost of Schweppence

42

Food & Drink

The first ice cream was a right royal treat, and ice cream continued to be an expensive luxury until American dairyman Jacob Fussell set up the first ice-cream factory, in 1851. Since then the introduction of cones, wafers and Eskimo Pies have made ice cream ever more popular.

ICE CREAM

TIMELINE

c.a.d. 50 The Roman Emperor Nero is reported as sending slaves to collect snow, which would then be flavored with honey, nuts and fruit

c.1770s The proprietor of the Parisian coffee house Le Caveau introduces ice cream to France, and in 1774 sculpts the arms of the Duke of Chartres in what he calls iced butter

1850 Ice cream is first sold in Canada, by confectioner Thomas Webb in Toronto, Ontario

1851 Jacob Fussell (U.S.A.) produces the first factory-made ice cream

1874 At the semicentennial celebration of the Franklin Institute in Philadelphia, Robert M. Green (U.S.A.) serves the first ice-cream soda

1890 The first ice-cream sundaes are served, in Wisconsin

1896 Italo Marcioni (Italy–U.S.A.) produces the first ice-cream cone, and in 1903 patents a special mould

1921 Christian K. Nelson (U.S.A.) sells the world's first Eskimo Pie

1922 Sausage and pie manufacturer Thomas Wall (England) produces Britain's first factory-made ice cream

1923 Frank Epperson (U.S.A.) patents the first iced lollipop, which he calls the Epsicle, a name that is later changed to Popsicle

Alexander the Great and the Roman Emperor Nero ate flavored snow or ice, but these were precursors of sorbet rather than ice cream, and probably the first people to enjoy dairy ice cream were English King Charles I and his courtiers during the 17th century. This delicacy was prepared by Charles's French chef, Gerald Tissain, the first person known to have made iced desserts using milk or cream.

For the next 200 years ice cream remained the preserve of the wealthy, until in 1851 dairyman Jacob Fussell of

Baltimore, MA, realized the best way of avoiding wastage of cream was to freeze the excess. His iced cream was so popular that he set up a factory, and on June 15, 1851 he made the world's first delivery of mass-produced ice cream, at less than a third of the price of his competitor's handmade ice cream. Within a year Fussell had set up factories in New York and Washington, and the popularity of ice cream soon spread across North America.

The first ice-cream cone was made by Italo Marcioni (Italian-American) in 1896, but the idea did not become popular until the 1904 St. Louis World's Fair, when it is said that E.A. Hamwi, a Syrian waffle-maker, rolled his waffles into cones so that the vendor at the next stall could fill them with ice cream.

The Eskimo Pie came about after American confectioner Christian K. Nelson had watched a boy in his shop agonizing over the choice between ice cream or chocolate. Nelson experimented with ways of combining the two, and in 1921 he launched the first Eskimo Pie.

DID YOU KNOW?

● Legend has it that the ice-cream sundae is so-called because an ice-cream seller in Wisconsin regularly ran low of supplies on a Sunday. To compensate for smaller portions he added chocolate sauce or fruit syrup, which was so popular that customers began to ask for "Sunday ice cream" during the week—the spelling was later changed in response to puritanical objections to the profane use of the name of the Lord's day

● In late 19th-century London Italian immigrants known as hokey-pokey men sold ice cream from carts in the street. They were so-called because of their familiar cry, *Ecco un poco*, meaning try a little. When Wall's ice-cream men began selling ice cream from tricycles in 1922, they adopted the cry, "Stop me and buy one"

● The Popsicle was an accidental invention. American lemonade salesman Frank Epperson left a glass of lemonade on a windowsill overnight with a spoon in it. The following morning it had frozen, and when he tried to remove the spoon he found himself holding the world's first Popsicle

Opposite top Popsicle, the frozen drink on a stick
Left French illustration from the early 19th century depicting the appropriate manners for eating ice cream
Below Electric ice cream van (1949)

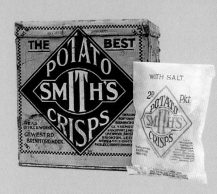
For nearly three centuries after it was introduced to Europe from the Americas chocolate was a drink. It wasn't until 1819 that eating-chocolate was produced in bars for the first time, by Swiss François-Louis Cailler, starting a trend that has become the curse of many a chocoholic.

Food & Drink

CHOCOLATE AND POTATO CHIPS

DID YOU KNOW?

● Chocolate is made from the seeds of the cacao tree, which, because of a spelling mistake or mis-pronunciation by English importers, became known as cocoa beans

● The name *Toblerone*® derives from the name of the Tobler chocolate firm and *torrone*, Italian for nougat

● Ganong Brothers Ltd. in St. Stephen, New Brunswick, introduced the first five-cent chocolate nut bar in 1910

Above Early packaging for Smith's Potato Crisps

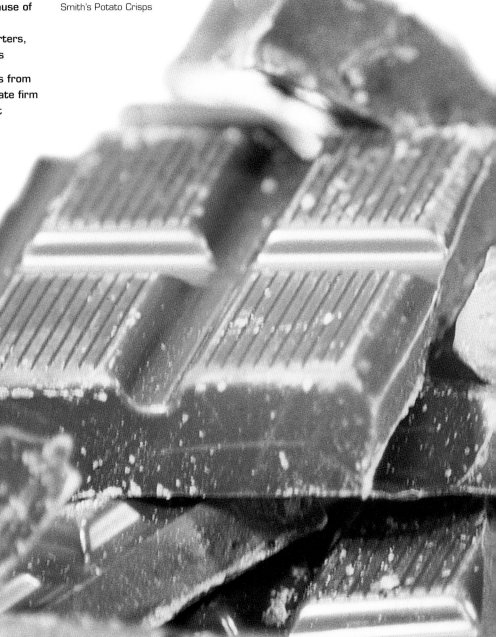

Chocolate

Chocolate was an important part of Mayan and Aztec culture, and was first introduced to Europe in 1528 by Hernando Cortés, the Spanish conqueror of Mexico. For hundreds of years it was prepared as cocoa or hot chocolate, until, early in the 19th century, French and Italian confectioners began producing chocolate for eating. In 1819 François-Louis Cailler began the commercial manufacture of eating-chocolate at Vevey in his native Switzerland, producing chocolate for the first time in solid blocks.

Potato chips

The first potato chips were served in 1853 at the Moon Lake House Hotel in Saratoga Springs, New York, where financier Cornelius Vanderbilt had complained that the fried potatoes were too chunky. The piqued chef, George Crum, reacted by slicing the potatoes as thinly as he possibly could and frying them until they were crisp. Despite his intention, these chips proved extremely popular, and Crum found that his act of defiance had turned into a culinary revolution.

Potato chips were introduced to England in 1913 by a grocer named Carter, who cooked them to a recipe he had brought back from France. They did not sell well until, in 1920, Carter's manager, Frank Smith, set up Smith's Potato Crisps Ltd. and succeeded in popularizing the snack throughout the country.

TIMELINE

1819 François-Louis Cailler (Switzerland) manufactures the world's first chocolate bars

1853 The first potato chips are served, at the Moon Lake House Hotel, Saratoga Springs, New York

1875 Cailler's son-in-law Daniel Peter produces the world's first milk chocolate bars

1885 Ganong Brothers Ltd. (Canada) introduce Chicken Bone, a chocolate center cinnamon hard candy

1900 Milton Snavely Hershey (U.S.A.) produces the first Hershey bar

1905 Cadbury's produces its first bar of Cadbury's Dairy Milk

1908 Cousins Emil Baumann and Theodor Tobler (both Switzerland) create the first *Toblerone®* bar

1909 *Toblerone®* is granted a patent for its chocolate recipe, and is marketed as "the first patented Swiss chocolate"

1922 Manufacturer Frank Smith (England) adds salt in blue paper twists to packets of chips for the first time

1923 Franklin C. Mars's (U.S.A.) Mar-O-Bar Company produces the first Milky Way (known as a Mars bar outside the United States)

1932 Forrest E. Mars leaves the United States and begins manufacturing Mars bars in Slough, England

1935 Kit Kat is launched in England as Rowntree's Chocolate Crisp

1936 Chocolate manufacturer John Mackintosh & Sons (England) introduces the Quality Street assortment

1960 Manufacturer Golden Wonder (Britain) introduces the first ready salted chips

1962 Golden Wonder introduces the first flavored chips (Cheese and Onion)

1991 Mars bars are exported to the U.S.S.R for the first time, where they are rationed to four per person

Clarence Birdseye is generally acknowledged as the father of the frozen food industry, although he was not the first person to freeze food. He was, however, the first to fully exploit its commercial potential, and the first Birds Eye frozen foods reached the shelves on March 6, 1930.

Food & Drink # FROZEN FOOD

Above Packaging for frozen fish fingers (1950s)

Left "Stop at your Birds Eye shop"

| **19th century** Meat is frozen for transportation from Australia, New Zealand and South America to Europe | **1912–15** Fur trader Clarence Birdseye (U.S.A.) observes Inuit in Canada preserving food by freezing | **1913** The first domestic refrigerator is manufactured, in Chicago, IL, and marketed as Domelre (Domestic Electric Refrigerator) | **1926** The Biological Board of Canada decides to investigate the market potential for high-quality frozen fish | **1927** Birdseye files a patent for "quickly freezing food for preserving and later defrosting" | **1929** 1 lb packs of frozen haddock known as Fresh Ice Fillets go on sale in Toronto, Ontario. It is the first time frozen fish has been available commercially |

TIMELINE

"That first winter I saw natives catching fish in 50° below zero weather, which froze stiff as soon as they were taken out of the water. Months later, when they were thawed out, some of those fish were still alive." Clarence Birdseye's pioneering ideas about frozen food were inspired by his observations of age-old Inuit practice while on a U.S. government survey of fish and wildlife in Newfoundland between 1912 and 1915. Birdseye also learned to preserve vegetables by freezing them in water.

However, Birdseye was not the first: apart from the Inuit practices, meat had been frozen for transportation since the mid-19th century, frozen fruit had been sold along with ice cream from as early as 1905, and a Canadian government department began marketing frozen fish (the first individually packaged frozen food) in 1929. But Birdseye pioneered two revolutionary new ideas. He discovered that a slow freezing process created large ice crystals, which in turn made the product soggy when it was thawed, so he devised a fast-freezing process that did not harm the food. And he also came up with the idea of freezing *prepared* fruit and vegetables and *portions* of fish, an idea later marketed as, "The modern way to shop and cook," with advertisements describing how the foods were "quick-frozen so their freshness, flavor and goodness is sealed in tight. All prepared ready to cook. No cleaning. No tiresome kitchen chores. That's all been done for you."

Birdseye set up the Frosted Food Company in 1924 to put his ideas into practice, and sold out in 1929 to the Postum Company (later the General Foods Corporation). Postum launched the first range of quick-frozen food in 1930, having agreed that the brand name for its products would be Birds Eye. At first, frozen food was slow to catch on—shoppers did not think to look in the ice-cream cabinets where it was kept, it was relatively expensive and, in Britain, few households had freezers. However, frozen fish fingers have been described as the greatest food revolution since the discovery of fire, and frozen food, for hundreds of years part of the Inuit tradition, is now an indispensable part of modern living.

Clarence Birdseye in 1943, preparing carrots for a dehydration process that he hoped would be as popular as his quick-frozen food

DID YOU KNOW?

● A would-be pioneer of frozen food was English philosopher and statesman Francis Bacon, who died in 1626 after catching cold while stuffing a chicken with snow in order to determine the effect of cold on the preservation of meat

● Clarence Birdseye, who is described with no apparent sense of irony as a biologist and fur trapper, was also an inventor, with more than 350 patents to his name

| **1930** Birds Eye launches its first range of frozen food, including vegetables, fruit and fish—the first time frozen vegetables have been available commercially | **1937** Frozen asparagus produced by S.W. Smedley of Wisbech becomes the first frozen food available in Britain | **1939** Birds Eye introduces the first precooked frozen meals (chicken fricassée and criss-cross steak) | **1953** Food manufacturer Gorton's (U.S.A.) introduces the first fish sticks | **1955** Birds Eye introduces fish fingers to Britain, test marketing Herring Savouries in South Wales and cod sticks in Southampton—cod proves more popular |

CANNED FOOD

Napoleon Bonaparte may seem an unlikely instigator of a worldwide revolution in food processing, but canned food came about as a direct result of the need to supply his army and the rapidly expanding French Navy at the end of the 18th century.

DID YOU KNOW?

● For 45 years users were instructed to cut cans of food open with a chisel and hammer, and it wasn't until 1855 that Robert Yeates invented the first can opener

● Heinz products already numbered more than 60 when Henry Heinz coined the slogan "57 Varieties" in 1896, and they now number more than 5,700 worldwide

● Cans of veal and carrots supplied to the Royal Navy in 1824 were found to be still edible when they were opened 112 years later in 1936 (though the taster's job was given to laboratory animals)

● Legend has it that the distinctive red and white label of Campbell's soups was inspired by the colors of the Cornell University football team

● The loss of the Franklin Expedition, who were searching for the Northwest Passage in Canada's Arctic in the mid 19th century, has been attributed to poisoning from lead cans

Above Heinz headquarters in Pittsburgh, PA
Right Advertising poster by Jean d'Ylen for Jambon Villettte tinned ham (1924)

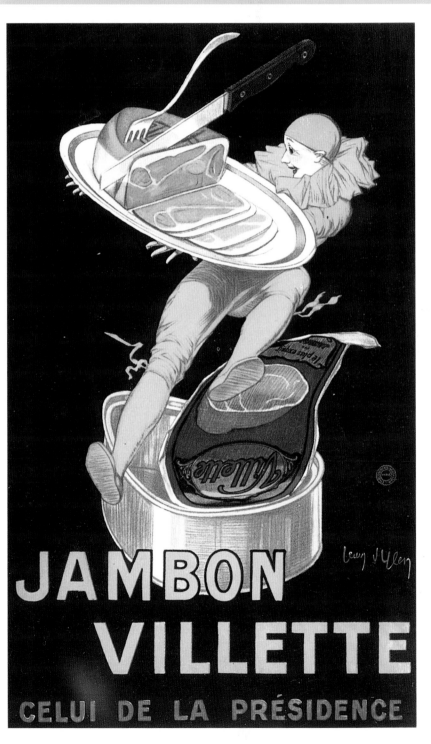

JAMBON VILLETTE
CELUI DE LA PRÉSIDENCE

Above A tin of roast veal packed in 1823 by Donkin, Hall & Gamble and supplied to the Royal Navy in 1824; when opened over 100 years later the veal was found to be edible
Right Campbell's Soup Banner by Andy Warhol

1804 The French Navy tests food preserved using a bottling and heating process pioneered by Nicolas Appert (France)

1810 Peter Durand (England) is awarded a patent by King George III for the use of "vessels of tin or other metals" for the heat-preservation of food

1812 Bryan Donkin and John Hall (both England) establish the world's first cannery, at Blue Anchor Road, Bermondsey, London

1839 The word "can" is coined by the bookkeepers of a cannery in Boston, MA, as an abbreviation for "canister"

1855 Robert Yeates (England) invents the can opener

1860s Messrs Reckhow and Larne (both U.S.A.) produce the first-known pictorial label for canned food, showing a dish of tomatoes against a plain background

1866 J. Osterhoudt (U.S.A.) invents a tin can opened by a key fixed to the top

1869 Joseph Campbell (U.S.A.) begins canning foods

1870 William Lyman (U.S.A.) invents the rotary can opener

1875 The world's first canned baked beans are produced by Burnham & Morrill Co. of Portland, ME

1895 H.J. Heinz Co. of Pittsburgh, PA, produces its first canned baked beans with tomato sauce

1905 H.J. Heinz introduce canned baked beans to Britain

1927 The wall can opener is invented by the Central States Manufacturing Co. of St. Louis, MO

1928 H.J Heinz begin manufacture of baked beans in Britain for the first time

1941 H.J. Heinz and ICI pioneer the self-heating can, incorporating a heating element lit by a match

I n 1795, in order to simplify feeding its armed forces, the French government offered a 12,000-franc prize for an improved method of food preservation. Fifteen years later, in 1810, Parisian chef and confectioner Nicolas Appert received the prize, having invented a method (later known as appertization) of sealing food in bottles and heating it to preserve it.

Until 1822 Appert used glass jars and bottles rather than tins, but his pioneering work means that he is generally seen as the father of canned food despite the fact that it was an Englishman, Peter Durand, who invented the tin can, in 1810. Durand sold the rights of his patent to fellow Englishmen Bryan Donkin and John Hall for £1,000, and in 1812 Donkin and Hall set up the world's first cannery, using Durand's can and Appert's technique. As in France, the main consumers were the armed forces, but Donkin and Hall also sent their products to the British Royal Family, and in 1813 received a report that their canned beef had been served "on the Duke of York's table where it was tasted by the Queen, the Prince Regent and several distinguished personages and highly approved."

During the 20th century Heinz convinced the world that Beanz Meanz Heinz, but in fact baked beans were canned for the first time in 1875, the year before the Heinz company was founded. Heinz did not begin canning baked beans until 1895, and introduced them to Britain in 1905 as a cheap and nourishing meal for the working classes. However, 19 years earlier Henry Heinz (U.S.A.) had identified the upper classes as his target market: in 1886 he took "seven varieties of our finest and newest goods" to Fortnum & Mason's, which became the first shop in London to stock Heinz canned foods when the purchasing manager famously told him, "I think, Mr Heinz, we will take the lot."

The first microwave oven came about as a by-product of wartime technology, and in 1946 a prototype was installed in a restaurant in Boston, MA. It proved to be a culinary development as revolutionary as the first iron stove nearly two millennia earlier.

OVENS

Top The first gas cooker, designed by James Sharp, who claimed that it could cook dinner for 100 people
Right Demonstration of the prototype Raytheon Raydarange microwave oven at the Waldorf Astoria Hotel, New York, NY, on June 7, 1947
Opposite The Aga Cooker, first invented in 1922

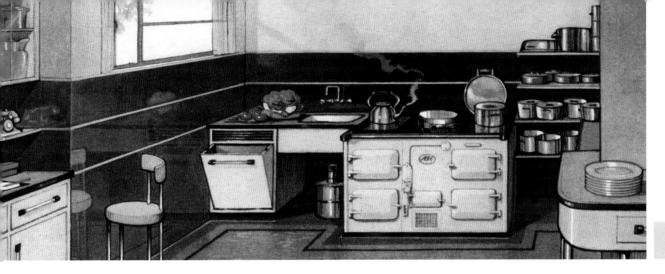

ooking practices were fairly restricted until the Chinese developed the first iron cooking stove some time between a.d. 100 and 200, and it was to be another 17 centuries before solid fuel stoves were replaced by gas or electricity. At first, gas was considered impractical for cooking, but in 1826 James Sharp, Assistant Manager of the Northampton Gas Company in England, installed the world's first practicable gas stove in his kitchen. He sold gas cookers to two local hotels, but did not commit himself to opening a factory until after a visit from Earl Spencer (an ancestor of the late Diana, Princess of Wales), who visited Sharp's home requesting a gas-cooked lunch, thus convincing Sharp that there was a market for gas stoves.

Electric cookers followed toward the end of the century, but it was the microwave oven that was to provide the next big change in cooking methods, using electromagnetic energy to cook rather than direct heat. This new type of oven arose from the use of microwaves in airborne radar during World War Two. After the war, Dr. Percy LeBaron Spencer (no relation to Diana, Princess of Wales), realized that the heating effect of the microwave beam could be put to good use.

Other engineers had noticed the heating effect (now known to be due to the excitation of molecules rather than the radiation of heat) and had dismissed it as an annoying side-effect, but Spencer investigated further, putting a bag of maize in the path of the microwave beam—seconds later he had a bag of popcorn. He demonstrated this to his colleagues at the Raytheon Mfg. Co. by cooking an egg. The egg exploded, but nonetheless the company went ahead with the project and in 1947 produced the first commercial microwave ovens, known as the Raydarange.

DID YOU KNOW?

● Gas cookers proved so efficient that the phrase "cooking with gas" entered the English language as a slang term describing anything that was progressing well. Microwave ovens, on the other hand, provoked so much suspicion that cooking with a microwave became known as "nuking" the food—a reference to destruction by nuclear weapons

● The first microwave ovens were 1.6 m (5 ft.) tall, weighed about 350 kg (770 lbs) and cost between $3,000 and $5,000

● Early research into domestic use of gas concentrated on keeping the flame cool, because gas was used for light and not heat

A good cup of tea once involved a great deal of preparation and ceremony, but the tea bag, popularized during the 1930s, made it a much simpler affair—to the chagrin of purists and the delight of workmen, office staff and convenience junkies the world over.

Food & Drink

TEA BAGS

Above Tabloid Tea, a late-Victorian invention—instant tea in the form of a tablet
Below The Boston Tea Party—Bostonians disguised as Native Americans throw tea into the harbor in protest at unfair taxation

The Portuguese are thought to have been the first Europeans to drink tea, bringing limited quantities into Lisbon from as early as 1580, but it was the Dutch East India Company that, in 1610, made the first commercial imports of tea to Europe. Tea-drinking became very fashionable in Holland, and soon spread across Europe and into North America. In 1773 British duty on tea being exported to the American Colonies sparked the Boston Tea Party, in which a group of Americans protesting against the taxes threw an entire cargo of tea into Boston Harbor—a significant step on the road to revolution and American Independence. Since then the United States has, as a nation, tended to shun tea in favor of coffee (Canada drinks four times as much tea per head), so it is perhaps surprising that it should have been an American who popularized the tea bag.

In 1896 a patent for the first tea bag was issued to Englishman A.V. Smith, but the idea did not take off in England, where traditional methods of tea-making were firmly entrenched. Eight years later, on the other side of the Atlantic, New York tea and coffee merchant Thomas Sullivan began dispatching samples of tea in silk envelopes rather than tins, and his customers discovered that the tea could be brewed in these bags. However, it was another American, Joseph Krieger, who introduced the first purpose-designed tea bags, which were made of muslin. Initially these were used only by caterers, but by the 1930s the majority of tea bags in the United States were being bought for use in the home, where they took the place of the metal tea egg or tea ball, which had perforated holes to allow tea to infuse.

Tea experts complain that tea bags produce a brew that is all strength and no flavor but, for some, strength is a virtue. Ex-First Lady of the United States Nancy Reagan famously said that, "A woman is like a tea bag. It's only when she's in hot water that you realize how strong she is."

| **c.1560** Priest Gaspar de Cruz (Portugal) is the first European to give an account of tea drinking | **1610** The Dutch East India Co. makes the first commercial import of tea to Europe | **1891** Samuel Rowbottom (England) patents the first automatic tea maker. The first electric kettle is marketed by Carpenter Electric Heating Manufacturing Co. of Minnesota | **1899** Theodore Estabrooks starts producing Red Rose tea in Saint John, New Brunswick | **1902** Gunsmith Frank Clarke (England) produces the first working automatic tea maker, a primitive machine involving matches, methylated spirits and a precarious tipping device to decant the boiling water |

TIMELINE

DID YOU KNOW?

● Japanese tradition has it that tea-drinking was discovered by the disciples of a Daruma, a Japanese Buddhist monk who visited China c.520 b.c. In order to stay awake during his meditation the revered teacher cut off his eyelids and a bush grew at the place where he threw them. Instead of cutting off their own eyelids, the master's followers brewed the leaves of the plant to stay awake, giving rise to the Japanese tea ceremony

● In October 2000, 227 years after the original Boston Tea Party, the ship *Spirit of Boston* hosted the world's largest tea party, on the Charles River in Boston, MA

● Paraguayans drink more tea per head than any other nationality, averaging nearly 15 cups per person per day

● Theodore Estabrooks started producing Red Rose tea in Saint John, New Brunswick in 1899

The Goblin Teasmade, first introduced in 1937

c.1904 Tea and coffee merchant Thomas Sullivan (U.S.A.) sends samples of tea in silk envelopes, and customers discover that the tea can be brewed in the bags	**1918** Benjamin Hirschorn (U.S.A.) files a patent for a tea bag	**c.1919** In San Francisco, Joseph Krieger (U.S.A.) introduces the first purpose-made tea bags	**1930s** Tea bags begin to be used in the home as well as by commercial caterers	**1937** British Vacuum Cleaner Co. (Goblin) introduces the Teasmade (initially marketed as the Cheerywake), designed by Brenner Thornton in 1936	**1953** The Tetley Group introduces tea bags to Britain

In 1930, hoping to stimulate sales, the Brazilian Coffee Institute asked Swiss company Nestlé to develop a coffee that was soluble in water and retained its flavor. Eight years later, in April 1938, Nescafé was launched as the first soluble instant coffee.

INSTANT COFFEE

offee originated in Ethiopia and spread to the Middle East c.a.d. 1000. Italian traders brought coffee to Europe for the first time in 1615, where it was drunk for more than three centuries before Nestlé produced the first soluble instant coffee. There had been precursors, such as liquid coffee essences and drinks made from pulverized coffee beans; in the latter, the coffee was held in suspension rather than being dissolved, and the drinker had to consume the grounds along with the drink itself. None of these "instant" coffees was a success and in 1930, in response to the request of the Brazilian Institute of Coffee, Nestlé scientist Max Mortgenthaler began researching ways of drying percolated coffee.

Seven years later Mortgenthaler produced powdered coffee using a technique known as spray-drying, and in 1938 Nescafé was launched. Spray-drying, a process still used today, involves spraying brewed coffee into a heated tower where hot air dries out the droplets of coffee as they fall, reducing the coffee to a powder by the time it reaches the bottom of the tower. Under modern methods, the powder is further processed into granules.

In 1964 Nestlé came up with a new technique for drying coffee, and in 1965 launched Nescafé Gold Blend as the first freeze-dried instant coffee. Freeze-drying is a far more complicated and expensive technique than spray-drying, but retains more of the flavor. The coffee is brewed, frozen in thin layers and then ground into particles, which are then placed in a vacuum chamber. Under low pressure the boiling point of water is reduced so, as the pressure in the chamber is reduced, the ice in the coffee evaporates without the need to apply heat, which would impair the flavor. The water vapor is then removed from the chamber leaving granules of freeze-dried coffee.

Above Nescafé, the first instant coffee
Left The Atomic coffeemaker, by A. & H.G. Sassoon of London, England (c.1950)
Opposite Contemporary engraving of a typical coffeehouse in London, England (c.1700)

DID YOU KNOW?

● The idea of tipping waiters and waitresses is said to have originated in 17th-century English coffeehouses, where boxes were provided for gratuities, marked, To Insure Promptness (TIP)

● Finns drink more coffee per head than any other nationality, averaging about five cups per person per day, well over twice the average of the United States

● Cappuccino is so-named because it is a similar color to the light brown robes of the Capuchin order of monks

C₂H₅OH, or alcohol, as it is more commonly known, is the oldest and probably the most widely used drug ever manufactured by mankind. There have been many alcoholic firsts since humans discovered the joys of fermentation in Mesopotamia some 7,000 years ago.

Food & Drink

WINES AND SPIRITS

Above Advertisement for Rhum Vieux (aged rum)
Right Film star Rock Hudson with a martini in a scene from *Man's Favorite Sport?*
Opposite Relief of Dom Pierre Pérignon, with champagne bottle, at Hautvillers Abbey in France

Mankind's first known laws, predating even the Ten Commandments, included the regulation of drinking houses in Babylon c.1770 b.c. It is thought that humanity's first contact with alcohol must have come from tasting fermenting fruit or honey (in which airborne yeasts had reacted with the natural sugars), and residues found during the excavation of a Neolithic village in what is now Iran show that by c.5000 b.c. man had learned how to ferment wine artificially.

The basic principles of wine-making remained fixed until c.1688, when Dom Pierre Pérignon, a monk at Hautvillers Abbey in France, made the first champagne. Pérignon was a renowned wine maker who, at first, tried to prevent the second fermentation induced by the local climate, but later turned it to his advantage. The second fermentation took place after the bottles were sealed, so the carbon dioxide produced was retained in the wine, making it sparkle. Pérignon was the first to make a virtue of

DID YOU KNOW?

● Calgary, Alberta bartender Walter Salin Chell invented the Bloody Caesar when he replaced the salt and tomato juice of a Bloody Mary with celery salt and Clamato juice in 1969

● The word whiskey comes from the Celtic *uisce beatha*, meaning "water of life" (or from the Gaelic *uisge beatha*); the name of the Scandinavian drink akvavit also means "water of life." Vodka comes from the Russian *voda* (water) and means "little water." Gin comes from *genièvre*, French for the juniper berry with which gin is flavored. Brandy comes from the Dutch *brandewijn*, from *branden*, meaning to burn, i.e. distil, and *wijn* (wine)

this phenomenon, using stronger English bottles and Spanish corks to produce a sparkling wine that he said tasted like stars.

After fermentation (used for producing wine, beer, cider and saké), the next big step was distillation, which was introduced to Western Europe from the Middle East in the 6th–7th century A.D. Brandy is thought to have been the first distilled drink (from grapes), since when spirits have been distilled from wine, cereal grains, sugar cane, potatoes and many other sources. One of the most popular is whiskey (or whisky), which has been distilled from cereal grains in Ireland and Scotland for centuries, though there are arguments about who was first: some claim that whiskey traveled to Scotland with Irish missionaries, others that the Scots discovered it independently using distillation techniques brought back from the Middle East by the Crusaders.

Whiskey means "water of life," and 18th-century Scottish writer James Hogg was sure that it could indeed lead to everlasting life: "If a body could just find out the exact proper proportion and quantity that ought to be drunk every day, and keep to that, I verily trow [truly believe] that he might live forever, without dying at all, and that doctors and kirkyards [churchyards] would go out of fashion."

THE BEST OF THE REST...

Drinking straws

Marvin Chester Stone (U.S.A.) manufactured the first drinking straws in 1886

Nonstick pans

Contrary to popular belief, nonstick pans were not a result of the space program. Teflon was discovered by Dr. Roy Plunkett of American chemical company DuPont as early as 1938. Teflon, or polytetrafluorethylene, is unaffected by corrosion, heat, electric current, acids or solvents, and has the lowest coefficient of friction of any substance yet discovered or manufactured. It has been used in applications ranging from medicine to electronics and architecture, but it wasn't until 1954 that Marc Grégoire (France) thought of using it as a nonstick surface for frying pans. The following year he set up the company Tefal, and in 1956 produced the first nonstick pan

Thermoses

The first vacuum flask was perfected by scientist Sir James Dewar (Scotland) in 1892. Known as the Dewar Vessel, it was used only for scientific experiments. A German student of Dewar's, Reinhold Burger, decided to manufacture vacuum flasks for domestic use and in 1904 produced the first Thermos flask. The name Thermos derives from the Greek word for heat and is a registered trademark, although it has become a generic term for vacuum flasks

Below Colored X-ray of a vacuum flask

Margarine

Margarine was invented when Napoleon III of France held a competition to find a cheaper, longer-lasting substitute for butter for use by the armed forces and "the less prosperous classes." On July 15, 1869 Hippolyte Mège-Mouriés patented a mixture of lard, skimmed milk, pork and beef scraps and bicarbonate of soda that he called margarine because of its pearly whiteness—*maragaron* is the Greek word for pearl. The Franco-Prussian War prevented production of his invention, and Jan and Anton Jurgens (Holland) produced the world's first margarine at their factory, after buying the rights from Mège-Mouriés

Breakfast cereals

The first ready-to-eat breakfast cereal was Shredded Wheat, produced by Henry D. Perky in Denver, Colorado, in 1893. Perky suffered badly from dyspepsia and introduced Shredded Wheat to aid digestion. The first flaked breakfast cereal was Granose Flakes, produced by Dr. John Harvey Kellogg at the Battle Creek Sanatorium, Michigan, and officially announced in the magazine *Food Health* in 1895; three years later Corn Flakes were introduced by Kellogg's brother, William

Restaurants

The first eating place to call itself a restaurant was the Champ d'Oiseau, Paris, France, in 1765. Its sign said *Venite ad me, omnes qui stomacho laboratis, et ego restaurabo vos* (Come to me all whose stomachs grumble, and I will restore you), and so restaurant owners are restaurateurs (restorers), not restauranteurs

Croissants

The croissant was invented in Vienna, Austria, by a Polish soldier called Kulyeziski, who had helped free the city from the Turkish army. Kulyeziski opened a café there and, in 1683, had a baker make the world's first croissants in their distinctive crescent shape to celebrate victory over the Turks (whose symbol is a crescent moon)

Chapter Three

Trade & Technology

The importance of money to economics has been likened to the importance of the wheel to mechanics. But money is not the same as cash, and banking developed in Mesopotamia more than 1,000 years before the first coins were officially stamped in Lydia (now part of Turkey) c.640 b.c.

MONEY

Above ECU (European Currency Unit) coins proposed for use in the Netherlands, Belgium, France and the U.K. and first issued as legal tender in Belgium in 1987
Left *Der Geldwechsler und seine Frau* (The money-changer and his wife) by Marinus van Reymerswaele (1539)
Opposite A German five million Mark note (1923)

| **c.640 b.c.** King Gyges (Lydia, now part of Turkey) issues the first officially stamped coins, whose value depends on their weight | **c.550 b.c.** King Croesus (Lydia) issues the first coins with fixed values | **c.a.d. 650** Emperor Yung Hue (China) issues the first paper money | **1574** The first paper money proved to have been used in Europe is issued by Burgomaster Pieter Andriaanszoon of Leyden (Netherlands) (coin presses were fed with paper due to a metal shortage) | **1661** The Riksbank of Stockholm (Sweden) issues the world's first banknotes, known as *Kreditsvedlar* (notes of credit) | **1686** Playing cards are used as the first paper currency in Canada |

▮TIMELINE

Money, as tokens representing wealth, developed from an ancient tradition of barter. Exchanging goods of equal value was not always practical, and early monetary tokens included amber, beads, salt, cattle, feathers and cowries (the shells of marine snails). Metal became a means of exchange in the Middle East, and in Lydia (now eastern Turkey) crude lumps of metal called dumps were stamped with the royal crest, and thus formalized into the first coins, during the reign of King Gyges.

The first paper money was issued in China to overcome a shortage of coins, but it was centuries before promissory notes such as letters of credit and goldsmith's receipts (which represented wealth deposited elsewhere) developed into formal banknotes. The check, which actually developed before the banknote, is a type of promissory note that has survived in its original form.

Cash is more than 2,500 years old, but it now plays second fiddle to "virtual" money in a world where an increasing number of financial transactions take place using credit cards or electronic transfers, with no exchange of physical tokens.

DID YOU KNOW?

● Dixie (or Dixieland), the nickname for the American South, is derived from a banknote issued by the Citizen's Bank of Louisiana in the 1830s. The bank used English and French on its notes and $10 bills were denoted *dix* as well as ten, and became known as "dixes." In 1860 songwriter Dan Emmett wrote, "I wish I was in the land of the dixes," which was corrupted to "the land of Dixie"

● The word salary, meaning a regular wage, derives from the salt rations, or *salarium*, issued to Roman soldiers and civil servants. When money began to be paid instead of the salt ration, the allowance kept the same name

| **1695** The Bank of England issues Britain's first banknotes | **1817** Canada's first bank, the Bank of Montreal, opens in Montreal | **1879** James and John Ritty (U.S.A.) patent the first cash register, for use in a saloon in Dayton, Ohio, to prevent pilfering by staff | **1891** American Express issues the first modern countersigned traveler's check. The first is cashed on August 5 at the Hotel Hauffe in Leipzig, Germany | **1967** Barclays Bank (England) installs the world's first cash dispenser at its branch in Enfield, London. The maximum withdrawal is £10 | **1999** The Euro is launched as what is intended to become the first pan-European currency |

The first charge card was the Diners Club Card (1950) and the first credit card was the BankAmericard (1958), later renamed Visa. Charge card holders must repay their card company on a specified date, while most credit card holders may repay the company whenever they like—at a price.

64

Trade & Technology

CHARGE CARDS AND CREDIT CARDS

Above Junior Diners Club Credit Card
Opposite Frank McNamara, inventor of the Diners Club Card

Charge cards

In 1950 New York businessman Frank McNamara was treating a group of guests to dinner when he realized that he had forgotten his wallet. Luckily, he was a regular customer, and he was allowed to leave his business card as an IOU—this inspired him to devise a card that would prove the holder's ability to pay. He launched his Diners Club Card that same year with an initial membership of 200, and so the world's first charge card was born.

The charge card was not a completely new idea, however, because, since the 1920s, American hotel chains and service stations (and later stores) had been issuing payment cards known as "shoppers' plate" for use in their own outlets in order to encourage customer loyalty. What made the Diners Club Card different was that it could be used in a number of different establishments, allowing members to dine in any one of 27 New York restaurants and use their card instead of paying cash. The Diners Club would then pay the restaurant, and the cardholder would pay the Diners Club at a later date. Half a century later the number of establishments accepting the card has grown to over eight million, and there are nearly eight million Diners Club Cardholders in over 200 countries.

Credit cards

Although the Diners Club and, later, American Express cards effectively gave credit to their holders, who were able to buy or eat now and pay later, both organizations required the entire balance to be paid each month. In 1958 the Bank of America became the first *bank* to issue a card, the BankAmericard (renamed Visa in 1976), and in this case holders could choose to pay only part of the balance, with interest being charged on the remainder, making it the first true credit card.

On October 1, 1958 the American Express Card was introduced in Canada. In 1959 American Express was the first company to issue a plastic credit card. Prior cards were made of index stock, which over time and repeated use crumbled, tore and sometimes disintegrated. In Canada, American Express released the Gold Card in 1964, the Corporate Card in 1970 and the Platinum Card in 1984. As early as 1964 a British bank manager announced: "It has been estimated that by the year 2000 credit cards will have taken over and money will only be used as petty cash."

1920s Payment cards known as "shoppers' plates" are introduced in the United States

1946 Flatbush National Bank, New York, launches the Charg-It system of cashless payment, a precursor of the modern credit card

1950 Frank McNamara (U.S.A.) launches the Diners Club card, the world's first charge card

1958 In California The Bank of America launches the BankAmericard, the world's first credit card, renamed Visa in 1976

1959 American Express issues the first plastic credit card

1984 Visa makes the first use of holograms on credit cards to prevent forgery

TIMELINE

Charge Cards

65

SUPERMARKETS

Problems of definition cloud the issue of which was the first supermarket, but it is possible to say for certain that the first shopping cart was the brainchild of Sylvan Goldman and went into action on June 4, 1937 at the Humpty Dumpty supermarket in Oklahoma City, OK.

Above 1960s' British supermarket
Below *Supermarket Shopper*, a model by superrealist Duane Hanson (1970). Hanson uses polyester and fiberglass to create uncannily lifelike statues of people in everyday situations

Supermarkets evolved from grocery stores with shop assistants and counter service into what is now instantly recognizable as a supermarket—a chain store with a huge shopping area, self-service aisles and check-outs rather than a counter. Self-service shopping began in California in 1912, when two independent grocers (Alpha Beta Food Market in Pomona and Ward's Grocetaria in Ocean Park) began to operate a self-service system in order to reduce staffing costs. Shortly afterwards the Bay Cities Mercantile Co. opened several self-service groceries known as Humpty Dumpty Stores, but all three companies (so far as is known) retained counter service for some goods.

Four years later Clarence Saunders (U.S.A.) patented a "self-serving store" that had all the features of a supermarket except for size: his patent described a turnstile entrance, self-service aisles and a layout carefully designed so that the customer had to pass in front of all the goods and then in front of a check-out before leaving. He called his stores Piggly Wiggly, and the first one opened at 79 Jefferson St., Memphis, TN, on September 6, 1916. Within a decade there were nearly 3,000 Piggly Wiggly stores across the United States and the chain is still in operation, though on a much smaller scale. Saunders had formulated the principles and basic layout of a modern supermarket, but the early Piggly Wigglies would today probably be classified as convenience stores rather than supermarkets, leaving the King Kullen food store on Long Island (1930) with a strong claim to be the first true supermarket, based on the size of its sales area.

Shopping cart

One thing missing from all these stores was the shopping cart, which did not make its appearance until 1937. Sylvan Goldman, manager of the Humpty Dumpty supermarket in Oklahoma City, realized that if his customers could carry more, they would buy more. He asked local handyman Fred Young to make a shopping basket on wheels and, on June 4, 1937, the shopping cart was born— in the form of a folding metal chair mounted on castors, with two baskets fitted to the front and the chairback serving as a handle. In case there was any doubt as to the purpose of these strange contraptions, Goldman paid people to push them around the shop filled with groceries in order to encourage his customers to do the same.

DID YOU KNOW?

● Sainsbury's supermarket in Greenwich, London, England, is the most energy-efficient in the world. Wind turbines and solar panels help to keep power consumption down to half that of a conventional supermarket of the same size

● A replica of what could be described as the first supermarket is in the Pink House Museum in Memphis, TN. The Pink House was intended as Clarence Saunders's home but, having made an initial success of his supermarket chain, he went bankrupt before he could live in the house

● In 1919 T.P. Loblaw and Justin Cork opened their first grocery store in Toronto, Ontario. They offered a wide variety of products at better prices using the self-serve policy. By 1947 Loblaw's was the largest supermarket company in Canada and third largest in North America

Despite the invention of the first mechanical calculator by Wilhelm Schickard in 1624, the slide rule remained the most common calculating aid for more than 300 years until the first commercial electronic pocket calculator was launched in 1970 by Texas Instruments in the United States.

Trade & Technology

CALCULATORS

DID YOU KNOW?

● Blaise Pascal, inventor of what for 300 years was thought to be the first mechanical calculator, was the son of the president of the local Court of Exchequer, and invented the pascaline to help his father complete his accounts. Pascal also initiated the world's first bus service, which was inaugurated in Paris in 1662

● As well as being an accomplished mathematician, John Napier was also a military inventor—for defence in the war against Spain he invented several war-machines including an armored chariot, which was effectively a primitive tank

Above Adding machines adorn the cover of *Fortune* magazine (February 1933)

The abacus (c.3000 b.c.) was the first calculating aid, and is still widely used in some parts of the world. However, evolution of the modern electronic calculator began in the 17th century when Scottish mathematician John Napier paved the way for mechanical calculating machines by inventing logarithms and by showing that multiplication and division can be performed as a series of additions and subtractions. The first tool to exploit Napier's findings was the slide rule (England, 1622), followed two years later by the first mechanical calculator, built by Wilhelm Schickard (Germany). Schickard's so-called "calculator clock" performed all four arithmetic operations, but his invention was forgotten until the discovery of his papers by German historian Franz Hammer in 1935. Shickard's papers were published in 1957 and Schickard was finally acknowledged as having built the world's first mechanical calculator, more than 300 years after that honor had been claimed for the pascaline built by Blaise Pascal (France) in 1642.

Another Frenchman, Charles Xavier Thomas de Colmar, produced the first commercially successful calculator, in 1820. This was followed by a number of desktop calculators and adding machines, but all of them were too unwieldy and too expensive to replace the convenience of the slide rule for general use—even the first all-transistor calculator (Japan, 1964) was the size of a typewriter and weighed 25 kg (55 lbs). The real breakthrough came when Jack Kilby (U.S.A.), inventor in 1958 of the first microchip, turned his attention to miniature electronic calculators as a means of exploiting his earlier invention. Together with two other engineers working for Texas Instruments, Kilby produced, in 1967, the first handheld electronic calculator. Three years later this had been made smaller, lighter and cheaper and was launched as the first commercial electronic pocket calculator, known appropriately as the Pocketronic.

c.3000 b.c. The abacus, thought to be of Babylonian origin, is the first mechanical calculating aid

1617 John Napier (Scotland) uses "Napier's Bones" to demonstrate that multiplication and division can be calculated as a series of additions and subtractions, paving the way for mechanical computation

1622 William Oughtred (England) invents the first slide rule

1624 Wilhelm Schickard (Germany) invents the first calculating machine, which he calls the "calculator-clock"

1642 Blaise Pascal (France) builds the pascaline, which for more than 300 years is thought to be the first adding machine

1820 Charles Xavier Thomas de Colmar (France) produces the first commercially successful calculator, the Thomas de Colmar Arithmometer

TIMELINE

Above A 1914 example of the first key-driven adding machine, the Comptometer, invented in 1885

Right The first handheld electronic calculator, built by Texas Instruments in 1967

A machine that performs only mathematical operations may seem to be the poor relation of the computer, but in fact this "dedicated functionality" (as well as small size and low cost) is what makes calculators such useful tools in their own right. One professor at the Massachusetts Institute of Technology pointed out in 1990 that "the calculator is as necessary in class as pen and paper." Another put it even more simply: "Calculators revolutionized calculating."

| **1885** Dorr Eugene Felt (U.S.A.) produces the comptometer, the first key-driven adding machine, patented late the following year | **1930** Vannevar Bush (U.S.A.) produces the first electromechanical calculator | **1964** Sharp Corporation (Japan) launches the first all-transistor desktop calculator, the CS-10A Compet | **1967** Jack Kilby, Jerry Merryman and James van Tassel (all U.S.A.), working for Texas Instruments, produce the first handheld electronic calculator | **1970** Texas Intruments (U.S.A.) in conjunction with Canon Inc. (Japan) launches Pocketronic, the first electronic pocket calculator | **1974** Hewlett-Packard (U.S.A.) produces the HP-65A, the first programmable handheld calculator |

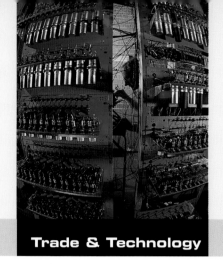

Trade & Technology

What is a computer? It is a vexed question, but two key factors are crucial to the modern definition: it must be programmable, and it must have stored memory. The first machine to fulfill both these criteria was first run at Manchester University in England on June 21, 1948.

COMPUTERS

DID YOU KNOW?

● The term debugging was coined after a problem with Harvard's Mk-1 computer was found to have been caused by a moth in the works

● Babbage's Analytical Engine (1835) failed to achieve the status of first programmable computer because it was not built—but it was the first computer to appear on a stamp

● The modern programming language ADA is named after mathematician Ada, Countess of Lovelace, daughter of Lord Byron and the world's first computer programmer; for several years the Microsoft certificate of authenticity was watermarked with an image of the countess

Above A technician enters data into Baby, the first stored-program computer
Below A Jacquard loom in operation

The computer was not a single invention; it evolved over a period of time. This makes it difficult to define the first, because many of the developments along the way were hailed as "the first computer." Charles Babbage (England) is considered to be the grandfather of computing, having designed the first programmable computer, the Analytical Engine, as early as 1835. Scientists consider that Babbage's engine, if built, would have been capable of performing the same tasks as early electronic digital computers, but the inadequacies of Victorian manufacturing techniques meant that it was not built. However, 20 years later George Scheutz (Sweden) built a simplified version, which he exhibited at the Paris Exposition of 1855.

Digital computers function using electronic switching to indicate 1 or 0 (on or off) in binary code. Konrad Zuse (Germany) pioneered this principle in his Z-1 computer of 1931 (although he used electromechanical relays rather than electronic switching), and some historians claim this to be the first programmable digital computer (Babbage's Analytical Engine was analog). However, Zuse's machine did not have stored memory, so the claim is disputed.

In 1939 John Atanasoff and Clifford Berry (both U.S.A.) produced the ABC computer, the first fully electronic digital computer. This machine was not patented and, from 1943 to 1946, John Mauchly and Presper Eckert (both U.S.A) developed it to produce ENIAC, the Electronic Number Integrator Analyser and Computer. Often claimed as the first programmable electronic computer, it had in fact been beaten to that title by Colossus (1943), which was developed in Britain and used at Bletchley Park during World War Two to decode German transmissions, but kept secret until 1976.

Memory

Although both these machines were programmable, neither of them had stored memory, which remained the holy grail of computing. The grail was found by Professor Freddie Williams (England), who discovered that cathode ray tubes could be used to provide electrostatic random access memory. He developed the Williams tube and, with Tom Kilburn, produced Baby, the world's first stored-program computer, which had 1,024 bytes of RAM. On June 21, 1948, Baby was programmed to find the highest factor of 218, and projected the correct answer onto a cathode ray tube. With that 17-instruction program, the first true computer was born.

Above The first laptop computer, the TRS-80 Model 100, launched in 1983 (available with 8 K or 24 K of memory, expandable to 32 K)
Right The world's first computer programmer, Ada, Countess of Lovelace (1815–52)

TIMELINE

1804 Joseph-Marie Jacquard (France) develops the first punched card control system (patent granted 1805), and the Jacquard Loom becomes the first programmable machine

1835 Charles Babbage (England) designs the Analytical Engine, the first programmable computer, but it is not built. The Countess of Lovelace (England) devises a program for it, thereby becoming the first computer programmer

1855 George Scheutz (Sweden) builds the first practical programmable computer, using a simplified form of the principles outlined by Babbage

1884 Dr. Hermann Hollerith (U.S.A.) patents the Hollerith Tabulator, the first machine designed for processing data (patents granted 1889)

1931 Konrad Zuse (Germany) produces the Z-1 computer, the first machine to use the presence or absence of electric charge to represent binary code

1939 Professor John Atanasoff and Clifford Berry (both U.S.A.) produce the first fully electronic digital computer

1943 The Colossus, formulated by Professor Max Newman and Alan Turing, and built by Thomas Flowers (all U.K.), becomes the first programmable electronic computer

1948 Professors Freddie Williams and Tom Kilburn (both England) build the first operational stored-program computer

1950 The Univac 1 (Universal Automatic Computer) becomes the first commercially manufactured computer, marketed by Remington Rand Inc. (U.S.A.)

1958 Jack Kilby, working for Texas Instruments (both U.S.A.), builds the first integrated circuit, or microchip (patent filed 1959, granted 1964)

1964 Douglas Engelbart (U.S.A.) produces the first computer mouse (patent filed 1967, granted 1970)

1983 Tandy Corporation (Radio Shack) launches the first laptop computer

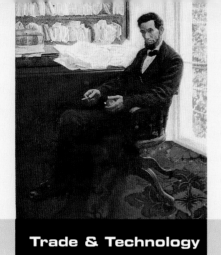

The first known patent for invention was granted to an Italian, Filippo Brunelleschi, in 1421, but the origins of trademarks are older. The first Trade Marks Registry was established in 1876 (in England), when the red triangle of the Bass brewery became the first registered trademark.

Trade & Technology

PATENTS AND TRADEMARKS

Patents

Modern patents are derived from Letters Patent, meaning open letters (the word patent comes from the Latin *patens*, meaning lying open). These public letters were first issued during the 15th century by the Italian city-states and, in England, by King Henry VI, granting the holder certain rights of monopoly. The first known patent for invention was granted by the city of Florence to architect, goldsmith and sculptor Filippo Brunelleschi (properly Filippo di Ser Brunellesco), for a method of conveying goods up the Arno River, allowing Brunelleschi to exclude all new means of transport on the river for a three-year period.

In England, Henry VI was concerned that his subjects were developing arms and technology without his knowledge, and agreed that if they disclosed their ideas to him the Crown would protect their interests. The first English patent for invention was granted to Flemish-born John of Utynam in 1449, allowing him a 20-year monopoly for making stained glass by a method that was new to England. He then used this glass to make windows for Eton College.

Trademarks

Some historians trace the roots of trademarks to the branding of cattle (which gave its name to the 20th-century phenomenon of product branding), but cattle-branding was an indication of ownership not manufacture. The first trademarks were the stamps and symbols used by ancient cultures, including the Egyptians, Greeks, Romans and Chinese, to indicate who had made goods such as pottery or bricks. Medieval European trade guilds extended this use to other products, and the Bakers' Marking Law of 1266 (England) is one of the earliest known pieces of legislation governing the use of trademarks.

1421 The first known patent for invention is granted by the city of Florence, Italy, to Filippo Brunelleschi (Italy)

1449 English King Henry VI grants the first English patent for invention to Flemish-born John of Utynam for a method of making stained glass

1641 The first patent law in the American Colonies is passed by the Massachusetts Bay Colony General Court, but applies only within the Colony. The first patent under this law is granted to Samuel Winslow (U.S.A.), for a process of manufacturing salt

1790 The first federal patent and copyright laws are passed in the United States. Samuel Hopkins, of Vermont, receives the first patent issued under this law for an improvement "in the making Pot ash and Pearl ash by a new Apparatus and Process" [sic]

1809 Mary Kies (U.S.A) becomes the first woman to be granted a patent in the United States

TIMELINE

Despite this early legislation, it was only during the 19th century that trademarks came to be seen not simply as a mark of origin but as the badge or signature of a particular trader, and therefore worth protecting. This led to the establishment of the world's first Trade Marks Registry, in London, England, in 1876, where on January 1 the red triangle of the Bass brewery became the first registered trademark.

Patents, trademarks and copyright exist to protect producers and consumers alike from fraudulent copies. Infringements are a form of flattery but, as intellectual property lawyer Richard Penfold (England) points out, "Flattery gets you nowhere—provided, of course, that a country has adequate copyright protection laws."

Opposite Abraham Lincoln in his office at the White House in 1865, by illustrator and writer Howard Pyle
Above *A Bar at the Folies-Bergère* by Edouard Manet (1882), showing the world's first registered trademark, the red triangle of the Bass brewery, on the bottles at either side of the bar

1876 The world's first Trade Marks Registry opens, in London, England. The red triangle of the Bass brewery is the first registered trademark

1893 Nancy Green (U.S.A.) becomes the first living trademark (as Aunt Jemima, cooking pancakes for the Aunt Jemima Mills Co.)

1927 Reginald Fessenden (Canada) becomes the first to patent the television

1940 Norman Breakey (Canada) becomes the first to patent the paint roller

1978 The first applications are received for European patents under the new European Patent Convention

1980 The first European Patent, EP 0000001, is granted to Klaus Adolf Busse (Germany), for a thermal heat pump

Hoover has become more than just a generic term for vacuum cleaners, it is also a verb defined in the *Oxford English Dictionary*. But William Henry Hoover did not invent the vacuum cleaner—the first "suction cleaning device" was the brainchild of Hubert Cecil Booth in 1901.

VACUUM CLEANERS

James Dyson (England) is scathing about the invention of the vacuum cleaner, describing it as "a fairly silly idea cooked up in response to a really silly one." The really silly idea was an American cleaner that used compressed air to blow the dust out of upholstery and carpets, but the idea cooked up in response revolutionized cleaning. English bridge engineer Hubert Cecil Booth saw the American machine in 1901 and suggested that it would be better to suck up the dust rather than blowing it away, an idea that he demonstrated by placing his handkerchief over a chair and sucking hard —the dirt covering the handkerchief showed that his idea worked.

On August 30, 1901 Booth patented the world's first vacuum cleaner. The motor and pump were so big that they were mounted on a horse-drawn carriage, and the vacuum cleaner itself remained in the street while hoses up to 244 m (800 ft.) long reached into the house that was to be cleaned—Booth later introduced clear tubes so that clients could watch the dirt being sucked out of their houses. Success was assured when Booth cleaned the carpets of Westminster Abbey for the coronation of Edward VII in 1902—the king was so impressed with the results that he ordered two vacuum cleaners, one for Buckingham Palace and one for Windsor Castle.

The first domestic vacuum cleaner was produced by Chapman and Skinner (both U.S.A.) in San Francisco in 1905, but it was William Henry Hoover who made vacuum cleaners a part of everyday life. Hoover was married to the cousin of an asthmatic janitor, James Murray Spangler (U.S.A.), who had made a homemade vacuum cleaner from a

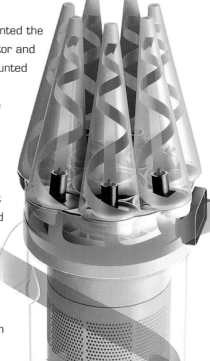

Opposite below Illustration of the principle behind Dyson Root⁸ Cyclone technology

Below Hoover's new vacuum cleaner shows its versatility (1940)

Right The Aspirator, "the Doom of the Duster, the Brush and the Broom" (1903)

THE **ASPIRATOR**

The DOOM of the DUSTER the BRUSH and the BROOM

THE ASPIRATOR

CLEANS EVERYTHING BY AIR SUCTION

APPLY-THE INTERNATIONAL ASPIRATOR COMPANY Ltd 353ª OXFORD ST. LONDON. W.

broom handle, a rotating brush, an electric fan and a pillowcase.

This was the first upright vacuum cleaner, and Hoover immediately spotted the potential, buying the rights in 1908 and marketing his machine the same year.

The shape changed, but the mechanics of vacuum cleaners remained basically the same until 1993, when James Dyson, having identified the least efficient part of the machine and dispensed with it, produced the first cyclonic vacuum cleaner. In his words, "I became determined to come up with a vacuum cleaner with a performance that did not stand or fall by the properties of a paper bag."

DID YOU KNOW?

● The prototype iron lung, produced in 1927, was made up of, among other things, two old vacuum cleaners

● Australian feminist author Germaine Greer once said that, "I didn't fight to get women out from behind the vacuum cleaner to get them onto the board of Hoover"

HOOVER

Washing machines were invented as labor-saving devices, but emptying them is now seen as a chore in itself. The first commercially produced dishwasher was invented by Josephine Cochran in 1885, and the first electric clothes-washing machine by Alva J. Fisher in 1907.

WASHING MACHINES

Below Advertisement for an early dishwasher

Opposite *Thor*, the first electric washing machine (1907)

Josephine Cochran's name is recorded with various spellings, which is said to be because she had social aspirations and was looking for a more refined way of spelling her surname. For the same reason she detested washing her own dishes, but she was equally annoyed when her servants chipped her dinner service, and so she set about inventing a dishwashing machine. She was not alone. Some 30 other American women patented mechanical dishwashers in the last 30 years of the 19th century, but Cochran's was the most successful and the first to be manufactured commercially. Domestic models used a hand pump, while the larger, steam-powered models sold to hotels and restaurants were reported as "washing, scalding, rinsing and drying from 5 to 20 dozen dishes of all shapes and sizes in two minutes."

Clothes-washing machines developed during the 19th century as mechanical versions of the age-old practice of pounding, stirring and wringing. The first electric washing machine was the *Thor*, designed by Alva J. Fisher (U.S.A.) and manufactured by the Hurley Machine Corporation in 1907—the same year that the Henkel company (Germany) produced the first washing powder, named *Persil* from its active ingredients *per*borate and *sil*icate. Fisher's machine pioneered the idea of a perforated drum within a water tub (still the basis of modern washing machines), and perpetuated the old idea that the clothes should be rotated first one way and then the other to avoid them tangling up into a mass.

But despite the advent of electric clothes-washing machines, the laundry still had to be carried to the machine, sorted, loaded, unloaded, folded, dried and ironed. It was a long way from the brave new world of the early *Persil* advertisements, which sold washing powder with the slogan: "Don't *wash* them ... *watch* them."

1885 Josephine Cochran (U.S.A.) files a patent for the first commercially produced dishwashing machine

TIMELINE

1907 The Hurley Machine Corporation (U.S.A.) markets the first electric clothes-washing machine, designed by Alva J. Fisher (U.S.A.) and known as the *Thor* (patented 1909). The Henkel company (Germany) produces *Persil*, the first washing powder

1924 The Savage Arms Corporation of New York manufactures the first domestic spin-dryer

1934 The *Washeteria* in Fort Worth, Texas opens as the first launderette equipped with electric machines

1982 Procter & Gamble (U.S.A.) introduces *Vizir*, the first clothes-washing liquid

In 1879, nearly 80 years after Sir Humphry Davy discovered the principle of incandescent light, Sir Joseph Swan demonstrated the first practical light bulb; less than a year later Thomas Edison demonstrated another one, leading to debate over who had actually invented the light bulb.

Trade & Technology # ELECTRIC LIGHT

Top Advertisement for Osram light bulbs
Above Satellite image showing the concentration of lights on earth at night. Urban areas emit artificial light, while the orange band across central Africa is from agricultural fires
Opposite First demonstration of electric street lighting, at the Place de la Concorde, Paris (1841)

Sir Humphry Davy made two far-reaching discoveries in the field of electric light, demonstrating incandescent light in 1801 and producing the world's first arc light in 1807. He took neither of these discoveries beyond the experimental stage, and it was more than 30 years before Messrs Deleuil and Archereau (both France) installed arc lighting in Le Quai Conti and La Place de la Concorde in Paris, France, making the capital the first place to be lit with electric street lighting.

Arc lights were not suitable for domestic lighting, so inventors began searching for a practical form of incandescent light (created by passing electricity through a filament until the filament glows brightly). James Bowman Lindsay (Scotland) produced the first experimental light bulb in 1835, after which some 17 inventors produced experimental bulbs before Joseph Swan (England) gave a public demonstration of the world's first practical incandescent light bulb on January 18, 1879, during a lecture in Sunderland, England. Meanwhile, in the United States, Thomas Edison had also been investigating the light bulb, and successfully tested Model No. 9 in his laboratory on October 21, 1879, 10 months after Swan's demonstration. Edison produced the first commercially viable light bulb in

TIMELINE

DID YOU KNOW?

• Thomas Edison was known as "the father of invention," having filed 1,093 patents during his lifetime. It was he who made the comment, "Genius is 1 percent inspiration and 99 percent perspiration."

• The Blackpool Illuminations, first lit on 18 September 1879, were the world's first seaside illuminations. The first electric advertising in Piccadilly Circus, London, England, was installed in 1890, and the first on Broadway, New York, USA, the following year. The world's first neon sign read *Le Palace Coiffeur*, and appeared above a barber's shop at 14, Boulevard Montmartre, Paris, France, in 1912, while the first neon advertisement read *Cinzano*, and appeared in Paris the same year

• Australia's first permanent installation of electric lights was, ironically, at the Apollo Stearine Candle Company in Victoria (1877)

1880, a few months before Swan, and shortly afterwards the two began legal proceedings against each other for breach of patent. However, they settled out of court and, in 1883, joined forces to form the Edison & Swan United Electric Co.

Later developments included electrical discharge lamps, in which electricity is discharged through a gas rather than a filament; these include the mercury vapor tube (England, 1901), the neon tube (France, 1910) and the fluorescent tube (U.S.A., 1930s).

Inventions and sales of electric lighting in the United States did not take long to cross the border into Canada. Electric streetlights were first used in Toronto in 1883. One of the most important companies to provide electric lighting in Canada was the Royal Electric Company, who brought lights to the streets of Montreal in 1886 with arc lamps; in 1888 the company began using incandescent lamps. The Royal Electric Company remained busy setting up 70 electric stations across Canada to supply arc lamps, and another 145 stations to supply incandescent lamps. Electric lighting arrived in Ottawa in 1885, Regina and Calgary in 1890 and Edmonton in 1891.

1801 Sir Humphry Davy (England) demonstrates the first electric incandescent light, by passing electricity through a strip of platinum

1807 Davy discovers the phenomenon of the electric arc and produces an experimental arc lamp

1835 *The Dundee Advertiser* describes the invention by James Bowman Lindsay (Scotland) of what appears to be an incandescent lamp powered by galvanic cells (effectively a battery-powered light bulb). It is the first experimental light bulb but it is not developed further

1841 Le Quai Conti and La Place de la Concorde, Paris, France, become the first places lit with electric street lighting

1857 Messrs Lacassagne and Thiers (both France) install electric lighting on La Rue Impériale in Lyons, France, the first street to be lit by a permanent electrical installation

1860 Sir Joseph Swan (England) patents an experimental incandescent light bulb

1879 JANUARY, Swan demonstrates the world's first practicable light bulb. OCTOBER, Thomas Alva Edison (U.S.A.) tests a light bulb that subsequently he patents on November 1

1880 OCTOBER, Edison begins commercial production of light bulbs. NOVEMBER, Swan patents an improved version of his light bulb, and begins commercial production early in 1881

1901 The Cooper-Hewitt Co. (England) produces the first electrical discharge lamp—the mercury vapor tube

1910 Georges Claude (France) produces the first neon tube George Elmer Inman (U.S.A.) patents the fluorescent tube, demonstrated by General Electric Co. (U.S.A.) in 1935

1963 Under the company name Crestworth (now Mathmos), Craven Walker (England, b. Singapore) produces the first "Lava-lamp" model, the Astro

Although not a particularly tall building by today's standards, the Home Insurance Building in Chicago, IL, had the distinction of being the world's first skyscraper. Only 10 stories high when completed in 1885, it had grown to 12 stories by the time it was demolished in 1931.

SKYSCRAPERS

The Home Insurance Building, designed by William Le Baron Jenney (U.S.A.), was the first building to be erected using skeleton construction, whereby the weight of the building is transferred to the ground not by load-bearing walls but by an internal frame that supports the building much as the skeleton of a mammal supports its body. The walls of such buildings transmit no load and are known as curtain walls because of the way they hang from the frame. Although at 10 stories the Home Insurance Building was extremely tall for its time, it is the type of construction rather than its height that earns it the accolade of first skyscraper.

Other engineers had experimented with the use of iron in building construction, including James Bogardus (U.S.A.), who is often regarded as the father of the skyscraper for the use of cast-iron columns and girders in his five-story Cast Iron building in New York City (1848). However, it was Jenney's first use of steel girders (being much stronger than iron), together with the skeleton frame and the curtain wall, which allowed him to build much higher than others had done. Jenney's ideas were developed by the "Chicago School" of architects, which included William Holabird and Martin Roche (both U.S.A.), whose Tacoma building (1887–8) was the first to have an all-steel skeleton (Jenney had used iron as well as steel); and Daniel Burnham and John Root (both U.S.A.), architects of New York's famous Flatiron Building (1902). The Flatiron Building (officially the Fuller Building) is often incorrectly cited as New York's first skyscraper but in fact that honor goes to the 12-story Tower Building (1889) on Broadway.

New York's 31-story Park Row Building was completed in 1899, the same year that William Archer wrote in *America Today*: "This is the first sensation of life in New York—you feel that the Americans have practically added a new dimension to space. When they find themselves a little crowded, they simply tilt a street on end and call it a skyscraper."

DID YOU KNOW?

● New York City has a greater number of skyscrapers (defined as a habitable building of over 152 m (500 ft.) than any other city in the world—more than twice as many as Chicago, which has the second most

● The upper part of New York's Empire State Building was intended as a mooring mast for airships, although it was never actually used for this purpose

● The Council on Tall Buildings and Urban Habitat has accepted the Petronas Towers in Malaysia as the world's tallest building despite controversy over the fact that its official height of 452 m (1,482 ft.) includes the spires, which are normally excluded from such measurements. Sears Tower in Chicago remains the building with the greatest number of stories (110), the highest occupied story, and the longest elevator ride—if its spire is included, it is also taller than the Petronas Towers, at 520 m (1,706 ft.)

● The prow of the Flatiron Building is reputedly the windiest corner in New York and, during the 1900s, peeping-toms would wait there for the wind to reveal a glimpse of flesh or stocking—in 1905 the building was even the subject of a racy docudrama entitled *The Flatiron Building on a Windy Day*

Opposite top The Home Insurance Building, Chicago, IL
Opposite below The first of the twin towers of the World Trade Center in New York under construction in the early 1970s
Right The tops of the twin Petronas Towers, Kuala Lumpur, Malaysia

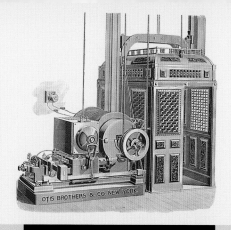

Trade & Technology

ELEVATORS AND ESCALATORS

Elisha Graves Otis is sometimes mistakenly credited as being the inventor of the elevator in 1852, but in fact the world's first passenger elevator was installed a century earlier for French King Louis XV at the Palace of Versailles, France, in 1743—what Otis invented was the safety elevator.

Above An Otis electrical elevator (c.1890)
Below Elevators and escalators give a modern slant to the board game Snakes and Ladders
Opposite The first hydraulic elevator, designed by Léon Edoux in1867

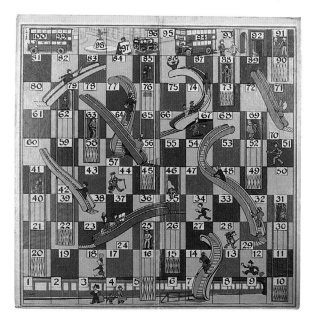

Elevators

Louis XV's "Flying Chair" gave him access to the rooms of his mistress on the floor above his own private apartments, using a system of counterweights to carry the king up the outside of the palace from his own balcony on the first floor to that of Madame de Châteauroux on the second. Eighty-six years later William George Horner (England) installed the world's first public elevator at the Regent's Park Coliseum in London. An 1835 visitors' guide commented: "Those that wish to ascend ... without the trouble of walking up stairs may, by paying sixpence, ascend by the moving apartment."

But elevators did not become part of everyday life until Elisha Otis (USA) brought them to the fore with a dramatic demonstration at New York's Crystal Palace in 1854. Otis stood in an elevator high above the crowd and called for the rope to be cut with an axe. The rope was cut—and nothing happened. It was the perfect demonstration of the safety lift that he had invented two years earlier, incorporating ratchets that locked into the guide frame in the event of any sudden downward movement. By the end of the decade elevators had been fitted in New York department stores and hotels, but the real impact of Otis's safety elevator (and the developments that followed) was that it allowed architects to build higher, making skyscrapers a workable proposition.

Escalators

The Otis Elevator Co. also played a significant role in the development of the escalator—indeed, the word escalator was originally a registered trademark of the company. In 1892 Jesse Reno and Charles A. Wheeler (both U.S.A.) filed separate patents for what are now known as escalators. Reno's inclined elevator was more like a sloping conveyor belt than a moving staircase, and the first one was installed in 1896 as a novelty ride at New York's Coney Island. Wheeler's design was improved by Charles D. Seeberger (U.S.A.), built by Otis in 1899 and exhibited in Paris in 1900. Two decades later, in 1921, Otis produced a moving staircase incorporating the best features of the Reno and Wheeler/Seeberger models, and the fundamental design of escalators has remained the same ever since.

TIMELINE

1743 The world's first passenger elevator is installed at the Palace of Versailles, France

1829 William George Horner (England) installs the world's first public elevator at the Regent's Park Coliseum, London, England

1852 Elisha Graves Otis (U.S.A.) builds the first safety elevator

1857 The first elevator in a department store goes into operation on March 23 at Haughwout & Co. on Broadway, New York, NY

1859 The first elevator in a hotel goes into operation on August 23 at the Fifth Avenue Hotel in New York, NY

1867 The first hydraulic elevator, designed by Léon Edoux (France), is used at the Paris Exposition, France, and later installed in the Eiffel Tower

1880 The first electric passenger elevators, manufactured by Siemens & Halske (Germany), are installed in the observation tower of the Mannheim Industrial Exhibition, Germany

1896 The first inclined elevator (acknowledged to be the first escalator, although it was not known by that name) is installed at the Old Iron Pier on Coney Island, NY

1898 Britain's first inclined elevator (escalator) is installed at Harrods department store in London, where customers are offered brandy or smelling salts when they reach the top

1899 The world's first moving staircase goes into operation at the factory of the Otis Elevator Co. in New York; the design is registered as the "Escalator"

1900 The first public moving staircase goes into operation at the Paris World's Fair in France, and is later installed at Gimbel's Department Store on 8th Street, Philadelphia, PA

1950 The first elevator with automatic doors is installed by Otis, at the Atlantic Refining building in Dallas, TX

1956 U.S. company Westinghouse produces the first talking elevator

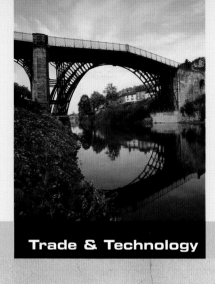

Trade & Technology

BRIDGES

Man's first bridges were prehistoric—beam bridges made from tree trunks and suspension bridges made from vines and creepers. The first written record of an individual bridge did not come until c.600 b.c., when Greek historian Herodotus described a bridge across the Euphrates.

Top Iron Bridge, Coalbrookdale, England, the first bridge made wholly of iron (1779–81)
Above Bird's-eye view of the Brooklyn Bridge, New York, NY, the world's first steel-wire suspension bridge (completed 1883)

There are five basic types of bridge, all of which began in antiquity. *Girder bridges* consist of beams or girders resting on piers, or pillars. These developed from the simple tree trunk laid across a stream to the iron, steel and concrete girder bridges developed from the 19th century onward. The first iron box-girder bridge was the Britannia Bridge in Wales (1850); one of the first steel box-girder bridges was the Elbe Bridge in Germany, completed in 1936, and the first match-cast concrete box-girder bridge was the Shelton Road Bridge, Connecticut (1952).

The first *suspension bridges* were simply vines or creepers tied across a river. The first written record of a chain-link suspension bridge dates from a.d. 630, and the first wire suspension bridge was the Wheeling Bridge, a

| **c.600 b.c.** Greek historian Herodotus provides the first written record of a bridge (a 600 ft. wooden beam bridge supported by stone pillars, spanning the Euphrates) | **a.d. 399** Chinese monk Fa Hsien provides the first written record of a suspension bridge (a footbridge across the River Indus) | **a.d. 630** Buddhist scholar Hsuan-Tsang provides the first written record of an iron chain-link suspension bridge, also across the Indus | **c.1218** The Twärenbrück, or Transverse Bridge, a chain-link bridge spanning the Schöllen Canyon in what is now Switzerland, becomes the first suspension bridge in the Western world | **1507** Pont Nôtre-Dame becomes the first stone bridge in Paris, France | **1727** Ralph Wood (England) builds the world's first railway bridge, known as the Causey Arch, near Tanfield, County Durham, England |

▎TIMELINE

300 m (985 ft.) iron-wire bridge in Ohio (1848). The longest marine span bridge in the world is Confederation Bridge, linking P.E.I. and New Brunswick. It measures 13 km (8 miles) long and was built with a curve to eliminate the hypnotic effect of a straight bridge.

The *arch bridge* is one of the most common types of bridge, and was widely used by the Romans for both bridges and aqueducts. The first all-iron arch bridge was the Iron Bridge in Shropshire, England (1781); the first steel truss-arch bridge was the St. Louis Bridge in Missouri (1874), and the first reinforced concrete arch bridge was the Stauffacher in Switzerland (1898–9).

Cantilever bridges, as the name implies, rely on the cantilever principle whereby an architectural projection is supported at one end only. In the case

The Britannia Tubular Bridge, Menai Strait, Wales. (Original oil painting, undated, for London Midland and Scottish Railway poster by Norman Wilkinson)

| **1755** The first bridge to incorporate iron girders is an arch bridge built across the Rhône River by M. Garvin (France), with one arch of iron and two of wood | **1779–81** The world's first wholly iron bridge (called Iron Bridge), designed by Thomas Pritchard and built by Abraham Darby (both England), is built across the Severn River at Coalbrookdale, England | **1801** The world's first rigid suspension bridge is built across Jacob's Creek, Pennsylvania, by James Finlay (U.S.A.) | **1804** A bridge over the Tank Stream in Sydney becomes Australia's first stone bridge | **1846–8** Charles Ellet (U.S.A.) builds the first wire suspension bridge, the Wheeling Bridge in Ohio. (The bridge collapsed in 1854 and was rebuilt by Ellet, reopening in 1860) |

Sydney Harbour Bridge, Australia

of bridges, a girder or truss bridges the span between cantilevers on each side of an obstacle. Cantilever bridges were known in ancient China but it was the advent of steel that allowed for cantilever bridges of significant length. The first steel truss cantilever bridge was the Fraser River Bridge in Canada (1886).

Another class of bridges is *movable bridges*, which work on many principles and include the drawbridge, swing bridge and vertical lift bridge. The drawbridge is an early type of bascule bridge, from the French word for seesaw, of which the most famous is Tower Bridge in London.

1850 Robert Stephenson (England) builds the first box-girder bridge, the Britannia Rail Bridge spanning the Menai Strait in Wales	**1866** M. Joret (France) builds the first steel bridge	**1869** Sir John Fowler (England) builds the first concrete bridge (temporary structure)	**1874** James Eades (U.S.A.) builds the first steel truss-arch bridge, the St. Louis Bridge over the Mississippi River in Missouri	**1877** The first permanent concrete bridge is built (at Seaton in Devon, England)	**1883** The Brooklyn Bridge in New York, NY is completed to become the world's first steel-wire suspension bridge. It was designed by John Roebling (U.S.A.) before his death in 1869 and completed by his wife, Emily, and son Washington Roebling

Gateshead Millennium Bridge

The Gateshead Millennium Bridge,
England, the world's first tilting bridge
(completed 2001)

DID YOU KNOW?

● The span of the Humber Bridge in England is so great that the towers are 36 mm (1.5 in) farther apart at the top than at the bottom to allow for the curvature of the earth

● The Sydney Harbour Bridge (1932) is based on the design of New York's Hell Gate Bridge (1916), which was the world's first "1,000 ft." steel arch bridge

● The cables of a modern suspension bridge are spun from thousands of strands of steel wire just a few millimeters thick

● San Francisco's Golden Gate Bridge has always been painted orange vermilion—or International Orange—because it blends in with the natural surroundings

1886 The Fraser River Bridge in British Columbia is completed to become the first steel-truss cantilever bridge

1898 Robert Maillart (Switzerland) builds the first reinforced concrete bridge, the Stauffacher arch spanning the Sihl River in Zürich, Switzerland

1952 Jean Muller (France) builds the Shelton Road Bridge, Con., the first match-cast concrete box-girder bridge

1955 Stormstrund Bridge in Norway is completed to become the first cable-stay bridge

2001 The Gateshead Millennium Bridge (England), designed by Wilkinson Eyre Architects, opens as the world's first tilting bridge

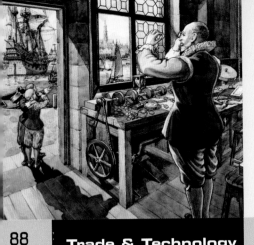

In 1590 eyeglass maker Hans Janssen put a lens at each end of a tube and called it a microscope, but he could find little use for it. Eighteen years later Janssen's townsman Hans Lippershey called the same arrangement a telescope and inspired Galileo's astronomical discoveries.

MICROSCOPES AND TELESCOPES

Microscopes

Hans Janssen was born in Middleburg (Netherlands, now part of Germany). With his son Zacharias, he created the first microscope in 1590, but at first no one, including Janssen, could see a use for it. It was treated as a novelty, and was not taken seriously as a scientific instrument until after the publication of *Micrographia* in 1665 by Robert Hooke (England), detailing his microscopic investigations into several branches of science. The book was praised by diarist Samuel Pepys (England) as "the most ingenious book I have ever read in my life," but popular opinion of microscopes remained sceptical—Hooke was ridiculed by Thomas Shadwell (England) in his play *The Virtuoso* as "one who has broken his brains about the nature of maggots...but never cares for understanding mankind." However, Hooke had the last laugh when Antoni van Leeuwenhoek (Netherlands) discovered protozoa in water (1674) and bacteria in the tartar of teeth (1676), the first of many microscopic discoveries that showed a great deal of "care for understanding mankind."

Above Hans Lippershey in his workshop; one fanciful story is that his children (seen in the doorway) invented the first telescope
Right Robert Hooke's improved compound microscope (i.e., with two or more lenses)
Opposite NASA astronauts work on the Hubble Space Telescope as it orbits the earth

Telescopes

Galileo (Italy) is often credited with inventing the telescope but in fact he heard of it in 1609 as the invention of "a certain Fleming," possibly Hans Lippershey, another eyeglass maker from Middleburg. Lippershey had demonstrated the idea to the Netherlands States General in 1608 (the first official demonstration of a telescope), but it is thought that Janssen may have realized before that date that with different lenses his microscope could act as a telescope. When Galileo heard of this invention he built his own telescope, and used it to make several discoveries that led him to affirm the Copernican theory that the earth moves around the sun. But while Hooke had suffered only ridicule for his discoveries, Galileo was taken before the Inquisition and forced to publicly recant his claim that the earth was not the center of the universe—Galileo is said to have qualified his recantation by muttering under his breath, "But it does move."

1590 Eyeglass maker Hans Janssen and his son Zacharias (both Netherlands) build the first microscope

1608 Eyeglass maker Hans Lippershey (Netherlands) makes the first official demonstration of a telescope

1668 Sir Isaac Newton (England) builds the first reflecting telescope

1937 James Hillier and Albert Prebus (both Canada) invent the electron microscope

1937 Grote Reber (U.S.A.) builds the first radio telescope, based on the discoveries of Karl Jansky (U.S.A.)

1990 The Hubble Telescope is placed into orbit to become the first space telescope

THE BEST OF THE REST...

Department stores

The world's first department store was the Marble Dry Goods Store opened by Alexander Turney Stewart (U.S.A.) in 1848 on Broadway, New York. Britain's first department store was Bainbridge's of Newcastle upon Tyne, opened by Emerson Muschamp Bainbridge and William Dunn (both England) in 1838 and departmentalized in 1849. The first department store in France was Au Bon Marché, opened by M. et Mme Boucicauts in 1852—Bon Marché was also the name of Britain's first purpose-built department store, opened by James Smith in Brixton in 1877

Bar codes

The first item to be sold with a bar code was a packet of Wrigley's chewing gum, on June 26, 1974 at the Marsh Supermarket in Troy, Ohio. The bar code (originally concentric rings) had, however, been patented in 1949 by Norman Woodland and Bernard Silver (both U.S.A.). Philco bought the rights in 1962, later selling them to RCA. Meanwhile Woodland, working for IBM, developed the 12-digit Universal Product Code used in the United States (Europe has a 13-digit European Article Number) and a foolproof method of scanning the code; IBM was thus first to market with a practical bar code and scanner

Chain stores

The world's first chain store (a series of stores owned by the same company and selling the same range of goods) was W.H. Smith & Son (England), which in 1848 began selling books and other goods at all stations belonging to the London & North Western Railway, the Midland Railway and, by 1862, five other railway companies. W.H. Smith did not open any high street stores until 1905. The Great Atlantic & Pacific Tea Co. (A&P) is generally acknowledged as the first retail chain in the United States, beginning operation in 1859 as the Great American Tea Co.

Aerosols

In 1926 Erik Rotheim (Norway) patented the aerosol as a means of dispensing liquid soap, paint, insecticide and cosmetics. Paint and polish manufacturer Alf Bjerke (Norway) produced the first commercial aerosols soon afterwards in Oslo, Norway. The first aerosols to have lightweight casings and plastic valves were manufactured in 1946 by Airosol Inc. in Kansas

Nuclear reactors

The first nuclear reactor was built in a squash court at the University of Chicago and produced the first chain reaction on December 2, 1942. The first electricity to be generated by nuclear power was produced in 1951 by the Experimental Breeder Reactor in Idaho. The first nuclear power station was at Obninsk, Russia, which began generating power on June 27, 1954. It produced just 5,000 kW. The first commercial-scale nuclear power station was at Calder Hall, Cumberland, England, with a capacity of 90,000 kW; it began generating power on August 20, 1956. The first nuclear power station in Canada opened in Rolphton, Ontario in 1962

Plastic

The first plastic was patented by Alexander Parkes (England) in 1855 and shown at the International Exhibition of 1862. He described it as a "beautiful substance for the Arts" and called it Parkesine, though it was later marketed as xylonite. In 1869 John Wesley Hyatt (U.S.A.) independently invented a very similar plastic, which he called celluloid and which was a far greater commercial success. The first fully thermosetting plastic (i.e., once set it does not soften with heat) was Bakelite, invented by Hendrick Baekeland (Belgium) in 1905 and dubbed "the material of 1,000 uses"

Electric batteries

The first electric battery was made in 1800 by Alessandro Volta (Italy), from whose name the electrical unit volt is derived. He is shown below demonstrating it to the Institut Française and the consul Napoleon Bonaparte on November 18, 1800

Chapter Four

Lifestyle & Leisure

The first cigarettes were smoked in 16th-century Spain, but it was to be three centuries before anyone lit one with a match—the store records of John Walker show that the world's first purchase of friction matches was made in Stockton-on-Tees, England, on April 7, 1827.

TOBACCO AND MATCHES

Opposite top Cuban revolutionary leader Fidel Castro, famous for his love of cigars, exhales smoke from a Cuban cigar in Havana, Cuba (1977)

Opposite below A match is not enough to light this meter-long cigar in Andorra, the country in which the largest cigars are made (1946)

Right "The filter tip will keep you fit!" Du Maurier advertisement (early 1930s)

The Filter Tip will Keep you Fit!

du MAURIER
ALSO PLAIN TIP IN THE BLUE BOX
10 for 6ᴰ   20 for 1ʹ⁻

DID YOU KNOW?

● Nicotine is named after Jean Nicot (France), who in 1561 introduced tobacco to France from Portugal, where he had been the French ambassador for two years

Tobacco

Tobacco was introduced to Europe in the 16th century, where it was smoked in pipes or as cigars until beggars in Seville, Spain, took to salvaging the tobacco from cigar butts, shredding it and rolling it in paper. The habit soon spread across Europe, and moved up-market in the process as people began rolling cigarettes (meaning "little cigars") with fresh, rather than used, tobacco. The world's first cigarette factory (hand-rolling) opened in France in 1843, and a hand-rolling factory in Cuba was equipped with steam-driven machines in 1853, becoming the first factory for mass-production of cigarettes.

Matches

Matches are a more remarkable invention than they seem to 21st-century sensibilities, because their arrival marked the first time since the discovery of fire that humans had found a quick and easy way of producing it. In 1680 Robert Boyle (England) had devised a crude form of match using sulphur-coated sticks that were lit by contact with phosphorous. These were impractical because phosphorous is so volatile, and it was to be nearly 150 years before chemist John Walker (England) invented the first friction match—not for the convenience of smokers, but for use with hunting guns.

Walker reputedly made his discovery by accident. He is said to have been mixing potassium chloride and antimony sulphide when he scraped his mixing stick across some stones to clean it and it burst into flames, leaving him holding the world's first friction match. The match had ignited because the friction had generated enough heat to raise the mixture to its relatively low ignition temperature. Walker did not patent his invention, and soon many other chemists were manufacturing their own matches, improving upon Walker's recipe by adding white phosphorous. A strip of sandpaper was usually included for striking the matches, but often they would ignite accidentally simply by rubbing against each other; the solution to this problem came in 1855 with the use of the more stable red phosphorous, a decade after its discovery, which Johan Edvard Lundström (Sweden) used to make the first safety matches.

TIMELINE

16th century The cigarette is invented by beggars in Seville, Spain

1680 Robert Boyle (England) produces the first crude matches

1827 Solicitor Mr Hixon (England) purchases a box of the world's first friction matches, invented the previous year by chemist John Walker (England)

1843 The Manufacture Française des Tabacs (France) opens as the world's first commercial cigarette factory

1853 Don Luis Susini's cigarette factory in Cuba is mechanized to become the first factory to mass-produce cigarettes

1855 Johan Edvard Lundström (Sweden) invents the safety match, first manufactured the same year. The British rights are bought by Bryant & May, who produce their first safety matches, also in 1855

1865 The Erie, manufactured by the Repeating Light Co. (U.S.A.), becomes the first pocket cigarette lighter

1883 Globe Cigarettes (Britain) begin printing pictures on cigarette cards, which had been introduced by Marquis of Lorne Cigarettes (U.S.A.) in 1879

1896 The Diamond Match Co., U.S.A., produces the first book matches, patented by Joshua Pusey (U.S.A.) in 1892

1909 Count von Welsbach (Austria) produces the first wheel-action cigarette lighter

1926 Du Maurier introduces the first filter cigarette

1931 Craven A becomes the first brand of cigarettes to be sold in a cellophane-wrapped packet

1971 The first ban on cigarette advertising comes into force, applying to U.S. radio and television

1986 Pharmacia Les Therapeutics AB (Sweden) introduces Nicoret, the first nicotine chewing gum

1992 Ciba-Geigy Pharmaceuticals (Switzerland) introduces the first nicotine skin patch (patented 1990)

Since businessman King Camp Gillette's death in 1932 it has often been said that he, in particular, did more than any other person to change the face of mankind. It was Gillette who patented the safety razor.

Lifestyle & Leisure

RAZORS

DID YOU KNOW?

● King Camp Gillette was a Utopian socialist who disapproved of waste—an ironic standpoint for the man who invented disposable razor blades. In 1910 he set up the World Corporation with the aim of promoting a globally planned economy

● The same year that Gillette patented his safety razor, another American, Thomas Ferry, invented a mustache guard "designed to hold the mustache away from the lips and to prevent the lodgement of food thereon while eating." However, Ferry was not the first: Harry Jones (England) patented an almost-identical device in 1872, and some 43 British patents for mustache guards were filed before the turn of the century, including several for cups and spoons with built-in mustache guards

"Invent something that will be used once and then thrown away. Then the customer will come back for more." This was sound advice from William Painter (U.S.A.), inventor of the disposable crown cork (see p.41), to his salesman King Camp Gillette (U.S.A.). Gillette could think of nothing that would lend itself to this throwaway ideal until it came to him while shaving one morning in 1895—razors.

Men had always shaved, at first with shells or bones, later with blades, and then with steel cutthroat razors, first produced in Sheffield, England, during the 18th century. Cutthroat razors had to be sharpened regularly, and Gillette realized that disposable blades would be the perfect fulfillment of Painter's advice. Steel manufacturers told Gillette that it would be impossible to make a blade of the type he envisaged but, undeterred, he established the American Safety Razor Co. Then, together with his only employee, William Nickerson, Gillette set about devising a flat, double-sided blade and a handle/blade holder in the familiar T-shape that is still the norm for razors more than a century later.

In 1926 Gillette wrote of the safety razor that: "There is no other article for individual use so universally known or widely distributed. In my travels, I have found it in the most northern town in Norway and in the heart of the Sahara Desert." Certainly no other invention has had the same impact on shaving, including the electric shaver, which was invented by Colonel Jacob Schick (U.S.A.) after he moved to Alaska for health reasons. When he realized how unpleasant it was shaving in ice-cold water, Schick tried to devise a means of dry shaving. His first attempt was something akin to barbers' clippers and was never manufactured but he went on to produce the first successful electric shaver, manufactured in 1931 by Schick Dry Shaver Inc. (U.S.A.).

In 1956 Wilkinson Sword (England) reversed the original intention of Gillette's disposable blades by producing the first long-life steel blade for safety razors, and in 1974 Gillette took its own first principles a step further by producing the first fully disposable razor, with a plastic handle/blade holder that is thrown away along with the blade.

Top A Gillette advertisement of 1903, showing just how safe the company considered its new safety razors to be
Left The Acme Moustache Guard. This 1892 advertisement in *Judge* boasted:

"Does not interfere with free use of mouth ... Every genteel person should have one"
Opposite Poster for BIC disposable razors, by Raymond Savignac (1978)

1901 King Camp Gillette (U.S.A.) forms the American Safety Razor Co. (a name changed in 1902 to the Gillette Safety Razor Co.) and patents the first double-edged safety razor, which is also the first razor to use disposable blades

1913 G.P. Appleyard (England) patents a "power-driven shaving appliance", but is unable to manufacture it because electric motors cannot be made small enough

1931 Schick Dry Shaver Inc. (U.S.A.) manufactures the first successful electric razor

1940 Remington (U.S.A.) produces the Duchess, the first electric shaver designed specifically for women

1956 Wilkinson Sword (England) produces the first long-life stainless steel blades

1975 BIC launch the first disposable razor; Gillette follows suit less than a year later

The fashion industry exists to create new trends, but these often turn out to be variations on what has gone before. However, some garments, such as jeans, dinner jackets, bikinis and top hats, were so revolutionary that history has recorded their creators or those who first wore them.

Lifestyle & Leisure   # CLOTHING

Hats

In 1797 English clothing dealer John Hetherington was arrested for a breach of the peace and fined £50 for the disturbance caused in London when he wore his new creation, the first top hat. About half a century later, in 1849, the world's first bowler hat was ordered from Lock's hatters of London, by William Coke, to protect his head while shooting—only later did it become *de rigueur* for office workers. It is named after Thomas and William Bowler, the hatters who make it, although Lock's still refer to it as a coke, after the man who ordered it. In North America the bowler is known as a derby, after Lord Derby, who first popularized it there. In 1882 Victorien Sardou (France) published the play *Fédora*, which gave its name to a hat, and 12 years later George Du Maurier (England, b. France) published the novel *Trilby*, whose eponymous heroine, Trilby O'Ferral, gave her name to a hat. The first trilby hats were worn by the cast of the stage production of the novel, and became popular soon afterwards. In 1932 film star Greta Garbo (Sweden, properly Greta Lovisa Gustafsson) became the first woman to wear a pillbox hat, created for her by costume designer Gilbert Adrian (U.S.A.) for the film *As You Desire Me*.

Pants

In 1850 during the San Francisco Gold Rush, Levi Strauss (Germany–U.S.A.) made the first pair of jeans, out of cloth intended for tents and wagon covers. Jeans take their name from a heavy twilled cotton called gene fustian, first made in Genoa, Italy (*Gênes* is the French for Genoa). Denim, now used for making jeans, derives from a serge made in Nîmes, France, and known in French as *serge de Nîmes*. The year after Strauss's invention, Amelia Jenks Bloomer (U.S.A.) started a brief fad for baggy Turkish-style trousers, gathered at the ankle and named after her.

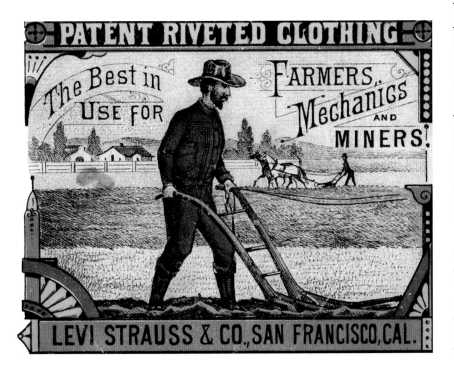

TIMELINE

1797 The first top hat is made

1849 The first bowler hat is made

1850s The first cardigan is made

1850 The first jeans are made

1851 The first bloomers are made

1865 The North British Rubber Co. (Scotland) manufactures the first rubber wellington boots (taking their name from a type of riding boot named after Arthur Wellesley, 1st Duke of Wellington [Britain])

1872 The first Alice band is worn by Alice, the heroine of Lewis Carroll's *Through the Looking Glass* (published 1872)

1873 Levi Strauss and Jacob Davis (both U.S.A.) patent the use of copper rivets at the stress points of jeans. Rivets are first used in 1874

1886 The first dinner jacket is made

1906 The first panama hat is worn by U.S. President Theodore Roosevelt during a tour of the Panama Canal

1932 The first lady's pillbox hat is made

1942 The U.S. Navy issues the specification for a new T-type undershirt, which, after the war, is worn as a shirt in its own right: the T-shirt is born

1946 The first bikini is made

1947 Orthopedic surgeon Klaus Maertens and engineer Herbert Funck (both Germany) produce the first shoes with air-cushioned soles, patented the previous year

1960 R. Griggs & Co. Ltd. (England) produces the first British-made Dr. Martens footwear (branded as AirWair and with Maertens's name anglicized)

Left Early advertisement for Levi's clothing
Opposite top Film star Greta Garbo, who in 1932 became the first woman to wear a pillbox hat, for the film *As You Desire Me*
Opposite below Marlon Brando in *The Wild One*, showing that jeans have moved on from work clothes to rebel fashion statement

Jackets

The first cardigans were military jackets worn by British soldiers during the Crimean War (1853–56) and named after James Thomas Brudenell, the 7th Earl of Cardigan (Britain), who survived the "valley of death" after being ordered to lead the infamous Charge of the Light Brigade. The first dinner jacket (modeled on a smoking jacket) was worn by Griswold Lorillard (U.S.A.), to the Autumn Ball of the Tuxedo Park Country Club in 1886. (In 21st-century France a dinner jacket is still known as *un smoking*.)

Bikini

There is evidence that the Romans wore two-piece swimsuits, but its modern use began in the United States during World War Two—textiles were in short supply so designers simply removed the midriff of the traditional one-piece. In 1946 Jacques Heim (France) created a tiny two-piece that he called the *atome*, but rival designer Louis Réard (France) upstaged him by introducing the even smaller *bikini* the same year, so-called because he said it would be as explosive as the atomic bomb tested four days earlier by the United States on Bikini Atoll in the Pacific Ocean. Dancer Micheline Bernardi (France) was the first person to wear a bikini in public, as a catwalk model for Réard's swimwear collection. Later that year Pat Riley was ordered by police to leave Bondi Beach, Sydney, when she became the first Australian woman to wear a bikini.

Above Michael Jackson sporting a military-style jacket
Right The latest fashions in swimwear, from the film *The Impossible Years* (1968)

Clothing styles may follow the dictates of fashion, but fashion is influenced by materials available. The inventors of synthetic fabrics, and of fastenings such as VELCRO® brand hook & loop, in 1941, and the zipper, in 1913, have had as much impact on style as have fashion designers themselves.

FASTENINGS AND FABRICS

Fastenings

Until the 19th century people used pins, laces, clasps, buckles or buttons to fasten their clothes. Then came the hook-and-eye (U.S.A., 1843), the snap fastener (France, 1855) and the press stud (England, 1860). Snap fasteners were often used several at a time in rows, and had to be fastened and unfastened individually—this gave Whitcomb L. Judson (U.S.A.) the idea for what he patented as a "clasp locker" (1893). Judson's invention used a sliding device to lock or unlock a row of clasps—an early form of zipper.

With Colonel Lewis Walker (U.S.A.), Judson set up a company to manufacture his fastening, and in 1913 company engineer Gideon Sundback (Canada) made the breakthrough that led to the modern zipper. Sundback's inventive leap was to use metal teeth on flexible tape with the slide fastener, an idea that was marketed as the Hookless No.2; this name was later changed, along with that of the company, to Talon.

The 20th century's other revolutionary fastening returned to the use of hooks, and reputedly came about because of a zipper that had jammed. George de Mestral (Switzerland) returned from a walk one day and noticed burrs sticking to his clothes. He examined the burrs under a microscope and discovered that they were covered with tiny hooks that had stuck to the loops in the fabric of his clothes. Remembering the jammed zipper, he sought to use the hook and loop principle to create a new, foolproof fastener—the result was VELCRO® brand hook & loop fasteners, which takes its name from the French *velours croché*, meaning hooked velvet.

Fabrics

The first synthetic fibers were used as decorative tassels and fringes, but in 1898 Charles Cross and C.H. Stearn (both England) produced viscose rayon, the first synthetic fiber that could be woven into a fabric. This artificial silk appeared in many types of garment (including, in 1910, the first synthetic stockings) but was not used on a wide scale until after World War Two, by which time DuPont (U.S.A.) had produced what it described as "the first man-made organic textile fiber wholly from new materials from the animal kingdom": nylon. The first items to be made from nylon fiber were toothbrush bristles in 1938, but the fabric woven from it soon revolutionized the hosiery industry, and before long stockings became known simply as nylons.

Above Wallace Hume Carothers, most famous for his discovery of the fiber-forming amides or nylons and in particular Nylon 6.6, which had much commercial success as a textile fiber. Despite his success, Carothers suffered from depression and, soon after his marriage, killed himself at the age of 41

DID YOU KNOW?

● The word zipper was coined by American company B.F. Goodrich, which launched a range of zipper-fastening galoshes in 1923. Legend has it that the company president said: "What we need is an action word…something that will dramatize the way the thing zips," providing himself with the answer in asking the question. Zipper Boots was registered as a trademark in 1925 but has since lost its trademark status

● Although Charles Mackintosh invented the first waterproof cloth, in 1823, he did not make the first raincoat—that honor went to François Fresnau, who made a raincoat, in 1747, by smearing an overcoat with rubber from the local trees in French Guiana

Above "These boots were made for zipping"
Below Raincoats are not always put to the uses for which they were intended

1747 François Fresnau (France) makes the first raincoat

1823 Charles Mackintosh (Scotland) patents the first waterproof cloth, made from cotton and India rubber

1883 While searching for an improved lightbulb filament, Sir Joseph Swan (England) produces the first synthetic fiber

1889 Comte Hilaire de Chardonnet (France) establishes the first factory for the production of synthetic fiber, having patented his process in 1884

1892 Charles Cross (England) patents a method of producing viscose

1898 Charles Cross and C.H. Stearn (both England) form the Viscose Spinning Syndicate and produce viscose rayon, the first synthetic fiber capable of being woven into a fabric. It is first produced commercially in 1905

1938 Nylon, developed by Wallace H. Carothers (U.S.A.) and patented in 1937, is manufactured commercially for the first time, by DuPont (U.S.A.)

1941 Polyester is produced for the first time, by Rex Whinfield and James Dickson (both England) of the Calico Printers Association, but its invention is declared a wartime secret

1946 The invention of Polyester is announced, and it is later manufactured (and branded Terylene) by ICI around the world except in the United States, where DuPont manufacture it under license as Dacron

1958 Fiber K (elastane) is produced for the first time by DuPont (U.S.A.), and in 1959 its name is changed to Lycra

1971 Kevlar (a fire-resistant synthetic fibre five times stronger than steel of the same weight), patented by Stephanie Kwolek (U.S.A.) in 1963, is manufactured commercially for the first time, by DuPont (U.S.A.)

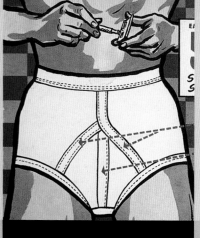

Fashion has affected underwear just as strongly as outerwear, especially at times when a particular shape has been desirable. Corsets were worn in Crete c.1800 b.c., and women were not freed from their strictures until Mary P. Jacob patented the first successful brassière in 1914.

UNDERWEAR

TIMELINE

c.1800 b.c. Minoan men and women (Crete) are known to have worn corsets

1893 Marie Tucek (U.S.A.) patents a "breast supporter" looking very much like a modern brassière. It is the first support to use shoulder straps rather than pushing up the bust from below, but the idea does not catch on

c.1906 Designer Paul Poiret (France) introduces his *soutien-gorge*, a precursor of the brassière

1910 The first stockings to be made from synthetic fiber are produced in Bamberg, Germany (from rayon)

1914 Mary Phelps Jacob (U.S.A., living in France) patents the first successful brassière and subsequently sells her patent to Warner Brothers Corset Co.

1934 Cooper Inc. (U.S.A.) produces the first Y-fronts, available to employees and launched publicly in 1935

1938 Y-fronts are manufactured under license in Britain for the first time, by Lyle & Scott

1939 The world's first nylon stockings go on sale in parts of the United States, launched nationally the following year

Above The Activity Center-Front was a variation on the Y-front theme (c.1965) **Right** "Health Braided Wire Dress Forms" **Opposite** The convenience of modern tights and bras does not stop stockings and corsets being worn on special occasions...

Bras

There is little wonder that 19th-century women had a tendency to faint, being strapped tightly into corsets that

were usually strengthened with whalebone. There were several precursors to the modern backless brassière (bra) but the move away from corsets really began in 1906, when French designer Paul Poiret popularized a more relaxed shape and claimed to have emancipated women, saying: "It was in the name of liberty that I proclaimed the fall of the corset and the adoption of the brassière ... Yes, I freed the bust." His fashions were indeed much softer-fitting but he continued to experiment with corset-like underclothes, and said that his bust-bodice, a precursor of the bra, would make the bosom "rise forth from the bodice like an enchanting testimonial to youth."

Perhaps not surprisingly, it was a woman who invented a bra that women were happy to wear. In 1913 Mary Phelps Jacob asked her maids to tie two handkerchiefs together to support her bosom, and then copied the idea for her friends. The following year she patented her brassière before selling the rights to Warner Bros Corset Co. (U.S.A.). It is ironic that during the 1960s the bra, once seen as a symbol of women's freedom from the corset, should itself have become a symbol of repression.

Y-fronts

Three years before the invention of the bra, a revolution was also taking place in men's underwear. Long johns were the norm, and in 1910 the Cooper Underwear Co., of Kenosha, WI, introduced the Kenosha Klosed-Krotch, which boasted an X-shaped flap to keep the crotch closed where previously the choice had been buttons or fresh air. In 1911 this new garment became the first item of male underwear to be advertised nationally in North America; it was an immediate success, but it was 1934 before X-fronts became Y-fronts. By then men's underwear had gone from long to knee-length to shorts, but it was a photograph of the trunks worn by a swimmer on the French Riviera that inspired Cooper in 1934 to produce the close-fitting Brief Style 1001, with its now famous inverted Y opening. Marketed under the name Jockey, Y-fronts were patented in 1935 and first sold at Marshall Field's department store in Chicago.

DID YOU KNOW?

● The Canadian-born inventor of X-flap underwear, Horace Johnson, was given the nickname Klosed Krotch Johnson

● Legend has it that when Y-fronts were manufactured under license for the first time in Britain (1938), left-handed men were advised to wear them inside-out

Sprinto non spinto. More feard than hurt.

FLUSHING TOILETS

The Minoans (Crete) had flushing toilets some 4,000 years ago, but the first modern toilet was not invented until 1589, by Sir John Harington. However, Harington's invention did not catch on, and it was another two centuries before toilets were manufactured commercially.

Above Illustration of a toilet from Sir John Harington's *The Metamorphosis of Ajax* (1596). Harington recommended that the toilet should be flushed once a day
Below A scene from the 1974 film *The Phantom of Liberty*, directed by Luis Buñuel (Spain)

Although she was Sir John Harington's godmother, Queen Elizabeth I refused to grant a patent for his invention of the flushing toilet on the grounds of propriety. Despite this refusal she did have a Harington toilet installed at Richmond Palace, but, because the idea was so far ahead of its time, the royal water closet and the one at Harington's country house in Kelston, Somerset, were the only two to be made. The problem was not so much public acceptance as the lack of a sewage system, which meant that there was nowhere for the toilet to discharge once flushed, and so it was to be nearly 200 years before flushing toilets were in common use. In 1596 Harington was banished from court for publishing a Rabelaisian satire entitled *The Metamorphosis of Ajax*, in which he described his toilet in great detail—his design was surprisingly modern, and included a cistern (which he depicted containing fish), an overflow pipe, a reservoir of water in the bowl, and a pull-up handle for flushing. In the title of Harington's controversial pamphlet, "Ajax" is a pun on "a jakes," the Elizabethan slang word for toilet.

The first patent for a flushing toilet was issued to Alexander Cumming (England) in 1775, but commercial manufacture of toilets did not begin until 1778, when cabinetmaker Joseph Bramah (England) patented an improvement on Cumming's design and started a business that was still manufacturing toilets more than a century later.

DID YOU KNOW?

● Sanitation in 17th-century London was not good. Samuel Pepys (England) records in his *Diary* that: "going down into my cellar ... I put my foot on a great heap of finds ... by which I find that Mr Turner's house of office is full and comes into my cellar, which doth trouble me"

● Queen Elizabeth I was unusually hygiene-conscious for her time, and was reported to take a bath at least once a month "whether she needed it or no"

DID YOU KNOW?

● A U.S. law requires that homes and businesses use low-flow toilets. But not all Americans are happy with the 1.6-gallon (6-liter) flush. As a result, 3.5-gallon (13-liter) toilets are sometimes smuggled across the border from Canada

NOT THE FIRST...

● The 19th-century plumber Thomas Crapper (England) was not the inventor of the flushing toilet. Neither is his name the origin of the word crap, which comes from a 15th-century word meaning chaff, itself deriving from the Old Dutch *krappe*

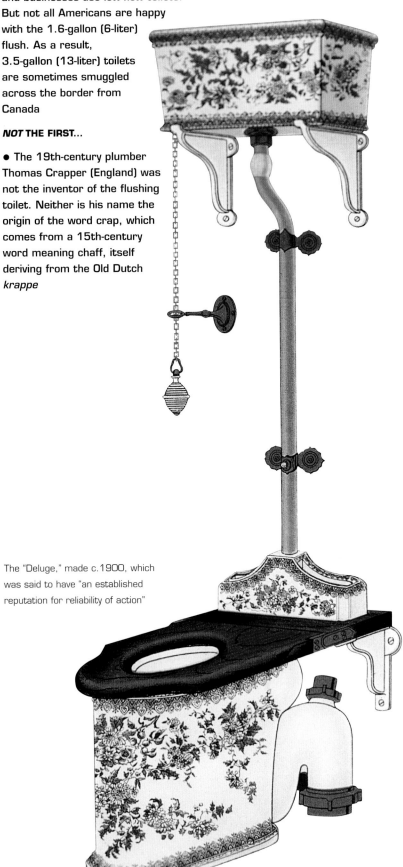

The "Deluge," made c.1900, which was said to have "an established reputation for reliability of action"

TIMELINE

c.2000 b.c. The Minoans (Crete) are the first people known to have had flushing toilets, using cisterns fed by streams, with levers to release the water

1589 Writer Sir John Harington (England) installs the first nongravity-fed flushing toilet, at his house in Kelston, Somerset

1596 Harington publishes his design for the first flushing toilet in his satire *The Metamorphosis of Ajax*

1775 The first patent for a flushing toilet is granted to Alexander Cumming (England)

1778 Joseph Bramah (England) improves Cumming's design and becomes the first manufacturer of toilets on a commercial scale. (An original Bramah is still in use in the House of Lords, England, 225 years later)

c.1811 Australia's first flushing toilet is a Bramah installed at Government House, Sydney, by Lachlan Macquarie (Scotland, Governor of New South Wales, 1811–21)

1852 The first public lavatory to contain toilets opens at 95 Fleet Street, London

1857 Joseph Cayetty (U.S.A.) invents the first toilet paper

1859 The "Old No.9" Pullman car goes into service on the Chicago & Alton Railroad (U.S.A.) as the first railway carriage to be equipped with toilets

1871 Seth Wheeler (U.S.A.) invents the first toilet paper on a roll

1883 Chester Cross (England) manufactures the first practical vacant/engaged bolt for toilet doors, patented the previous year by A. Ashwell (England)

1884 Jennings's of Brighton (England) produces the first pedestal toilet (previously the bowl had been boxed in)

1913 Sikorsky passenger plane *Russky Vitiaz* (U.S.S.R.) is the first airplane to be fitted with a toilet

1978 The world's first flushing toilets for dogs open in Paris, France

LAWN MOWERS

Until the aptly named Edwin Budding invented the lawn mower in 1830, lawns had to be kept in trim using a scythe. The first recorded sale of a lawn mower was to a Mr. Curtis, who was the Head Gardener of Regent's Park Zoo in London, in 1831.

"Gentlemen may find, in using the mower themselves, an amusing, useful and healthful exercise." This was Edwin Budding's (England) optimistic opinion of his invention but it was to be another 40 years before lawn mowers were in common use. Budding, the son of a farmer, worked in a textile mill—a combination of influences that led him to think that the rotating cutters being used to trim the nap of velvet could be adapted to cut grass. He took his idea to local businessman and manufacturer John Ferrabee, and together they developed the first lawn mower. It was a cylinder mower with a spiral blade, and looked very similar to the cylinder mowers available 170 years later.

Lawn mowers developed through horse-drawn and steam-powered models to gasoline and electric machines. The first rotary-blade lawn mowers were introduced in the 1930s, after which the next major development came in 1963 with the first hover mower. Inspired by the hovercraft (invented by Christopher Cockerell (England) and first launched in 1959), Swedish inventor Karl Dahlman used the same principle of a fan and skirt to create a mower that would hover above the grass and take the weight out of mowing. The patent specification for this revolutionary mower, known as the Flymo, described "blades shaped to give downdraft" and a fan to "produce an air cushion below the housing to support the mower clear of the ground." Dahlman had paid Cockerell the ultimate compliment of taking inspiration from the hovercraft, but it is not known whether Cockerell ever returned the compliment by using a Flymo to cut his lawn.

DID YOU KNOW?

● Early lawn mowers were often pulled along by horses or donkeys, which were often fitted with padded boots to prevent their hooves damaging the lawn

● During the 1950s single-rotating blade mowers outsold reel mowers 9 to 1 in North America

Opposite top Edwin Budding's patent lawn mower, as manufactured by John Ferrabee at the Phoenix Foundry, near Stroud, England
Opposite below A push mower being pulled by a donkey
Below German advertisement in the 1970s showing an electric rotary mower and his-and-hers garden work clothes

Package tours, caravans, holiday camps and air charters progressively brought annual holidays to the masses, but at first they were only for the lucky few. The first package holiday departed England in 1862 and the first air charter holiday took off from England for Switzerland in May 1932.

Lifestyle & Leisure # HOLIDAYS

Top Thomas Cook, "servant of the traveling public"
Above Gazing at the Mediterranean
Opposite Sunshades on the beach at Deauville, France

Thomas Cook (England) described himself as "the willing and devoted servant of the traveling public." He almost single-handedly created the travel industry, setting up one of the first tourist travel agencies and operating with few competitors for a quarter of a century after his first holiday excursion in 1845. Foreign tours followed a decade later, and in 1862 Cook made the travel arrangements for the world's first package tour; the difference from previous tours was that he advertised a complete "package deal," with one fee to cover accommodation and meals in addition to the usual fare payment.

In 1898 Cook was the coorganizer of the first coach tour but, in the meantime, another new form of holidaymaker had taken to the roads. In 1885 Dr. Gordon Stables (England) took delivery of *Wanderer*, the first caravan to be built specifically for holidaying in rather than as living accommodation. Stables traveled 1,300 miles around Britain and later wrote a book about the tour, entitled *The Cruise of the Land Yacht Wanderer*. Dr. E.E. Lehwess (Germany), owner of the first motor caravan, was equally romantic, calling his vehicle *Passe Partout* and hoping to become the first

DID YOU KNOW?

● At the end of the 19th century Thomas Cook's foreign tours were so famous that travelers to the Middle East were known to the locals not as tourists but as "Cookii"—and they were referred to disparagingly in the monthly periodical *Blackwood's Magazine* as "i Cucchi." When Cook's cheaper package tours became popular, the wealthy complained that "places of rare interest should be excluded from the gaze of common people"

man to drive around the world. He made it across Europe but sadly his plans were shattered when he had to abandon the caravan in a snowdrift in Nizhniy-Novgorod, Russia.

Thomas Cook saw travel as a means of education and edification rather than simple enjoyment, and so it was with the first holiday camp. J. Fletcher-Dodd (England) opened Dodd's Socialist Holiday Camp in 1906 with a regime of exercise and sports for the health of the body, followed by evening lectures and debates for the health of the mind. Other delights included being summoned to meals by a bugle, expulsion for talking loudly after 11 p.m. and, later, fines for untidiness.

In May 1932 the first air charter holiday took off from Croydon Airport, England, flying to Basle, Switzerland, with Imperial Airways. By the end of the year the Polytechnic Touring Association had taken nearly 1,000 tourists to Europe—without a single case of air rage being reported. Similarly, Thomas Cook reported after his early package tours to France that "not a single case of misbehavior had come under the argus eyes of one of the most vigilant police systems ever established." How things have changed.

TIMELINE

1841–45 Thomas Cook (England) organizes railway excursions to Temperance Society meetings and then, in 1845, a holiday excursion from Leicester to Liverpool and North Wales, thereby establishing the earliest surviving travel agency

1855 On Thomas Cook's first continental tour he (reluctantly) offers travelers the option to buy vouchers in advance for accommodation and meals, a precursor of the full "package deal"

1862 Thomas Cook organizes the first full "package holiday," with one ticket to cover travel, meals and accommodation

1871 Pierre Collignon (France–U.S.A.) patents the first folding deck chair

1872 George Livesey (England) of the South Metropolitan Gas Co. provides the first holidays-with-pay for manual workers. Yellowstone National Park becomes the world's first national park

1885 Banff National Park, Canada's first, is open for the public to enjoy its hot sulfur springs, ice-capped peaks, glaciers and abundant wildlife

1897 Prince Oldenburg (Russia) takes delivery from Jeantaud (France) of the first caravan designed to be motor-hauled; the two-wheel caravan is towed by a steam tractor

1898 Thomas Cook & Son (England) and the Compagnie Nationale d'Automobiles (France) jointly organize the first coach tour, which takes six days to travel through France

1902 Sir Henry Lunn organizes the first winter sports package holiday. Dr. E.E. Lehwess (Germany) takes delivery from Panhard & Levassor (France) of the first motor caravan

1919 Thomas Cook becomes the first travel agent to offer tourist trips by air

1920 Frei-Sonnenland opens at Motzener See, Germany, in 1920 as the first official nudist camp

THE BEST OF THE REST...

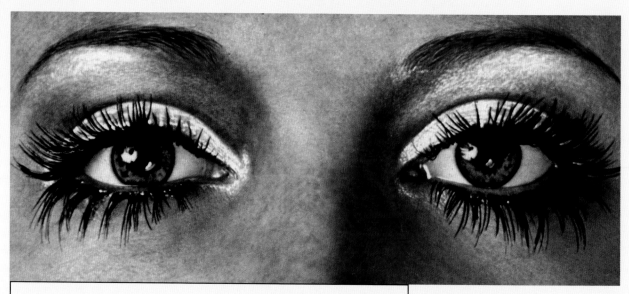

False eyelashes

False eyelashes were used for the first time in 1916, when they were worn by actress Seena Owen in D.W. Griffith's silent Hollywood epic *Intolerance*. Hollywood makeup artists David and Eric Aylott (U.S.A.) developed the first consumer false eyelashes in the late 1940s, launched as Eyelure, and Eric later went on to produce the first false fingernails

Avon calling

Avon Products, made famous by the slogan "Avon calling," was founded by David McConnell (U.S.A.) in 1886 as the California Perfume Company (though it was based in New York). In 1939 McConnell renamed the company in honor of his favorite playwright, William Shakespeare of Stratford-upon-Avon

Diapers

The disposable diaper was first sold by Saks Fifth Avenue, New York, in 1948. Procter & Gamble test-marketed disposable diapers in the late 1950s, finally launching the first mass-produced disposable diapers in 1961, under the name Pampers®

Wall plug

The first wall plug (for fixing into masonry) was the Rawlplug, invented by John J. Rawlings (patented in 1919). The plugs (known as fiber plugs) were made from twisted jute soaked in pig's blood and baked until hard. Rawlplugs replaced the traditional method of fixing into masonry: chisel a hole, plug it with wood and screw into the wood. In 1934 Rawlplug Ltd patented an expanding bolt called the Rawlbolt

Black&Decker®Workmate®workbench

The first Black&Decker®Workmate®workbench was patented as the Minibench by ex-Lotus Cars designer Ron Hickman (South Africa) and first manufactured by his company Mate-Tool in 1968. Black & Decker (England), who turned down Hickman's idea in 1967, bought the rights in 1972 and launched the workbench in North America in 1975

Baby carriages

The first folding metal baby carriage, known as the Allwin, was manufactured by Liddle Co. (U.S.A.) in 1904. The first lightweight aluminium pushchair that could be folded using one hand was the Maclaren baby buggy, patented by ex-aeronautical designer and test pilot Owen Finlay Maclaren (England) in 1965 and produced in 1967

Emulsion paint

The first emulsion paint was Spred Satin, first marketed by Glidden Co. (U.S.A., now part of ICI) in 1949 and advertised as "A new Wonder Paint almost beyond belief"

Polyfilla

The first decorator's filler was Polyfilla, invented by Dr. Saloman Neumann (Czechoslovakia, working in England) in 1956 and first manufactured by Polycell Products the same year

Brillo pad

The first steel-wool cleaning pad was Brillo, patented in 1913. Brillo pads were the brainchild of an aluminum kitchenware salesman called Brady and his brother-in-law, a jeweler named Ludwig (both U.S.A.). The name Brillo was suggested by Milton B. Loeb (U.S.A.), cofounder and first president of the company

Safety pin

The first safety pin was invented by Walter Hunt (U.S.A.) as a means of settling a debt. His creditors, William and John Richardson (U.S.A.), agreed to cancel the debt and pay a small fee if Hunt could create a useful invention from a piece of wire. Hunt patented the safety pin, which he called a dress pin, on April 10, 1849, assigning the patent rights to the Richardsons.

Above A man from the Danis tribe wears a safety pin through his ear in the Baliem Valley, Irian Jaya, Republic of Indonesia

Chapter Five

Transportation

English father and son George and Robert Stephenson are the names most readily associated with railway firsts, but in fact it was fellow countryman Richard Trevithick who built the first steam railway locomotive, which was first demonstrated in Wales on February 29, 1804.

Transportation

RAILWAYS

TIMELINE

c.500 b.c. The ancient Greeks operate a rail system to carry boats across the approximate route of the current Corinth Canal

1430 A mine railway in Germany is the first recorded railway

1650 Two boys are "slain with a wagon" on a wooden mine railway in County Durham, England, becoming the first recorded railway fatalities

1767 The first cast-iron railway tracks are laid (on the Coalbrookdale–Horsehay railway, England)

1804 Richard Trevithick (England) builds the first steam railway locomotive.
FEBRUARY, Trevithick's locomotive runs on the Pen-y-Darren ironworks railway, Wales, and takes the world's first railway passengers to be drawn by steam.
JUNE, an Act of Parliament establishes the Oystermouth Railway, England, which in March 1807 becomes the first passenger railway (using horse-drawn wagons)

1812 Matthew Murray and John Blenkinsop (both England) pioneer the first commercial use of steam railway locomotives, on the Middleton Railway, Yorkshire, England

1815 In the first fatal steam railway accident, 16 people are killed at Philadelphia, County Durham, England, by a boiler explosion

1825 The Stockton & Darlington Railway (England) opens as the world's first public steam railway to carry passengers, as well as freight

The railway is a highly efficient means of transportation that vastly reduces the amount of power required to move a given load compared with a road. The first known use of rails for transport was c.500 b.c. when the ancient Greeks operated a rail system to carry boats across the approximate route of the current Corinth Canal. Modern railways developed from wooden mine railways on which the wagons were pushed by miners or pulled by horses, the first recorded example being in Germany c.1430. The first use of cast-iron rails was on the Coalbrookdale-Horsehay Railway, England, in 1767, and the first steam locomotive was built in 1804 by Richard Trevithick (England); it first ran in February of that year on the Pen-y-Darren ironworks railway in Wales. In June 1804 the Oystermouth Railway in Wales was established by Act of Parliament, and in March 1807 it became the first railway to carry fare-paying passengers (using horse-drawn wagons).

In 1825, George Stephenson's Stockton & Darlington Railway (England) opened as the world's first public steam railway to carry passengers as well as freight, and from then on development was very rapid. In May 1830 the Canterbury & Whitstable Railway, England, inaugurated the world's first regular steam railway passenger service and in September the Liverpool & Manchester Railway opened as the world's first intercity railway.

Commuters

The issue of the first railway season tickets in 1834 led to the concept of "commuters"—to commute actually means to exchange, and for season ticket holders the commutation, or exchange, was the payment in advance for their ticket. The first "commutation" tickets issued on the Liverpool & Manchester Railway in 1842, but the word did not become common until the 1960s, by which time it had been generalized to mean anyone who traveled regularly to and from work, even if it was by car.

Opposite top George Stephenson Centenary Medal
Opposite below "Train crossing Chat Moss Bog," *Coloured Views on the Liverpool and Manchester Railway*, T.T. Bury (1831)
Below New York Elevated Railway (the El) at Fourth Avenue (c.1900)

DID YOU KNOW?

● **The colony of British Columbia joined Canada in 1871 on condition that a transcontinental railway be built to link the west coast province with the east. The railway was completed in 1885**

1829 The Rocket, designed and built by George and Robert Stephenson (England) sets the first official rail speed record at 29.1mph (46.8km/h)

1830 MAY, the world's first regular steam railway passenger service is inaugurated by the Canterbury & Whitstable Railway, England. SEPTEMBER, the Liverpool & Manchester Railway opens as the world's first intercity railway

1834 The Canterbury & Whitstable Railway offers the first recorded season tickets (the Stockton & Darlington Railway also offers season tickets during the 1830s but the exact date of the first is not recorded)

1835 Belgian State Railways opens as the world's first state-owned railway

1836 The Champlain & St. Lawrence Railroad build Canada's first railway between Laprairie and St. Jean, Quebec

1837 Thomas Edmondson (England), a booking clerk on the Newcastle & Carlisle Railway, devises and issues the first preprepared, serially numbered railway tickets. Australia's first railway line opens, in Tasmania

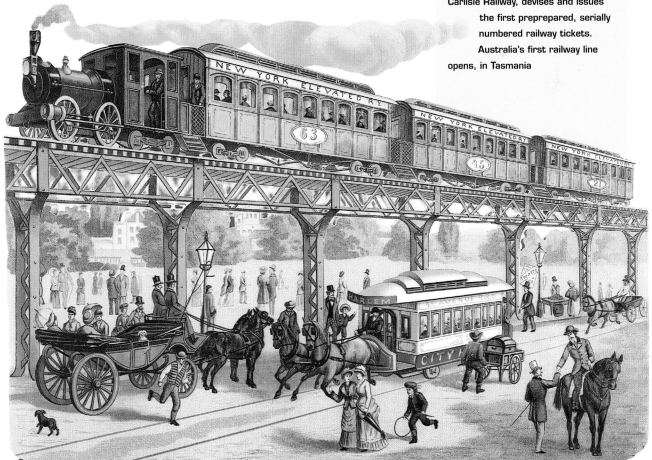

1838 The word timetable is first used, by the London & Birmingham Railway, and derives from maritime "tide tables"

1839 *Bradshaw's Railway Companion* is published in Manchester, England, as the world's first national railway timetable. (Bradshaw begins publishing *Bradshaw's Monthly Railway Guide* in 1842.) The Baltimore & Ohio Railroad operates the first (experimental) electric train to run on standard gauge track

1841 The world's first semaphore signals are installed, by Sir Charles Hutton Gregory (England), at New Cross Gate on the London & Croydon Railway, England

1850 The Edinburgh & Northern Railway inaugurates the world's first train-ferry service

1857 The first recorded use of steel rails is made on the Midland Railway at Derby, England

1861 Canada's first street railway begins operation in Toronto, Ontario

1863 The Metropolitan Railway opens to passengers in London, England, as the world's first underground passenger railway; it runs from Paddington (Bishop's Road) to Farringdon Street

1867 Colonel Charles T. Harvey (U.S.A.) opens the world's first elevated railway (the El) in New York, a system later developed by Rufus Gilbert (U.S.A.)

1869 North America becomes the first continent to have a coast-to-coast railway when the Union Pacific and Central Pacific Railroads (authorized by Congress in 1862) meet at Promontory, Utah, to complete the Pacific Railroad

1879 A train shown by Werner von Siemens (Germany) at the Berlin Trades Exhibition is the first electric train to pick up an external current (in this case from a third rail), now acknowledged as the beginning of practical electric traction (see 1839)

1883 The Orient Express train makes its first journey between Paris, France, and Istanbul, Turkey

1885 The Canadian Pacific Railway completes Canada's first transcontinental railway at Craigellachie, BC

1893 The world's first electric automatic signalling system is installed on the Liverpool Overhead Railway, England

1899 Charles Brown of Brown Boveri (Switzerland) builds the first AC electric locomotive

1912 The world's first diesel locomotive is built by the Swiss company Sulzer for the Prussian–Hessian State Railway, but is never put into regular service

1917 Australia's first transcontinental railway opens between Sydney and Perth. The 478-km (300-mile) stretch across the Nullarbor Plain is the longest in the world without a curve

1921 The first diesel locomotive to go into regular service goes into operation with Tunisian Railways

1960 The Middleton Railway Trust becomes the first standard-gauge railway preservation society to begin operation (see 1758 and 1812)

1964 The Tokaido *Shinkansen* (new main line) between Tokyo and Osaka, Japan, opens as the first purpose-built high-speed passenger line

1965 The Bullet Train, operating on the Tokaido *Shinkansen*, provides the world's first regular railway service to average more than 100 mph (160 km/h). (*Shinkansen* now refers to the Bullet Train itself rather than simply the line)

1975 Britain's experimental Advanced Passenger Train is tested as the first "tilting train," but never goes into regular service

1994 The Channel Tunnel is officially opened, and trains run beneath the English Channel between England and France for the first time

Above *Shinkansen* train yard, Japan (1996)
Opposite Trial trip on the Metropolitan Line in North London in 1862—a train passing Portland Road Station. The line opened to the public in 1863
Left Silent film star Harold Lloyd finds commuting a bit of a squeeze

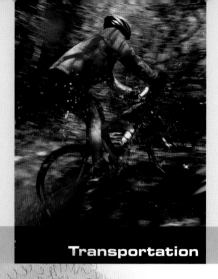

The bicycle, one of the most energy-efficient forms of transportation ever invented, evolved from its beginnings to a recognizably modern form over a period of about 70 years—but it is surprising, given that the wheel has been in use for some 6,000 years, that it did not evolve sooner.

BICYCLES

It was not until about 1790 that the first precursor of the modern bicycle appeared, a two-wheeled wooden frame invented by the Count de Sivrac (France), known as a *célérifère*, or wheeled horse. This machine was reinvented c.1817 as the *draisienne*, named after its inventor Baron Karl von Drais (Germany). The rider leaned forward across a padded support and rode the machine by simply taking huge strides as the wheels turned.

In 1839 Scottish blacksmith Kirkpatrick Macmillan invented the first mechanically propelled bicycle. However, it was French coachbuilder Pierre Michaux who really set the wheels of bicycle development in motion. In March 1861 Michaux was repairing a *draisienne* when he came up with the idea of fitting a cranked axle to the front wheel to see if the machine could be driven by pedals. Michaux's son Ernest carried out the work, which proved so successful that they set up a prosperous business as the world's first commercial bicycle manufacturers, building *vélocipèdes*, which soon became known as boneshakers.

Because the pedals of the *vélocipède* were fixed directly to the front wheel, the rider had to pedal very quickly to build up any speed. This problem was overcome in 1870 by English sewing-machine manufacturer James Starley, who realized that if he made the front wheel bigger the bicycle would travel farther for each revolution of the pedals. For practical reasons the rear wheel had to remain small, and the result was the Ariel, which became known as the Penny-Farthing after the coinage of the day, with the large penny-piece in front and the small farthing behind.

With the saddle up to 1.4 m (4.5 ft.) off the ground, the Penny-Farthing was not only difficult to mount and dismount, it was a dangerous machine to ride. Then in 1873 H.J. Lawson (England) came up with the idea of driving the rear wheel indirectly by a chain, allowing the force of the pedals to be geared and there was no longer any need for a large front wheel; the modern safety bicycle was born. Lawson's model was not a commercial success, but James Starley's nephew John exhibited the Rover safety bicycle in 1885, setting a pattern for bicycle design that remains basically the same today.

Above Opening of the new Rütt-Arena, Berlin. Ex-champion Paul Leinart on his historical ordinary bicycle (1926)
Below From *The Pedestrian Hobbies, or the Difference of Going Up and Down Hill*; published by J. Tegg (1819)

TIMELINE

1790 Count de Sivrac (France) invents a two-wheeled wooden frame known as the *célérifère*

c.1817 Baron von Drais (Germany) invents a two-wheeled wooden frame known as the *draisienne*, or hobbyhorse

1839 Kirkpatrick Macmillan (Scotland) invents a treadle-driven two-wheeler, the first mechanically propelled bicycle

1842 Macmillan knocks over a child, thereby committing the world's first cycling offense, for which he is fined 5 shillings

1861 Pierre and Ernest Michaux (France) build the first rotary pedal bicycle, the *vélocipède*, or boneshaker

1867 The Liverpool Vélocipède Club becomes England's first cycling club

1869 Gym owner C. Spencer becomes Britain's first cycle dealer, importing *vélocipèdes* from France. The world's first international cycle race is won by Ernest Michaux at Crystal Palace, London

1870 James Starley (England) patents the Ariel lightweight bicycle, the first of the Ordinaries, or Penny-Farthings

1873 H.J. Lawson (England) builds the first chain-driven safety bicycle

1885 John Kemp Starley (England) produces the first commercially successful safety bicycle, setting the pattern for modern bicycles

1887 John Dunlop (Scotland) develops the first air cycle tires and goes on to found the Pneumatic Tyre Co. (later the Dunlop Rubber Co.)

1891 Eduoard Michelin (France) patents the first removable air cycle tire

1903 The First Tour de France cycling race is won by Maurice Garin (France)

1950 Alex Moulton (England) develops the first folding bicycle

1979 Richard Forrestal and David Gordon Wilson (both U.S.A.) patent the first recumbent bicycle

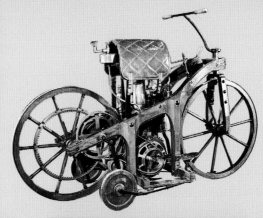

The first motorcycle, built in 1885, was little more than a push-bike with an engine fitted. Although it was designed simply as a way of testing what was to become a car engine, the motorcycle soon became a means of transportation in its own right.

MOTORCYCLES AND SCOOTERS

1869 Bicycle manufacturers Michaux and Perreaux (France) build a steam-powered *vélocipède*, a precursor of the motorcycle

1884 Edward Butler (England) patents a motor tricycle, built 1887–88

1885 Wilhelm Maybach and Gottlieb Daimler (both Germany) build the first motorcycle, the Einspur. Paul Daimler becomes the world's first motorcyclist

1888 Mrs. Butler (England) becomes the first female motorcyclist (see 1884)

1894 Heinrich and Wilhelm Hildebrand and Alois Wolfmüller (all Germany) produce the first commercially manufactured motorcycle, the Motorrad

1899 George Morgan (England) becomes the first person to die as a result of a motorcycling accident

1902 Georges Gauthier (France) produces the first motor scooter, the *autofauteuil* (motorized armchair)

1904 George Hendee and Oskar Hedstrom (both U.S.A.) introduce the first twist-grip throttle control

1907 The first Isle of Man TT (Tourist Trophy) Race is held

c.1910 Sidecars begin to come into use

1946 Aircraft manufacturer Piaggio (Italy) produces the first internationally successful motor scooter, the *Vespa*

Motorcycles

Wilhelm Maybach and Gottlieb Daimler (both Germany) designed an internal combustion engine in 1884 and, the following year, mounted it in a boneshaker-style bicycle in order to test it. The bicycle, with a wooden frame and wooden wheels, was much cruder than the engine, but it had the honor of being the world's first motorcycle. The saddle was placed above the centrally mounted engine, which was not an ideal arrangement—in the process of becoming the world's first motorcyclist, Daimler's son Paul had to jump off the machine when the saddle caught fire!

Daimler and Maybach's priority was car engines, and it was three other Germans—Heinrich and Wilhelm Hildebrand and Alois Wolfmüller—who in 1894 produced the first commercially manufactured motorcycle. Seven years later, in 1901, Werner Frères (France) established a design with the engine as an integral part of the frame where the bottom bracket of a pedal-bike would be. Apart from the mechanical advantages, this also gave the machine a low center of gravity, making it more stable, and placing the engine in this position became standard practice for all modern motorcycles.

Motor scooters

A motor scooter is defined as "a small-wheeled motorcycle with a protective shield curving back to form a support for the feet," although the concept of a scooter comes from the much earlier child's toy with a footboard and tall handlebar. Strangely, the first motor scooter fits the more modern idea: it was the French *autofauteuil* or motorized armchair (1902), which had the definitive small wheels and protective shield forming part of an open frame that allowed the rider to sit on rather than straddle the machine. However, the Auto-Ped, produced in New York in 1915, better fits the description motorized scooter: like the child's toy, it had no seat and the rider stood on a low footboard to drive it.

Scooters went out of fashion during the 1920s, and were not revived until 1946, with the arrival of the Vespa. Corradino d'Ascanio (Italy), an engineer at Enrico Piaggio's aircraft factory, made a prototype in 1945 that set the pattern for modern scooters: open frame with flat footboard, enclosed engine and small wheels.

Opposite above The world's first motorcycle (1885)
Below left Motorcycle with sidecar (c.1910)
Right Model with a Vespa (1955)

For three centuries Frenchman Blaise Pascal was held to have built the first mechanical calculator. An earlier calculator has since been discovered, but in 1661, the year before he died, Pascal initiated a first that has not been discredited—the first bus service.

BUSES, STREETCARS AND TAXIS

1662 The world's first bus service goes into operation in Paris, having been proposed by Blaise Pascal (France) the previous year

1819 Jacques Lafitte (France) inaugurates the first bus service to operate in the 140 years since the demise of Pascal's pioneering service c.1680

c.1823 Stanislas Baudry (France) applies the word omnibus to public coaches for the first time

1825 John Greenwood (England) inaugurates Britain's first bus service, between Manchester and Pendleton

1829 George Shillibeer (England) inaugurates Britain's first regular, scheduled bus service

1831 Goldworthy Gurney and Sir Charles Dance (both England) inaugurate the first steam-powered bus service (between Cheltenham and Gloucester)

1832 John Stephenson (U.S.A.) establishes the first urban streetcar service (in New York)

1837 The first steam streetcars go into service (in New York)

1852 Emile Loubat (France) establishes the first urban streetcar service to use rails embedded in the roadway (in the United States)

1861 The Toronto Street Railway Company (Canada) is the first company to offer public transportation in Toronto, Ontario

Blaise Pascal (France) is more famous as a mathematician, physicist and philosopher than as the father of public transport, but in 1661 he proposed that a number of coaches should "circulate along predetermined routes in Paris at regular intervals regardless of the number of people" and pick up passengers for the price of five sous. The coaches, which went into service in March 1662, were known as *carrosses à cinq sous* (literally "coaches for five sous"). However, the immediate popularity of this novel scheme proved to be a fad rather than a lasting success, and there is no record of any other bus service until 1819 when the idea was resurrected by Jacques Lafitte (France), again in Paris.

The word omnibus (from which bus derives) was first applied to public coaches c.1823 by coach operator Stanislas Baudry (France), who reputedly took the name from a local shop called Omnes Omnibus, meaning Omnes For Everything (Omnes being the name of the store owner). Baudry realized that omnibus could just as well be translated as "for everyone" and applied the name to his coaches because anyone could join the coach along its route, unlike stage coaches, which had to be prebooked.

The first coaches for hire to individuals for specified journeys (17th century) were known as hackney carriages, although nothing to do with Hackney in London: the name came from the French *hacquenée*, a horse that was hired out for journeys. By the 19th century these had been replaced by *cabriolets de place*, or cabs, another French innovation—one of the most famous was the Hansom cab, the first of which hit the streets in 1834 and was named after its inventor Joseph Hansom (England). Many cab drivers used taximeters (to measure mileage and calculate the fare) to show that they were charging a fair price. Motorized cabs fitted with this device became known as taxis, as celebrated in the music hall song *The Taximeter Car*, whose chorus was "You can do it in style for eightpence a mile."

DID YOU KNOW?

● The first double-decker buses (1850s) were single-deckers with passengers sitting on the roof. Then "knifeboard" seats were provided, on which passengers sat back to back facing outward, later superseded by "garden" seats, as in the modern arrangement. "Decency boards" were placed along the sides of the top deck to prevent young men glimpsing the ankles of ladies riding on the top deck

1881 The world's first electric streetcar goes into service in Germany

1888 A Daimler streetcar goes into service in Stuttgart, Germany, as the first gasoline-driven streetcar. Frank J. Sprague (U.S.A.) demonstrates the United States' first practical electric streetcar in Virginia

1895 A Benz "enclosed landau" driven by Hermann Golze (Germany) goes into service as the first gasoline-driven bus

1896 Herr Dütz (Germany) establishes the world's first motorized taxi service, in Stuttgart, using two gasoline-driven Benz cars. The first electric taxis appear in Philadelphia, PA, later the same year

1897 Friederich Greiner (Germany) establishes a second Stuttgart cab service, using the first motorized taxis to be fitted with taximeters. The London Electric Cab Co. begins operating as Britain's first motorized taxi company. The Yorkshire Motor Car Co. inaugurates Britain's first motorized bus service. The world's first motoring fatality involving a taxi occurs when 9-year-old Stephen Kempton (England) tries to steal a ride and is crushed after his coat gets caught in the chain-drive of the taxi

1900 A De Dion-Bouton steam omnibus (France) becomes the first bus to run on air tires

1905 The first regular motorized bus service in the United States begins (in New York)

1909 Widnes Corporation (England) introduces the first closed-top double-decker buses

1925 The first diesel buses go into operation, in Germany for the Bavarian post office

125

Opposite above Advertising poster for London's Tramways (1929)
Opposite below A streetcar in Amsterdam, Holland
Left Mid-19th-century horse-drawn omnibus in Paris, France

Horseless carriages were discussed as early as the 13th century, but the first steam carriage did not appear until 1769 and the first car until 1862, both in France. The development of road transportation also brought such joys as parking meters, traffic cops and speed cameras.

Above Sketch of Lenoir's proposed first automobile as illustrated in *Le Monde Illustré*, June 16, 1860
Below A gasoline-driven automobile by Benz & Co., capable of 16km/h (10 miles/hr). From *Der stein der Weisen*, Leipzig (c.1895)
Opposite Top-of-the-range Panhard et Levasuor (c.1895)

The quest for self-propelled road vehicles led first to the use of steam. After a shaky start with Nicolas Cugnot's *fardier*, or gun carriage (France, 1769), there were a number of very successful steam carriages before the advent of the motor carriage, or car. The world's first motorcar had a gas-fueled internal combustion engine and was built in 1862 by Étienne Lenoir (France) who, having proved that the concept worked, turned his attention instead to motorboats. The first gasoline-driven motorcar was built in 1883, also in France, but the chassis proved too flimsy for the weight and power of the motor. It was Karl Benz (Germany) who built the first successful motorcar in 1885, becoming the father of the car industry.

From then on development was remarkably fast, including the surprisingly early development of disc brakes (1902), catalytic converters (1909) and power steering (1926). One of the most significant developments in the history of the car industry was the invention of the three-point lap and shoulder seat belt by Volvo engineer Nils Bohlin (Sweden) in 1958—Volvo did not enforce its patent rights, believing that all motorists should have the right to the potentially life-saving benefits of the seat belt. Bohlin, who developed aircraft ejector seats for Svenska Aeroplan AB before he became Volvo's first safety engineer in 1958, said: "Sometimes I get a call from some grateful person who has survived thanks to the belt. It warms my heart and shows that I really have been able to do something for mankind."

1769 Nicolas Joseph Cugnot (France) builds the first self-propelled road vehicle, a steam-powered gun carriage or *fardier*. This unstable vehicle tips over and hits a wall in the first accident involving a self-propelled vehicle	**1801** Richard Trevithick (England) builds the first successful steam carriage	**1862** J.J. Étienne Lenoir (France) builds the first motorcar with an internal combustion engine	**1863** Lenoir makes the world's first motorcar journey, a round trip of 12 miles at an average 4 mph (6 km/h)	**1867** Henry Seth Taylor (Canada) builds a steam-powered motorcar, the first car built in Canada	**1879** George B. Selden (U.S.A.) files the first U.S. patent for a motorcar with an internal combustion engine (the patent is not granted until 1895, and the car is never built)	**1883** Edouard Delamere-Deboutteville and Charles Malandin (both France) build the first gasoline-driven motorcar

■ MANUFACTURING TIMELINE

1885 Karl Benz (Germany) builds the first successful gasoline-driven motorcar, a three-wheeler acknowledged as the beginning of the commercial development of motorcars

1886 Benz makes the first public demonstration of his motorcar. Gottlieb Daimler (Germany) builds the first four-wheeled gasoline-driven car

1888 Emile Roger (France) becomes the first person to buy a motorcar (from Rheinische Gasmotorenfabrik Karl Benz of Mannheim, Germany)

1894 Benz produces the *Velo*, the first series-production motorcar

1895 Edouard Michelin (France) develops the world's first air motorcar tires. Britain's first air motorcar tires are made the following year by the Dunlop Co. for car manufacturer Frederick Lanchester

1898 Louis Renault (France) produces the first motorcar with a fully enclosed body

1901 Ransom Eli Olds (U.S.A.) begins manufacture of the first mass-produced motorcars

1927 The Philadelphia Storage Battery Co. (U.S.A.) produces the first commercially manufactured car radio, the Philco Transitone

1938 Oldsmobile (U.S.A.) produces the first automatic-transmission motorcar (described as Hydromatic Drive)

1947 B.F. Goodrich Co. (U.S.A.) markets the first commercially successful tubeless tyres

1958 Nils Ivar Bohlin (Sweden) of Volvo AB patents the first three-point safety belt

1959 The Volvo PV544 becomes the first car to be fitted with a three-point safety belt as standard

1968 Volvo introduces the inertia-reel to the three-point safety belt

1969 Czechoslovakia becomes the first country to make the wearing of safety belts compulsory

1974 Airbags are fitted to cars for the first time, first fitted to the Mercury company cars of the Allstate Insurance Company (U.S.A.), and then made available to the public as an optional extra on several Oldsmobile models

1981 Ron Dork (U.S.A.) of General Motors develops the first satellite navigation system and fits it to his Buick

1982 Bosch (Germany) produces the first anti-locking brake system (ABS)

1985 Volvo introduces the first anti-skid electronic traction control (ETC)

1990 The first commercial satellite navigation system for cars is launched by Pioneer Electronic Corporation (Japan)

Above The aim of the "clunk, click, every trip" public safety campaign was to convince people that wearing a seat belt was as important as closing the door. Here, a model shows how it's done
Left Sir Bibendum: "My strength is the strength of ten because my rubber is pure." Michelin poster (c.1905)
Opposite Mercedes Jellinek

● The Mercedes marque was created by the Daimler company, and named after the daughter of board member Emil Jellinek (Austria)—her name was first used as a pseudonym for a Daimler car during a speed trial in 1899 and adopted as the tradename for all Daimler cars from 1902

● In 1898 August Horch (Germany) founded Horch cars and 12 years later he established a second company and used the Latinized version of his name, which derives from the German *horchen*, "to listen" —the new company was called Audi

The joys of motoring

Cars brought with them a number of other things that motorists love to hate, including parking meters, traffic cops and traffic lights—although the first traffic light was actually installed to control horse-drawn traffic. It was a revolving lantern with red and green signals lit from within by a gas lamp, and installed near Parliament Square in London to make it easier for MPs to enter the houses of parliament. It remained there from 1868 until it was removed in 1872, 22 years before the first motorcar was imported to Britain. It is easy to forget that traffic lights were invented for safety rather than as an annoyance for motorists; Garrett Augustus Morgan (U.S.A.) received a U.S. government award for road safety after inventing the first electric traffic lights, which were installed at the corner of Euclid Avenue and 105th Street in Cleveland, OH, in 1914 (he patented a later version in 1922).

The first parking meter was installed in Oklahoma City, OK, in 1935, the invention of newspaper editor Carlton Magee, who established the Dual Parking Meter Company (now POM Inc.) to manufacture his invention—the name of the company reflected the meter's dual purpose of restricting parking and raising revenue for the city. Magee's delightful invention brought peace

PERIPHERALS TIMELINE

1834 In Scotland, five people are killed in the first fatal road accident to involve a self-propelled vehicle (a steam coach)

1868 The world's first traffic light (gas lit) is installed near Parliament Square, London, England

1889 Britain introduces the first Vehicle Excise Tax, which applies to all four-wheeled steam and motor vehicles

1893 The world's first motor vehicle registration plates are introduced, by an ordinance of the Paris Police applying within the Department of the Seine

1895 NOVEMBER 1, the American Motor League becomes the world's first motoring organization. NOVEMBER 12, the Automobile Club de Paris (France) becomes Europe's first motoring organization. DECEMBER 10, the Self Propelled Traffic Association becomes Britain's first motoring organization

1896 Mrs. Bridget Driscoll (England) becomes the first motoring fatality when she is run over in the grounds of the Crystal Palace, London, by a Roger-Benz being driven at 4 mph by Arthur Edsell. Walter Arnold (England) becomes the first motorist to be convicted of speeding—for exceeding the 2 mph limit in a built-up area

1897 The world's first collision between two motor vehicles occurs on Charing Cross Road, London. Taxi-driver George Smith (England) becomes the first motorist to be convicted of drunk-driving (drunk-in-charge of an electric cab). George Innes becomes the first Australian to be convicted of a motoring offense (speeding at 8 mph).

1898 Henry Lindfield (England) becomes the first car driver to be killed as a result of a motoring accident, dying of shock the day after crashing his electric car on the way home to Brighton from London

1899 The Munich police issue Germany's first motor vehicle registration plate, to Herr Beissbarth for his Wartburg

1901 The first motor vehicle registration plates in the United States are introduced in New York State. The world's first multistorey car park opens on Denman Street, near Piccadilly Circus, London

1902 Edgar Purnell Hooley (England) patents "tar macadam" road surfacing and forms a company called TarMacadam (Purnell Hooley's Patent) Syndicate Ltd—a name shortened in 1905 to Tarmac Ltd.

1903 France becomes the first nation to adopt standardized traffic signs throughout the country

1911 River Road in Trenton, Michigan, becomes the first road to be painted with a white center line

1912 Norway becomes the first country to introduce compulsory third party motor insurance

1914 The world's first electric traffic lights are installed (in Cleveland, Ohio)

1918 The world's first three-color traffic lights (manually operated) are installed in New York

1921 The Avus autobahn in Berlin, opens as the world's first motorway

1923 The Milano-Varese autostrada, Italy, opens as the first intercity motorway

1925 The Bronx River Parkway opens in New York as the first highway in the United States

and goodwill to all motorists and later gave rise to another great favorite, the traffic cop, first unleashed on unsuspecting motorists in New York City and London in 1960.

Edgar Purnell Hooley (England) used the name of an earlier inventor for his contribution to motoring history. In the early 19th century John Loudon McAdam (Scotland) pioneered the use of crushed stone and gravel to create macadamized roads. These roads were a vast improvement on unmade roads but remained prone to ruts. Then, in 1901, county surveyor Hooley found a stretch of road with no ruts. He discovered that a barrel of tar had fallen off a wagon, and that slag from a local ironworks had been used to cover the tar. He patented a process for making "tar macadam" in 1902 and registered the trademark Tarmac in 1903. The use of iron slag explains why roads made using this process became known as "metalled" roads.

Left The first traffic lights, in Paris, France (c.1900)
Below "Beat the Warden," an autombile dice game
Opposite A spaghetti junction—well known to all drivers

DID YOU KNOW?

• Henry Seth Taylor, inventor of the first steam-powered motorcar in Canada, unveiled his prize at a fair in 1867; it promptly broke down. Taylor was later involved in Canada's first automobile accident. His brakeless car sped down a steep hill, careened out of control and crashed. Frustrated by the problems, Taylor turned his attention to building a steam-powered yacht

• London's traffic wardens issued 344 fixed-penalty parking tickets on their first day in operation (September 19, 1960), the first being slapped on a Ford Popular belonging to Dr. Thomas Creighton—who at the time was treating a patient suffering from a heart attack. After an outcry in the press, the doctor was excused from paying his £2 fine

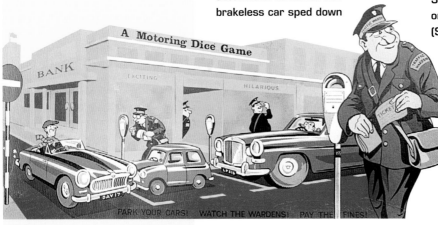

A Motoring Dice Game
BANK
EXCITING
HILARIOUS
PARK YOUR CARS!   WATCH THE WARDENS!   PAY THE FINES!

1928 Australia's first traffic lights are installed in Melbourne

1932 Carlton Magee (U.S.A.) patents the parking meter (the classic meter is an improvement patented in 1935)

1935 JULY, the world's first parking meter is installed, in Oklahoma City, OK AUGUST, Reverend North (U.S.A.) becomes the first driver to be fined for overstaying at a parking meter. Percy Shaw (England) patents Catseyes reflecting road studs

1939 Queen Elizabeth Way, linking Toronto and Hamilton, opens as Canada's first highway

1950s Rally driver Maurice Gatsonides (Netherlands) develops the first speed camera in order to test his performance

1956 Britain's first parking meters are installed in London as an experiment, before being adopted in earnest in 1958

1958 Britain's first motorway, the Preston by-pass (now part of the M6), is opened by Prime Minister Harold Macmillan

1960 JUNE, New York Mayor Robert Wagner (U.S.A.) introduces the first meter maids.
SEPTEMBER, the London Borough of Westminster introduces Britain's first traffic wardens

Steam power, screw propellers and internal combustion engines revolutionized water transport during the 18th and 19th centuries, while the 20th century saw the first diesel, nuclear- and solar-powered vessels, as well as a new first for wind power—Windsurfer, the first commercial sailboard.

SHIPS AND BOATS

1783 The Marquis de Jouffroy d'Abbans (France) builds the first practical steamboat, propelled by a paddle wheel

1785 Lionel Lukin (England) files the first patent for a lifeboat. The first lifeboat station opens in Bamburgh, Northumberland, the following year, with a Lukin lifeboat

1809 Canada's first steamship, *Accommodation*, is launched in Montreal

1819 Paddle-steamer *Savannah*, built in Savannah, Georgia, becomes the first steamship to cross the Atlantic Ocean

1833–36 Robert Wilson (England), Frédéric Sauvage (France), John Ericsson (Sweden; U.S. citizen from 1848) and Francis Pettit Smith (England) all independently develop early screw propellers

1836 Francis Pettit Smith files the first patent for a screw propeller. Six weeks later Ericsson files a patent for a different type of screw propeller

1838 SS *Great Western* (England) begins the first regular transatlantic paddle-steamer service. *Archimedes* (England) is launched as the first purpose-built propeller-driven ship

1845 SS *Great Britain* (England) makes the first transatlantic voyage by a propeller-driven iron ship

1861 The American barge *Parke Curtiss* is converted to tow and launch balloons, thereby becoming the world's first aircraft carrier

With a few experimental exceptions, boats were powered by human effort or by the wind until the Marquis de Jouffroy d'Abbans (France) built the first practical steamboat in 1783. Just over half a century later, in 1838, the first regular transatlantic paddle-steamer service was inaugurated, in the same year that the first propeller-driven ship was launched. The ship was named *Archimedes* because propellers, often referred to as screws, are based on a machine invented by Archimedes (Greece) in the 3rd century b.c.

The Archimedes Screw is used to raise water by turning a large-threaded screw inside a cylinder. During the 1830s, several inventors experimented with reversing this principle, pushing water backwards with the screw to provide momentum. They soon realized that the length of the screw was irrelevant; in fact, only the tips of the thread were required, which is why propellers do not look much like the screws from which they derive.

Steam remained the only source of power for boats until 1864, when Frenchman Étienne Lenoir (who in 1862 built the first motorcar) built the first boat powered by an internal combustion engine. The first gasoline-driven motorboat was built in 1886 by Gottlieb Daimler (Germany), who had built the first motorcycle (1885) and the first four-wheeled gasoline-driven motorcar (1886).

DID YOU KNOW?

• When Gottlieb Daimler built the first gasoline-driven motorboat in 1886, people considered gasoline engines to be so dangerous that Daimler had to add cables and insulators to make the boat look as if it was electrically powered

• In 1845 the British Admiralty organized a tug-of-war between two frigates, which were tethered stern to stern and driven full ahead to determine whether paddle wheels or screw propellers were more efficient. HMS *Rattler*, with the propeller, easily outpulled HMS *Alecto*

1864 J.J. Étienne Lenoir (France) builds the first motorboat

1886 Gottlieb Daimler (Germany) builds the first gasoline-driven motorboat

1896 The American Motor Co. produces the first outboard motor (only 25 are made)

1897 *Turbinia* (England) is launched as the first ship to be powered by steam turbine

1902 Canal boat *Petit-Pierre* (France) is launched as the first diesel-engine vessel

1910 U.S. Navy cruiser *Birmingham* is fitted with a temporary flight deck to become the first airplane-carrying aircraft carrier (see 1861)

1958 Peter Chilvers (England) builds the first known sailboard

1959 Russian icebreaker *Lenin* is launched as the first nuclear-powered surface vessel

1960 U.S. merchant ship *Savannah* (named after the first steamship to cross the Atlantic) is launched as the first nuclear-powered merchant vessel, making its maiden voyage in 1962

1968 Hoyle Schweitzer and James Drake (both U.S.A.) are granted the first patent for a sailboard, registering the trademark Windsurfer in 1974 (their application for a GB patent is not upheld—see 1958)

1973 The first sailboarding world championships are held; won by Stephan van den Berg (Netherlands), who went on to become the first person to win five world titles

1975 A.T. Freeman (England) builds the first solar-powered boat, the aptly named *Solar Craft I*

Sailboards

In 1968 businessman-surfer Hoyle Schweitzer and aeronautical designer James Drake (both U.S.A.) filed the first patent for a sailboard, but they were not in fact the first to produce one. Peter Chilvers (England) had built the first known sailboard in 1958 when he was 12, while S. Newman Darby (U.S.A.) had built a sailboard in 1964 and had written an article for *Popular Science Monthly* entitled "Sailboarding: An Exciting New Water Sport for High Speed Water Fun." Schweitzer and Drake's GB patent was revoked in January 1984, the year that sailboarding first became an Olympic sport, but their commercial success is illustrated by the fact that sailboards are almost universally known by Schweitzer's trademark, Windsurfer.

Opposite top *Comet*, the first commercial passenger steamboat in Europe, designed by Henry Bell (Scotland) and launched from Glasgow in 1812

Left A sailboarder takes to the air
Above An icebreaker in the Ross Sea, Antarctica

Human flight began with balloons, gliders and airships. During the 20th century powered flight developed phenomenally quickly: Orville Wright's famous first flight in 1903 covered less distance than the wingspan of the Boeing 747 Jumbo Jet, which first flew in 1969.

FLIGHT

MANUFACTURING TIMELINE

1783 OCTOBER, Jean-François Pilâtre de Rozier makes man's first (tethered) ascent, in a hot-air balloon manufactured by Joseph and Étienne Montgolfier (all France).
NOVEMBER, de Rozier and the Marquis d'Arlandes (France) make the first manned free flight, in a Montgolfier balloon.
DECEMBER, the first manned flight in a hydrogen balloon is made by Jacques-Alexandre-César Charles and Marie-Noël Robert (both France)

1849 Sir George Cayley (England) builds a triple-winged glider that carries a 10-year-old boy on the world's first manned flight by a heavier-than-air craft

1852 Henri Giffard (France) achieves man's first powered controlled flight, in his steam-powered airship

1853 Cayley builds the first glider capable of carrying a fully-grown person (designs published the previous year). It is test-flown by Caley's coachman

1890 Clément Ader (France) makes the first takeoff in a heavier-than-air powered aircraft (powered by steam)

1903 Orville Wright (U.S.A.) makes what is generally accepted as the first airplane flight

1907 Paul Cornu (France) builds the first helicopter to leave the ground carrying its pilot

1908 Samuel Cody (U.S.A.) makes Britain's first officially recognized airplane flight. First airplane flights are made in Belgium, Germany and Italy

It is tempting to think that the history of flight began with the Wright brothers (U.S.A.), but in fact man had been venturing into the air for more than a century before Orville and Wilbur Wright shifted their attention from bicycles to airplanes. In 1783, exactly 120 years before the Wright brothers made their famous flight, Frenchman Jean-François Pilâtre de Rozier became the first human to ascend into the air, in a tethered hot-air balloon manufactured by his countrymen Joseph and Étienne Montgolfier. The following month de Rozier and the Marquis d'Arlandes (France) made man's first free flight, again in a Montgolfier balloon.

Just one year after the excitement of the balloon ascents, a model helicopter built by two more Frenchmen, Messrs Launoy and Bienvenu, became the first heavier-than-air powered aircraft to fly, but it was to be more than half a century later before anyone built a heavier-than-air craft capable of carrying a person: in 1849 Sir George Cayley (England) built a triple-winged glider that carried a 10-year-old boy on the world's first manned flight by a heavier-than-air craft. This achievement was quickly followed by man's first powered controlled flight, achieved in 1852 by Henri Giffard (France) in his steam-powered airship. The year after that Cayley built the first glider capable of carrying an adult; it was test-flown by Cayley's coachman, who handed in his notice immediately afterwards, reportedly saying: "I was hired to drive, not fly."

So, free flight and powered controlled flight had been achieved by the mid-19th century in lighter-than-air craft, and Cayley, often referred to as the father of the airplane, had shown that flight in heavier-than-air craft was possible—but the holy grail

Above Famed Nazi pilot Hanna Reitsch flies the Focke-Wulf FW-61 helicopter *inside* Berlin's Deutschlandhalle to demonstrate its control and maneuverability. From *Illustrazione del Popolo* (February 27, 1938)
Right Wilbur Wright watches his brother Orville pilot what is generally accepted to be the first airplane flight (December 17, 1903)
Opposite top Montgolfier's *experience aerostatique* at Versailles, carrying a sheep, a rooster and a duck, "in the presence of their majesties and the royal family" (1783)

...was powered controlled flight in a heavier-than-air craft. French aviator Clément Ader made the first take-off in a heavier-than-air powered aircraft as early as 1890, but he was unable to achieve sustained controlled flight. In 1901 the *Bridgeport Sunday Herald* of Connecticut, reported that Gustave Whitehead (born Weisskopf, Germany–U.S.A.) had made the first sustained controlled flight in a heavier-than-air powered aircraft, but the claim was not substantiated or officially recognized. Another unsubstantiated claim was made on behalf of Richard Pearse (New Zealand), who may or may not have made the first airplane flight, in March 1903.

But, whatever the claims and counter claims, the first documented, substantiated, manned, powered, sustained and controlled flight by a heavier-than-air craft, generally accepted as the first airplane flight, was the 12 sec, 120 ft. (36 m) flight made by Orville Wright in the *Wright Flyer* at Kill Devil Hills, North Carolina, at 10:35 a.m. on December 17, 1903.

1783 Sebastien Lenormand (France) makes the world's first "parachute descent," jumping some 4 m (13 ft.) from the Montpelier Observatory in Paris, France (see 1797)

1785 Balloonists François Pilâtre de Rozier and Jules Romain (both France) become the first people to die in an aeronautical accident, two years after de Rozier became the first human to ascend in flight

1794 A Company of Aérostiers is formed under Captain Coutelle (France) as part of the French Artillery Service, carrying out reconnaissance from balloons to become effectively the world's first air force. The first use of an aircraft (a balloon) in battle takes place at Fleurus, Belgium, in the same year

1797 André-Jacques Garnerin (France) makes the first parachute descent from an aircraft at a considerable height, 680 m (730 ft.) (a balloon over Parc Monçeau, Paris)

1858 Gaspard Félix Tournachon (France) takes the first aerial photograph (from a balloon over Val de Bièrre, Paris)

1907 The Aeronautical Division of the U.S. Army Signal Corps is established and in 1908 becomes the first air force to be equipped with an airplane (see 1794)

1908 MAY, Charles W. Furnas (U.S.A.) becomes the first airplane passenger, piloted by Wilbur Wright.
JULY, Thérèse Peltier (France) becomes the first female airplane passenger.
SEPTEMBER, Lt. Thomas Selfridge (U.S.A.) becomes the first person to die in an airplane accident; the pilot, Orville Wright, survives the crash

1909 Count Ferdinand von Zeppelin (Germany) forms Deutsche Luftschiffahrt Aktiengesellschaft (Delag), the first commercial airline. In Nova Scotia J.A.D. McCurdy flies the *Silver Dart* in what is the first flight of an airplane in Canada

1910 Sir Charles Rolls (of Rolls-Royce fame) becomes the first British pilot to be killed in an air accident. Eugene Ely (U.S.A.) makes the first takeoff from a ship

Left A would-be stewardess at the British Overseas Airways Corporation (BOAC) training school in Hendon, serving a mock-up in-flight meal to qualified stewards and stewardesses as part of her assessment
Top Count Ferdinand von Zeppelin, German soldier, aviator and airship pioneer. Poster for Internationale Luftschiffart-Ausstellung (an international aeronautics art exhibition), Frankfurt (1909)
Above Cartoon inspired by French aeronaut André-Jacques Garnerin, who made the world's first parachute descent from an aircraft (a tethered balloon) over Paris in 1797

1911 Eugene Ely makes the first landing on a ship, which was at anchor

c.1912 Heinrich Kubis (Germany) becomes the first airline steward, serving on board Zeppelin airships (he later survives the *Hindenburg* disaster)

1914 The St. Petersburg–Tampa Airboat Line (Florida) becomes the first airline (with the exception of Delag, 1909) to establish a scheduled service. The first full meal is served on an airplane, on the Sikorsky airliner *Ilya Mourometz I* over Russia

1917 Squadron Commander E.H. Dunning (England) makes the first airplane landing on a moving ship

1918 Britain's Royal Flying Corps (army) and Royal Naval Air Service are amalgamated to form the Royal Air Force, the first air force independent of its nation's army or navy

1919 FEBRUARY, Deutsche Luft-Reederei (Germany) begins the first sustained daily passenger services. MARCH, Lignes Aériennes Farman (France) begins the first regular international passenger services

1925 The first in-flight movie is shown, on an Imperial Airways flight over Europe

1930 Ellen Church (U.S.A.) becomes the first air hostess, for Boeing Air Transport, which becomes part of United Airlines in 1931. The first recorded hijacking of an airplane occurs

1947 Pan-Am's *Clipper* magazine becomes the first in-flight magazine

1952 BOAC inaugurates the first jet airline service

1961 TWA becomes the first airline to introduce regular in-flight movies

1969 The Boeing 747 "Jumbo Jet" is introduced as the first wide-bodied airliner

THE BEST OF THE REST...

Caterpillar tracks

The first patent for what are now known as caterpillar tracks was filed by Richard Edgeworth (England) in 1770, for "a portable railway, or artificial road, to move along with any vehicle to which it is applied." However, it was the 20th century before anyone built a vehicle that could run on such tracks. In 1903 David Roberts (England) of Ruston Hornsby & Sons created the first "crawler tractor," an oil-powered machine with a continuous belt of track. Benjamin Holt (U.S.A.) produced his Steam Traction Engine No.77 in 1904, with continuous tracks on the rear wheels and a single conventional wheel at the front. Holt later bought the rights to the Hornsby patent, beginning the chain of events that saw the Holt Manufacturing Co. become the Caterpillar Tractor Co., now known simply as Caterpillar

Trucks

The first practical motor truck (defined as a self-propelled goods vehicle capable of carrying freight rather than pulling it) was a six-wheeled steam wagon built in 1870 by John Yule (Scotland) to carry ships' boilers from his factory in Glasgow to the city docks. The first gasoline-powered truck was completed by Panhard et Levassor (France) in February 1895, and the first commercially manufactured gasoline-powered truck was produced by the Daimler Co. (Germany) the following year. The first articulated truck was a steam-powered tractor unit with a two-wheeled trailer, built in 1898 by Thornycroft (England). The first diesel truck was built by Benz (Germany) in 1923

Hovercraft

The first hovercraft was the SRN1, built by Saunders-Roe (England) and launched on May 30, 1959. The hovercraft was invented by Sir Christopher Cockerell (England) and patented in 1955 after experiments using a cat food tin inside a larger coffee tin, with the nozzle from a vacuum cleaner blowing air into the gap between them. Cockerell discovered that the downward pressure of the air leaving the tins was three times that coming out of the nozzle, and applied the principle to create the first hovercraft. On the 50th anniversary of Blériot's first cross-Channel flight, SRN1 made the first hovercraft crossing of the Channel. The first scheduled hovercraft passenger service began in 1962 (Cheshire, England to Flint, Wales), and the first cross-Channel hover-ferry service was inaugurated in 1968

Submarine

The first submarine was built in England by Cornelius Drebbel (Netherlands) c.1624. It had a wooden frame, a leather casing, and was propelled by 12 oars protruding through ports in the casing. *Le Plongeur*, launched at La Rochelle, France, in 1863, was the first self-propelled submarine, and was driven by compressed air. The first nuclear-powered submarine (also the first nuclear-powered seagoing vessel) was U.S..S *Nautilus*, launched in 1954, first used its nuclear engines in 1955. In 1958 *Nautilus* became the first submarine to pass beneath the North Pole

Radar

The first practical radio detection equipment was developed by Dr. Rudolf Kühnold (Germany) in 1933 and demonstrated in Kiel Harbour in 1934. This equipment could not find the range of its target and therefore was not a fully-fledged radar, the final "r" of which denotes "ranging." The first radar to detect targets and provide their range was demonstrated by Sir Robert Watson-Watt (Scotland) in 1935. Radar was developed independently in the United States in 1936 where, about four years later, U.S. Navy Commander S.M. Tucker coined the term Radar, meaning radio detection and ranging. The first ship to be fitted with radar was the *Welle* (Germany) in 1935, and the first warship was the *Graf Spee* (Germany) in 1936. The first aircraft to be fitted with radar was a Heyford bomber tested by the RAF in 1936, and the first operational air-to-surface radar was in use with the RAF by 1939

Chapter Six

Arts & Entertainment

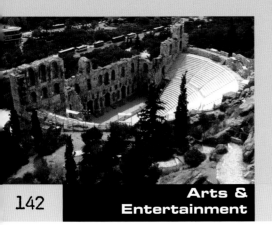

The first actor to be recognized for his talents was Thespis, who won the world's first drama competition in 534 b.c.. For Thespis, fame lasted more than 15 minutes—2,500 years later, actors are still often referred to as Thespians, or thesps, in his honor.

THEATER

The Ancient Greeks pioneered most of theater's firsts—the first playrights, the first plays, the first actors, the first theaters, the first actors' union (4th century b.c.) and the first drama competition, instituted in 534 b.c. by the Athenian ruler Peisistratos and won by the actor Thespis (the prize is thought to have been a goat). After the Romans, theater went into decline in the western world but thrived in India, Japan and also in China, where Emperor Ming Huang established the first-known drama school during the 8th century a.d. The school was in a pear garden and, even today, Chinese actors are sometimes referred to as "children of the pear garden."

European theater reemerged in the Middle Ages, when national variations of the religious mystery plays began to develop into secular drama. Europe's first covered theater was a room in l'Hôpital de la Trinité, Paris, where the Confrérie de la Passion theater company performed mystery plays from 1402; by the end of the 15th century King Henry VII of England was employing Britain's first professional actors to perform secular interludes at court (1493).

The next 200 years was the golden age of European theater, with the first permanent public theater since Roman times built in Malaga, Spain, in 1520, and the Comédie Française established in Paris in 1680 as the world's first national theater company.

Above The Herodeon Odean of Herodes Atticus in Athens (a.d. 3)
Right Theater poster for Fred R. Hamlin's musical extravaganza *The Wizard of Oz*, by Morgan Russell (1903)

534 b.c. Thespis (Greece) wins the world's first drama competition	**4th century b.c.** The Artists of Dionysus is formed as the first professional actors' union	**8th century a.d.** Emperor Ming Huang (China) establishes the first-known formal drama school	**1402** The Confrérie de la Passion theater company (France) is founded by Charles VI and gives performances in a room at l'Hôpital de la Trinité in Paris, which thereby becomes Europe's first covered theater	**1493** King Henry VII (England) employs Britain's first professional actors, known as the Players of the King's Interludes	**1520** The first permanent public theater in post-Roman Europe opens in Malaga, Spain

▌TIMELINE

Julius Caesar at the Globe Theatre, Southwark, London. The Globe Theatre is a faithful reconstruction of the open-air playhouse designed in 1599, where Shakespeare worked and for which he wrote many of his greatest plays

1539 Robert Coppyng (England) leases the Game Place House in Great Yarmouth for the performance of plays; though not exclusively used for drama, it is the first building in Britain used as a public theater

1606 Marc Lescarbot writes and stages North America's first play, at Port Royal, in Arcadia (now Nova Scotia)

1680 The Comédie Française is founded by Louis XIV as the world's first national theater co. (housed permanently in Paris 1792)

1758 The world's first revolving stage is built at the Kado-za doll theater in Osaka, Japan

1887 The Princess Theatre in Melbourne, Australia, opens as the first theater to have a sliding roof that can be opened during hot weather

1924 The Abbey Theatre in Dublin (founded 1904) becomes the first state-subsidized theater in the English-speaking world

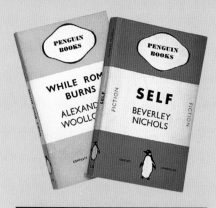

Modern bookstores provide a bewildering choice of literature ranging from worthy hardcovers to throwaway romance. The first paperbacks were designed to be just that—throwaway. Intended as disposable books for railway tourists, the first paperback was published in Germany in 1841.

Arts & Entertainment

LITERATURE

Above 1930s' Penguin paperbacks
Below "The Ourang-Outang commits horrific murder." An illustration by Arthur Rackham for Edgar Allan Poe's *Murders in the Rue Morgue* (1935)
Opposite *Voyages Extraordinaires. De la Terre à la Lune. Autour de la Lune,* Jules Verne (*Extraordinary Journeys. From the Earth to the Moon. Around the Moon*) (1860s)

Literature evolved out of the retelling of myths, legends, romances, folk tales and epic poems. It is impossible to pinpoint the firsts of many forms of literature, but some modern genres can be given an exact date. *Waverley*, by Sir Walter Scott (Scotland) and published in 1814, was the first novel to be set in an identifiable historic period describing the manners and personalities of the time. Other authors followed Scott's lead and *Waverley* is now recognized as the first of a new genre, the historical novel.

Frankenstein, by Mary Shelley (England) and published in 1818, is sometimes held to be the first work of science fiction, but in fact it was firmly rooted in the established genre of Gothic horror. Jules Verne (France) is the first true sci-fi author, creating an entirely new genre of fiction, with adventures based around the imaginative possibilities of emerging science. His first novel was *Five Weeks in a Balloon* (1863), but it was *A Journey to the Center of the Earth* (1864) and *From the Earth to the Moon* (1865) that really established the genre.

The first detective story, by Edgar Allan Poe (U.S.A.), was published in *Graham's Magazine* in 1841, the same year that the world's first paperback novel was published in Germany. That year Christian Bernhard Tauchnitz (Germany) began publishing his *Collection of British and American Authors*, a series of English-language paperbacks catering for English and North American tourists to continental Europe. The first of the series, and the world's first paperback book, was *Pelham*, by Edward Bulwer-Lytton (England).

Paperbacks were not produced for the mass market until 1935, when Allen Lane (England) founded Penguin Books. Legend has it that the directors were discussing a shortlist of ten animals and

1814 The first historical novel—*Waverley* by Sir Walter Scott (Scotland)—is published

1841 The first work of detective fiction—Edgar Allan Poe's (U.S.A.) *The Murders in the Rue Morgue*—is published. Christian Bernhard Tauchnitz (Germany) publishes the first paperback book: *Pelham* by Edward Bulwer-Lytton (England)

1864 The first science fiction novel—*A Journey to the Center of the Earth* by Jules Verne (France)—is published

1875 A.P. Watt (Scotland) establishes the world's first literary agency

1901 The first Nobel Prize for Literature is awarded to Sully Prudhomme (France) for his poetry

1903 The first Prix Goncourt (a French prize for literature) is awarded by the Académie Goncourt, founded in the will of novelist Edmond de Goncourt (France, d. 1896)

1917 The first Pulitzer Prizes are awarded (U.S.A.)

1924 Talking books for the blind are recorded for the first time

1932 Britain's National Book Council introduces the first book tokens, marketing them with the slogan, "The gift is mine, the choice is thine"

1935 Sir Allen Lane (England, originally Allen Lane Williams) launches Penguin Books, the first mass-marketed paperback books. Penguin's first title is *Ariel*, a life of Shelley by André Maurois (France, pseudonym of Émile Herzog)

1969 The first Booker Prize for Fiction is awarded (Commonwealth)

2002 Yann Martel (Canada) wins the 2002 Man Booker Prize for Fiction for his novel *Life of Pi*. Richard Russo (U.S.A.) wins the 2002 Pulitzer Prize for Fiction with *Empire Falls*

birds as possible names for the new imprint, when typist Jean Clark suggested "penguin." Designer Edward Young then spent the afternoon at the penguin pool in London Zoo sketching penguins and, the following morning, produced the famous penguin logo. Allen Lane described the penguin as the perfect choice of logo because of its "air of dignified flippancy."

DID YOU KNOW?

● The world's most overdue library book was returned 288 years late. A biography of the Archbishop of Bremen, Germany, was borrowed from the library of Sidney Sussex College, Cambridge, England, in 1668, and was returned in 1956 after being discovered at Houghton Hall, Norfolk, England

● Jules Verne wrote opera libretti before becoming the world's first science fiction writer

Humans have been making music since the Stone Age, but the first public concert before a paying audience was not performed until 1672. Since then recordings (1878), radio broadcasts (1906), radio DJs (1911) and music charts (1913) have all helped to make music ever more popular.

MUSIC

The first public concert for a paying audience was organized in 1672 by violinist John Banister (England), who had recently been sacked as Leader of the Court Band for impertinence to King Charles II. The concert took place in London, before an audience of 42 people, and Attorney-General Roger North recorded the fact that there was "a large raised box for the musitians, whose modesty required curtaines. The room was rounded with seats and small tables, alehous fashion. One shilling was the price … there was very good musick…"

TIMELINE

c.4500 b.c A Sumerian harp is the first-known stringed instrument

1672 John Banister (England) organizes the first public concert before a paying audience

c.1700 Johann Christoph Denner (Germany) adapts the traditional *chalumeau* (a reed pipe) to produce the first clarinet (the modern Boehm clarinet is patented in 1844)

c.1709 Harpsichord-maker Bartolomeo Cristofori (Italy) produces a harpsichord that plays soft and loud—the first piano

1780 Anselm Weber (Germany) of the Berlin Opera becomes the first conductor to use a baton

1846 Adolphe Sax (properly Antoine Joseph Sax, Belgium) patents the saxophone

1857 Edouard-Léon Scott de Martinville (France) invents the *phonautograph*, the first machine to record sound

1877 Thomas Alva Edison (U.S.A.) invents what he patents as the "phonograph or speaking machine;" it is the first machine that is able to record and reproduce sound

1878 Cornetist Jules Levy (England–U.S.A.) records *Yankee Doodle,* the first piece of music known to have been recorded

1887 Using the trademark "Gramophone," Emile Berliner (Germany–U.S.A.) patents the first machine to use a disc rather than a cylinder for recording

• The famous trademark depicting a fox terrier listening to his master's voice originally showed the dog, Nipper, listening to the artist's recently deceased brother on an Edison cylinder machine. In 1899 the Gramophone Company offered to buy the painting if the phonograph was replaced with a disc-playing gramophone, so the painting was duly reworked and the Gramophone Co. (later part of EMI) adopted the tradename His Master's Voice (HMV) the following year

• The composer of *God Bless America* was born in Russia—Irving Berlin was born Israel Baline in Siberia in 1888. He emigrated to the United States as a child, where he wrote more than 900 songs, including *White Christmas*

Recording

The first machine to record sound was the *phonautograph*, invented by Edouard-Léon Scott de Martinville (France) in 1857. It responded to sound by tracing a line on a cylinder of paper, literally creating a sound track. But the *phonautograph* could not reproduce the sounds it recorded; the first machine to be able to do both was the phonograph, invented by Thomas Alva Edison (U.S.A.) in 1877. A recording stylus made indentations on a tinfoil cylinder, and, for playback, a second stylus retraced the indentations, reproducing the sounds originally recorded. A decade later Emile Berliner (Germany–U.S.A.) trumped Edison's invention with the Gramophone, which used a disc for recording and which eventually rendered the phonograph obsolete.

All music was performed live until 1878, when Jules Levy was recorded playing *Yankee Doodle* on the cornet. It was the first piece of music known to have been recorded, marking the birth of the record industry. Levy's recording, like those played on the first jukebox (U.S.A., 1889), was made on a phonograph cylinder rather than on the disc that was to take over during the 20th century. The first recorded music to be broadcast on the radio was

Opposite top Caricature of Adolphe Sax with his invention, the saxophone
Opposite below The jukebox. Although it was invented in 1889 the first printed reference to it did not appear until 1939, in *Time* magazine
Below Nipper, listening to his master's voice on an Edison disc machine

1889 The first coin-operated jukebox is installed, in the Palais Royal Saloon, San Francisco

1898 Valdemar Poulsen (Denmark) files a patent for the Telegraphone, the world's first magnetic recorder

1900 Paper record labels are used for the first time, issued by the Consolidated Talking Machine Co. (later part of RCA Victor, U.S.A.)

1906 The first music broadcast on the radio is Gounod's *O Holy Night*, played on the violin by radio engineer Reginald Aubrey Fessenden (U.S.A., b. Canada) and broadcast by his transmitter in Massachusetts. The first record to be broadcast is Handel's *Largo*, in the same program

1910 *Cavalleria Rusticana* and *I Pagliacci* become the first operas to be broadcast (from the Metropolitan Opera House, New York by the De Forest Radio Telephone Co.). This is also the world's first outside broadcast

1911 Dr. Elman B. Meyers (U.S.A.) becomes the first disc jockey

1913 *Billboard* magazine (U.S.A.) publishes the first music charts

1914 Sybil True (U.S.A.) broadcasts her *Little Ham* program, becoming the first female disc jockey

1917 Leo Sergeivitch Thérémin (Russia) develops the first electronic instrument, known as the Thérémin (publicly demonstrated 1920, patents filed in Germany 1924 and the United States 1925). Moses Baritz (England) becomes Britain's first disc jockey

c.1920–24 Lloyd Loar (U.S.A.), working for Gibson, produces the first microphone adapted for use with a guitar, a precursor of the electric guitar

1928 Dr. Kurt Stille (Germany) builds the first magnetic recorder to use tape rather than wire

1931 RCA Victor produces the first 33.3 rpm long-playing disc, a recording of Beethoven's Symphony No. 5. New equipment is required to play such records, so the venture fails and long-players are not revived until 1948

1933 EMI produces the first (experimental) stereo record for single pick-up, using a technique patented in 1931 by Alan Dower Blumlein (England)

1934 *Billboard* magazine publishes the first pop music chart of the most-played songs on network radio (followed in 1935 by a chart of record companies' lists of bestsellers). AEG (Germany) produces the Magnetophone, the first commercially successful tape recorder and the first to use plastic tape

1935 Adolf Rickenbacker (Switzerland–U.S.A., b. Rickenbacher) produces the first electric guitar, the Electric Vibrola Spanish Guitar, which has a built-in microphone

1939 *Time* magazine provides the first printed record of the term "juke-box," originally from the Deep South where jook means dance

1941 The first Golden Disc, awarded for sales of one million records, goes to Glenn Miller for *Chatanooga Choo Choo* (RCA Victor)

1945 *Billboard* magazine publishes the first album chart, with the King Cole Trio at No.1. Hugh Le Caine (Canada) invents the synthesizer

1947 Guitarist Merle Travis commissions Paul Bigsby to produce the first electric guitar with direct amplification of the strings

1948 Columbia produces the first vinyl long-playing disc, developed by Peter Goldmark (U.S.A.), and coins the term LP. The first LP recordings include Mendelssohn's Violin Concerto, Tchaikovsky's Symphony No. 4 and the musical *South Pacific*

1950 Recording Associates (U.S.A.) market first prerecorded (reel-to-reel) music tapes

1952 *New Musical Express* (NME) publishes the first British Record Hit Parade, with *Here in My Heart* by Al Martino at No.1

1955 EMI markets the first stereo prerecorded (reel-to-reel) music tapes

heard on Christmas Eve 1906, by which time the disc was more popular.

In the meantime, a rival medium was being developed: magnetic recording. In 1898 Valdemar Poulsen (Denmark) built the Telegraphone, which recorded sound magnetically on a wire. His patent stated that a preferable recording medium would be "a strip of insulating material such as paper covered with magnetizable metallic dust," which is exactly where the future of magnetic recording lay. In 1928 Dr. Kurt Stille (Germany) produced the first tape recorder (using metal tape), and in 1934 AEG (Germany) produced the Magnetophone, the first commercially successful tape recorder and the first to use plastic tape. Early tape machines used open reels but in 1958 George

Below Leo Thérémin demonstrating his invention, the Thérémin
Opposite Roger McGuinn of The Byrds playing a 12-string Rickenbacker at the Mount Tamalpais Music Festival, Marin County, CA, 1967. The Byrds made the chiming sound of the Rickenbacker famous in their cover of Bob Dylan's *Mr. Tambourine Man*

DID YOU KNOW?

● Leo Thérémin, inventor of the first electronic instrument (1917) moved to the United States from Russia in 1927, but in 1938 he and his wife were kidnapped by the NKVD (the Soviet state security agency) and forcibly returned to the Soviet Union

● In 1952 John Cage (U.S.A.) "composed" a piece entitled 4' 33", which consists of 4 minutes and 33 seconds of silence, indicated by a blank score to be played by any instrument or group of instruments. Usually it is performed by a pianist who sits at the piano for exactly 4 minutes and 33 seconds

1956 George Eash (U.S.A.) produces the first tape cassette and player but both are too bulky to be a commercial success (see 1963)

1957 The first (demonstration) commercial stereo discs are played in Los Angeles

1958 Commercial stereo discs are marketed for the first time, by Audio Fidelity (U.S.A.) in MAY, and in JUNE by Pye (Britain)

1963 Philips (Netherlands) exhibits the first compact cassette at the Berlin Radio & TV Exhibition

1964 Robert Moog (U.S.A.) produces the first prototype Moog synthesizer, which he describes as "voltage-controlled electronic music modules." Philips introduces the first compact cassette recorder, the Model 150 Carry-Corder

1967 Ray Dolby (U.S.A.) introduces the first tape-noise reduction system

1978 During their tour of North America, the Rolling Stones become the first band to gross over $1 million for a concert

1979 Sony (Japan) produces the first commercially successful personal stereo, known as the Walkman

1980 The first compact disc (CD) is shown by Sony (Japan) at the Japan Audio Fair after joint development by Sony and Philips (Netherlands)

1981 Satellite channel MTV (music television) is launched as the first dedicated music television channel. The first music video to be shown on MTV is *Video Killed the Radio Star*, by the Buggles

1982 The first CD player goes on sale (in Japan; CD players are first marketed in Europe the following year)

1987 Aiwa (Japan) launches the first digital audio tapes (DAT)

Eash (U.S.A.) produced the first tape cassette, which was followed five years later by the familiar compact cassette, developed by Philips (Netherlands).

Compact Discs

In 1982 the first CD (compact disc)-player went on sale in Japan, developed jointly by Philips (Netherlands) and Sony (Japan). CDs provided a revolution in music reproduction, overcoming public resistance to buying new equipment and quickly taking the lion's share of the market from the existing formats. CDs provided a huge improvement in sound quality, particularly after new recording techniques evolved to compensate for an initial lack of ambience: there cannot be much higher accolade than the approval of world-famous conductor Herbert von Karajan, who declared that, compared with CDs, "All else is gaslight."

DJs

Discs gave their name to two other 20th-century phenomena – the discotheque, which emerged during the 1960s, and the disc jockey (DJ). The first person to play a record on the radio was Reginald Fessenden (U.S.A., b. Canada) in 1906, but the first true disc jockey was Dr. Elman B. Meyers, who began broadcasting a regular 18-hour program from New York, in 1911. In 1920 the first regular radio broadcasting in Canada began in Montreal, Quebec at CFCF station. The first broadcast of the Canadian Broadcasting Corporation (CBC) was on July 1, 1927—the diamond jubilee of Canadian confederation.

December 28, 1895 is generally acknowledged as the birthday of cinema. On that day, nine months after making the first-ever public screening of a motion picture, the brothers Lumière made their first commercial screening, at the Grand Café, 14 boulevard des Capucines, Paris.

MOVIES

Without doubt, France is the birthplace of cinema. It is not clear just who was the first to build a motion picture camera, but the discussion centers on two Frenchmen, Louis Aimé Augustin Le Prince and Étienne Jules Marey. The first public screening of a motion picture was made in March 1895 by the brothers Lumière in Paris. And the medium is named after the first practical film projector, the Lumière's *cinématographe*.

But North America also had its part to play. Inspired by Étienne Jules Marey's moving images, Thomas Edison had William Kennedy Laurie Dickson (both U.S.A.) build a motion picture camera (Kinetograph) and a peephole viewer (Kinetoscope) in 1891, and it was the Kinetoscope that inspired Louis Lumière to build his *cinématographe*. Just as Edison's phonograph was rendered obsolete by the Gramophone, so the peephole Kinetoscope was made redundant by the big-screen *cinématographe*, but Edison is remembered for a number of other significant cinema firsts: his company was the first to use celluloid film for motion pictures (1889), the first to use 35 mm as a standard size of film, the first to use perforations to control the speed of the film, and in 1893 they built the world's first film studio.

Opposite top Éttienne Jules Marey's cine camera (chambre chrono-photographique), the first cine camera, being used to study the movement of creatures in an aquarium
Opposite below Woody and Buzz, the central characters of *Toy Story*, the first wholly computer-generated feature film
Below A film projected using Thomas Edison's Vitascope, with live orchestral accompaniment

DID YOU KNOW?

● The word cinema derives (via the French *cinématographe*) from the Greek *kinema*, meaning "motion," and *graphein*, meaning "write" or "represent"

● Silent film star Gladys Smith was better known as Mary Pickford, "America's sweetheart." Ironically Pickford was not an American, she was born in Toronto, Ontario in 1892

1910 *Det Danske Statens Arkiv for Historiske Film og Stemmer* (The Danish State Archive for Historical Film and Sound) is established as the first film archive

1911 David and William Horsley (U.S.A.) establish Nestor Studios, the first film studios to be located in Hollywood (Selig's 1909 studio, the first in Los Angeles, was in Edendale)

1922 *Der Brandstifter* (The Arsonist, Germany) is shown at the Alhambra cinema, Berlin, as part of the first public screening of a program of sound-on-film productions

1925 In Berlin, *Das Mädchen mit den Schwefelhölzern* (The Little Match-Girl, Germany) is screened as the first sound-on-film feature film. It closes after two days because of poor sound quality

1927 MAY, the Academy of Motion Picture Arts and Sciences is founded. OCTOBER, *The Jazz Singer*, starring Al Jolson, becomes the first successful "talkie" feature film (sound-on-disc)

1929 Academy Awards are presented for the first time

1931 The Academy Awards are christened Oscars after Academy librarian Margaret Herrick exclaims: "Why, he looks just like my Uncle Oscar"

1932 The world's first film festival is held in Venice, Italy, as part of the International Art Festival

1933 Richard Hollingshead (U.S.A.) opens the first drive-in cinema, in Camden, New Jersey

1948 The British Film Academy is founded (becoming the British Academy of Film and Television Arts [BAFTA] in 1975). *The Best Years of Our Lives* (U.S.A.) wins the first BAFTA Best Film Award

1953 Fox's *The Robe* premières at Grauman's Chinese Theater in Hollywood as the first feature film to be shot in CinemaScope

1995 *Toy Story* is released as the first wholly computer-generated film

The first film star was created not in Hollywood but in Germany. Early film performers were anonymous, but the 1909 film *Das Liebesglück der Blinden* (*The Love of the Blind Girl*) was such a success that the producer was persuaded to reveal the name of its writer and lead actress, Henny Porten (Germany). In her next film, Porten became the first performer to have her name appear on the credits. By the same definition, Florence Lawrence (U.S.A.) became North America's first film star the following year.

Throughout the century, filmmakers attempted to synchronize recorded sound with projections, but the first successful feature film to have the sound on the film itself was *The Jazz Singer*. Two years later Alfred Hitchcock (England) reshot his silent film *Blackmail* as the first British "talkie," the two versions providing the perfect comparison between old and new forms. *The Times* newspaper declared that "the comparison is very much in favor of the silent version" and went on to say that "the talkie is an unsuitable marriage of two dramatic forms … we cannot believe that it will endure."

Arts & Entertainment

TELEVISION

Vladimir Zworykin and John Logie Baird both patented television systems in 1923. Baird's was obsolete within 15 years but Zworykin's principle is still used today. Baird is the more famous, however, because he was the first person to publicly demonstrate the phenomenon of "seeing by wireless."

TIMELINE

1884 Paul Nipkow (Germany) patents an optical scanning disc, which he describes in his patent as an *elektrisches teleskop*

1897 Ferdinand Braun (Germany) introduces the first cathode ray oscilloscope

1907 Boris Rosing (U.S.S.R.) achieves the first transmission of images through the air

1908 Alan Archibald Campbell Swinton (Scotland) publishes the first article proposing an electronic television system using cathode rays (independently of Rosing)

1923 JULY, John Logie Baird (Scotland) files a patent for a mechanical television system.
DECEMBER, Vladimir Zworykin (U.S.S.R.–U.S.A.) files a patent for a cathode ray television transmitting tube

1924 Zworykin files a patent for a cathode ray receiving tube

1925 William Taynton (England) becomes the first human being to appear on television (in an experiment by John Logie Baird [Scotland])

1926 Baird makes the world's first public demonstration of moving television images. Baird files the first patent for a video recorder (recording on wax Gramophone discs), demonstrated the following year

1927 Philo T. Farnsworth (U.S.A.) makes the first demonstration of electronic television. The world's first (experimental) cable television

The first person to transmit an image through the air was Russian scientist Boris Rosing in 1907. Rosing succeeded in transmitting crude static images of geometric shapes, but technical limitations prevented him from progressing further. Sixteen years later, John Logie Baird (Scotland) filed a patent for a "system of transmitting views, portraits and scenes by wireless telegraphy," using an improved version of an image-scanning disc patented, but never built, by Paul Nipkow (Germany, 1884). Then, one Friday in October 1925, Baird rushed from his room and grabbed William Taynton, an office boy working one floor below his London workshop, the first person he saw. "I placed him before the transmitter and went into the next room to see what the screen would show. The screen was entirely blank, and no amount of tuning would produce any result. Puzzled, and very disappointed, I went back to the transmitter, and there the cause of the failure at once became evident. The boy, scared by the intense white light, had backed away from the transmitter." Baird gave Taynton a small payment to remain in place and then, "Going again into the next room, I saw his head on the screen quite clearly. It is curious that the first person in the world to be seen by television should have required a bribe to accept that distinction." Or perhaps not. Most television personalities now require much more than a small payment for their services.

Baird used Nipkow discs for scanning as well as receiving and in January 1926 he made the world's first public demonstration of moving television images. Baird is remembered to this day for that first demonstration, but the mechanical system he invented was extremely limited and was rendered obsolete in February 1937. Among afficionados, Vladimir Zworykin (U.S.S.R.–U.S.A.) is considered the father of television for his pioneering work in electronic (not mechanical) television systems.

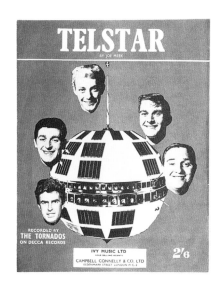

Above John Logie Baird with his Televisor
Left Sheet music for *Telstar* by the Tornados, inspired by the launch of the first successful telecommunications satellite (1962)

DID YOU KNOW?

- Film producer Sam Goldwyn (Poland–U.S.A., originally Samuel Goldfish) once said, "Why should people pay good money to go out and see bad films when they can stay at home and watch bad television for nothing?"

- Film director Alfred Hitchcock (England) clearly approved of the small screen, saying that, "Television has brought murder back into the home—where it belongs." Actor, playwright, composer and wit Noël Coward (England) had a slightly lower opinion, announcing, "Good heavens, television is something you appear on, you don't watch," while U.S. architect Frank Lloyd Wright described television as "chewing gum for the eyes"

A former pupil of Rosing, he emigrated to the United States in 1919, where he developed a cathode ray transmitter (which he called the iconoscope) and a cathode ray receiver (the kinescope). Zworykin made a public demonstration of his system in 1929, but by then Philo T. Farnsworth (U.S.A.) had already made the world's first public demonstration of electronic television, using his "image dissector." Zworykin had again been beaten to a "first," but ultimately his cathode ray system won out over the image dissector. Meanwhile, electronic television was also being developed in Canada, where, in 1934, F.C.P. Henroteau (Canada) invented the television camera.

In the late 1920s Baird made the first video recording, the first color transmission and the first transatlantic television transmission. But the death

transmissions are made, between Washington and New York by the Bell Telephone Co. (U.S.A.). Comedian A. Dolan (Ireland–U.S.A.) becomes the first televised professional entertainer (in a short one-off transmission by AT&T from New Jersey)

1928 Baird makes the first transatlantic television transmission (by land line to an international radio transmitting/receiving station). Baird makes the first color television transmission.
JULY, Daven Corporation (U.S.A.) produces the first commercially manufactured television receivers.
SEPTEMBER, New York television station WGY broadcasts *The Queen's Messenger*, the first television play (adapted from the stage version).

1929 The BBC (British Broadcasting Corporation) allots Baird a transmitter, and the first experimental BBC television broadcasts are made

1931 *People I Have Shot*, presented by photographer Howard Stein (U.S.A.), is broadcast by W2XCD as television's first chat show. The Baird Co. makes television's first outside broadcast (scenes from outside the company's studio in Long Acre, London)

1932 The BBC begins its first regular television broadcasts. New York television station W2XAB broadcasts television's first educational program

1934 Ursula Patzschke (Germany) becomes the first announcer to appear on television, introducing programs transmitted daily by the Reichspost from Berlin (announcements for Baird's early broadcasts were made off-camera)

1935 Reichs Rundfunkgesellschaft (Germany) inaugurates television's first regular high-definition service

1936 The BBC inaugurates Britain's first regular high-definition television service, from Alexandra Palace, London (mechanical and electronic broadcasts alternating weekly, the former being abandoned in FEBRUARY 1937

1937 Marcel Boulestin (France) becomes the first television chef, with his BBC program *Cook's Night Out*

1938 BBC's *News Map* is broadcast as television's first current affairs program. BBC's *Spelling Bee* is broadcast as the first panel game

1939 NBC (National Broadcasting Company, U.S.A.) starts the first regular high-definition television service in the United States

1941 An advertisement for Bulova Watches transmitted by WNBT (U.S.A.) becomes the first television advertisement to be broadcast (a 1930 advertisement for Eugène Permanent Waves was shown on CCTV only at a trade fair and was not broadcast). WNBT and WCBS (both U.S.A.) begin broadcasting television's first regular news bulletins

1947 *A Woman to Remember* (U.S.A.) becomes the first television soap opera

1951 CBS (Columbia Broadcasting System, U.S.A.) begins the world's first regular color television service (after making experimental transmissions as early as 1940)

1952 The Canadian Broadcasting Corporation (CBC) begins transmitting

1956 Ampex (U.S.A.) launches the first practicable video tape recorder and 3M (U.S.A.) produces the first magnetic videotape. Both are used in November by CBS to make the first retransmission of a television program

1960 DECEMBER 9, 7pm, the first episode of *Coronation Street* (Britain's, and now the world's, longest-running television soap opera) is broadcast

1962 *Telstar 1* goes into orbit as the first successful telecommunications satellite; the first transatlantic television broadcasts to use a satellite are made by AT&T the same year. Gay Byrne (Ireland) hosts the first *Late Late Show* (on Irish channel RTE 1), now the world's longest-running talk show

1966 Color television is introduced in Canada

1967 BBC2 begins Europe's first regular color television service, with coverage of the Wimbledon tennis championships forming the bulk of the first day of broadcasting

knell was sounded for mechanical scanning in 1936 when the Shoenberg and Baird systems were compared by the BBC in alternate weekly broadcasts. Within six months the Baird system was abandoned, confirming electronic television as the way forward. By then Baird might well have been in agreement with C.P. Scott, editor of the *Manchester Guardian*, who is attributed as saying:

"Television? The word is half Greek and half Latin. No good will come of it."

Programming

The first professional entertainer to appear on television was comedian A. Dolan (Ireland–U.S.A.), who was paid by AT&T to appear in an experimental transmission in April 1927, the first public demonstration of television in the United States. The first commercially manufactured television receivers were not available until the following year, so the only people to have seen Dolan's performance would have been those enthusiasts who had built their own sets, often from kits.

Entertainment developed alongside information: the first television documentary and the first television play appeared within months of each other in 1928, the first chat show in 1931 and the first educational program in 1932. The first television chef appeared as early as 1937, and then game shows and current affairs programs appeared together in 1938. Soap operas, so-called because they were sponsored by washing powder manufacturers, began on radio in 1932, but the first television soap opera was not screened until 1947. The formula remained the same as for radio soap operas—"never-ending stories of extraordinary events befalling quite ordinary folk with extraordinary frequency."

1969 The Canadian Broadcasting Corporation (CBC) discontinues tobacco advertising

1972 Philips (Netherlands) launches the first practicable domestic video cassette recorder, the N1500

1975 JVC (Japan) launches the first VHS format video cassette recorder

1979 The Canadian Broadcasting Corporation (CBC) begins live coverage of the Canadian House of Commons in Ottawa

1980 Philips (Netherlands) demonstrates the first video disc read by laser

Opposite "And now for the weather"
Below A German family gathers round the television to watch the coronation of Queen Elizabeth II, broadcast from England (June 2, 1953)

The introduction of plastics and injection molding in the 20th century gave impetus to a number of new toys, including the LEGO brick, Airfix models and the Frisbee® Disc, which was reputedly based on the aerodynamic qualities of a 19th-century pie tin from the Frisbie Baking Company.

Arts & Entertainment

TOYS

TIMELINE

1760 Joseph Merlin (Belgium) makes the first known use of roller skates, at a masquerade in London, England, where he rolls into a mirror, breaking the mirror and severely injuring himself

1816 Sir David Brewster (Scotland) invents the kaleidoscope

1863 James Leonard Plimpton (U.S.A.) patents the first four-wheeled roller skates, which he calls parlor skates

1866 Plimpton opens the first roller-skating rink, at the Atlantic House Hotel in Newport, Rhode Island

1897 William Harbutt (England) first manufactures Plasticine, which is first produced for sale in 1900 as a colored and more pliable form of modeling clay

1899 The first electric model cars are manufactured by Carlisle & Finch (U.S.A.)

1901 Meccano is patented by Frank Hornby (England)

1912 C.E. Richardson & Co. (England) patents the Ska-cycle (from skate-cycle), the first commercially manufactured scooter. (The generic name "scooter" is adopted later, and derives from a 19th-century word for a small sculling boat that "scooted" across the water.) Lionel Racing Automobiles is launched in the United States as the first electric slot-car racing game (see 1957)

Silly Putty

On March 30, 1943 Rob Roy McGregor and Earl Warwick (both U.S.A.) of Corning Glass filed the first patent for a method of "treating dimethyl silicone polymer with boric oxide," better known as Silly Putty. Silly Putty might never have seen the light of day but for the determination of an advertising agent and the intrigue of a journalist. Neither Corning Glass nor General Electric, which both independently tried to produce rubber from silicone and boric acid, could find a use for the flexible, bouncy substance they produced. Peter Hodgson (U.S.A.) saw the substance and exhibited it at the 1950 International Toy Fair as Silly Putty, which he registered as a trademark in 1952. It didn't sell until it was written about in the "Talk of the Town" column of the *New Yorker*, after which Hodgson was swamped with orders, ultimately making him a multimillionaire.

Opposite top The exasperating Rubik's Cube
Opposite below A Tokyo schoolgirl keeps an eye on her Tamagotchi electronic pet (1997)
Above 1960s' artwork promoting LEGO System

Frisbee®

In 1948 Walter Frederick Morrison and Warren Franscioni (both U.S.A.) developed the first plastic flying disc, calling it Morrison's Flyin' Saucer. In 1955 Morrison sold the idea to the Wham-O Manufacturing Co., who marketed it in 1957 as the Pluto Platter and relaunched it in 1958 as the Frisbee. Legend has it that the name Frisbee® originated with the pie tins of the Frisbie Baking Company of Connecticut, although this is hotly disputed. The company was founded by William Russell Frisbie in 1871 near Yale University, where students reputedly made a sport of throwing the empty tins.

Airfix

The Airfix company was founded by Nicholas Kove (Hungary) in 1939 as a manufacturer of air-filled rubber toys, hence the name. During the war the company was forced to make combs, and in 1947 bought the first machine in Britain for plastic injection molding. Production of model construction kits began the following year with a Fergusson tractor; the first Airfix ship, the *Golden Hind*, followed in 1952 and the first Airfix airplane, a *Spitfire*, in 1953.

The LEGO brick

In 1958 Godtfred Christiansen (Denmark) filed patents in Denmark, Britain and the United States for the first stud-and-tube system of building bricks, the LEGO brick. Godtfred was the son of carpenter Ole Kirk Christiansen, who made wooden toys and during the 1930s had set up a company called LEGO, taking its name from the Danish *leg godt*, meaning "play well." In 1947 the company bought the first machine in Denmark for plastic injection molding and began making plastic toys, including "automatic binding bricks." These were later improved to make the familiar LEGO brick, patented in 1958.

1943 Rob Roy McGregor and Earl Warwick (both U.S.A.) of Corning Glass file the first patent for what becomes Silly Putty

1945 Richard James (U.S.A.) files a patent for Slinky® (granted 1947); the name is coined by his wife Betty. Slinky® is first demonstrated at Gimbels department store

1948 Walter Frederick Morrison and Warren Franscioni (both U.S.A.) develop the first plastic flying disc, calling it Morrison's Flyin' Saucer. Airfix produces its first model construction kit

1957 Scalextric slot-cars are introduced by B.F. Francis (England) as an electric version of the Scalex cars first launched in 1952 by his company, Minimodels

1958 Godtfred Christiansen (Denmark) files patents for the first stud-and-tube system of building bricks, the LEGO brick. Richard Knerr and Arthur "Spud" Melin (both U.S.A.) of the Wham-O Manufacturing Co. launch the plastic Hula Hoop®, after hearing of Australian children exercising with bamboo hoops. Father and son surf-store managers Bill and Mark Richards (U.S.A.) produce the first commercially manufactured skateboards and christen the resultant new sport "terra-surfing"

1964 The first American National Skateboard Championships take place in Anaheim, California

1967 The LEGO Group (Denmark) introduces the DUPLO brick, larger bricks for smaller children

1975 Professor Erno Rubik (Hungary) patents the Rubik Cube, marketed in W. Europe and the United States in 1979

1996 Tamagotchi (electronic virtual pet) is invented and released by Bandai Japan, and becomes available worldwide the following year; sales eventually top 40 million

1997 The LEGO Group introduces LEGO MINDSTORMS, bricks programed to carry out various activities

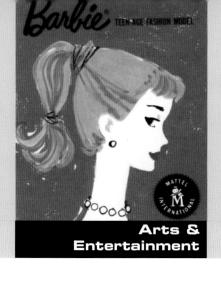

DOLLS

The first dolls were made from wood, clay, wax or sometimes ivory and by Classical times rag dolls and dolls with movable limbs had appeared. But only in an age of mass-production and television advertising could dolls such as Barbie or Action Man become a global phenomenon.

Above "Barbie—teenage fashion model"
Below "G.I. Joe, Action Soldier. America's *movable* fighting man" (1964)

Teddy bears

Stuffed animals were nothing new in 1902, but when Morris Michtom (Russia–U.S.A.) combined the idea of stuffed animals with the movable limbs of traditional dolls, he started a phenomenon. Inspired by a Clifford K. Berryman newspaper cartoon recording the fact that President Theodore "Teddy" Roosevelt had refused to shoot a young bear cub while on a hunting trip in Mississippi, Michtom called his toy "Teddy's Bear"; the more familiar term "teddy bear" first appeared in print in 1906, in the trade magazine *Playthings*. In 1903 Richard Steiff (Germany) of Steiff Co. showed a toy bear at the Leipzig Toy Fair. He later claimed that the Steiff Co.'s 1902 prototype predated Michtom's bears, making it the first stuffed toy bear with movable limbs. Neither Steiff nor Michtom had any proof of his claim, leaving historians divided on the issue of which was the first to produce a bear with movable limbs, but fairly certain that Michtom, whose company became the Ideal Toy Co., was the first to associate "Teddy" with bears.

Barbie, Ken, G.I. Joe and Action Man

In 1959 Mattel shocked the toy world by launching Barbie, the first children's doll to have an adult physiology. Many people disapproved of a doll with womanly curves, and New York's *Village Voice* referred to Barbie as "Boobs in Toyland." Barbie was named after the daughter of Ruth and Elliot Handler (U.S.A.), cofounders of Mattel. In 1961, two years after her launch, Barbie met her first boyfriend—it was a somewhat incestuous relationship as the new doll was named after the Handlers' son, Ken.

Although Ken was a male doll, he was aimed at Barbie's market. The first doll to have a target market of boys was

1558 The first recorded doll's house is made, for Duke Albrecht V of Bavaria (Germany)	**1902** Morris Michtom (Russia–U.S.A.) markets the first stuffed toy bear with movable limbs	**1913** Rose O'Neill (U.S.A.) patents the Kewpie doll, derived from the name Cupid	**1915** Cartoonist Johnny Gruelle (U.S.A.) creates and patents the first Raggedy Ann doll, publishing *Raggedy Ann Stories* in 1918. *Raggedy Andy Stories* follows in 1920

TIMELINE

G.I. Joe, launched in 1964 by Hasbro (U.S.A.), who claimed that G.I. Joe's face "comprised the faces of 20 Medal of Honor recipients." Two years later G.I. Joe was manufactured under license in Britain by Palitoy and marketed as Action Man, whose name was a play on a popular television series of the time called *Danger Man*. In North America G.I. Joe succumbed to a "G.I. Joe Must Go!" campaign in the wake of the Vietnam War, but in Britain Action Man went from strength to strength, with the addition of realistic cropped hair in 1970, gripping hands in 1973, Eagle Eyes in 1976 and plastic joints in 1979.

Elvis Presley, who had a massive hit with the song *Teddy Bear*

DID YOU KNOW?

● Action Man's realistic hair was achieved by spraying his head with glue, placing him in an electrostatic chamber and filling the chamber with nylon filaments. Because of the static charge, the filaments stuck to the head end on, like iron filings to a magnet

| **1959** Mattel launches Barbie, the first children's doll to have an adult physiology | **1961** Pedigree (Britain) launches the first Sindy doll, initially as part of a range of five Mam'selle Dolls | **1964** Hasbro (U.S.A.) launches G.I. Joe, the first doll to have a target market of boys | **1966** G.I. Joe is manufactured under license in Britain by Palitoy and marketed as Action Man | **1983** Sculptor Xavier Roberts (U.S.A.) introduces the first Cabbage Patch Dolls, previously known as Little People | **1984** Hornby Hobbies launches the first Flower Fairies dolls | **1993** Ty Warner (U.S.A.) of Ty, Inc. launches the first Beanie Babies® |

Out of the American Depression of the 1930s came two of the world's bestselling board games—Scrabble and Monopoly. The success of these games finally disproved the words of Lady Emily Lytton who, in 1892, wrote of "the most exciting game that ever was invented, called Tiddlywinks."

GAMES AND PUZZLES

Board games

In 1931 architect Alfred Mosher Butts (U.S.A.) devised the word game Scrabble (which he called Lexico), but his patent application was refused. Butts made a few sets by hand and in 1948 one owner, James Brunot (U.S.A.), acquired the rights, changed the name to Scrabble and began manufacturing the game. In 1953 Brunot licensed production to Selchow & Righter for North America and Australia, and to J.W. Spears (Britain) for the rest of the world. In 1954 James and Helen Brunot filed a patent application, which was granted in 1956. The first World Scrabble Championships took place in London, England, in 1991 and was won by Peter Morris (U.S.A.).

Three years after Butts devised Scrabble, Charles Darrow (U.S.A.) came up with the property board game Monopoly, using charms from Mrs. Darrow's

1934 Charles Darrow (U.S.A.) devises the property board game Monopoly

1944 Anthony E. Pratt and his wife (England) devise the whodunnit board game Cluedo, manufactured by Waddington's. The first public game is played in Waddington's managing director's office in 1947 and the game is first marketed in 1949

1947 Peter Adolph (England) devises the table football game Subbuteo

1970–71 Mordecai Mairowitz (Israel) invents the logic game Mastermind, launched commercially by Invicta Plastics (England) in 1973

1973 Gary Gygax (U.S.A.) founds TSR Hobbies to manufacture and market Dungeons and Dragons (launched 1974), devised by Gygax and his friend Dave Arneson

1974 Goro Hasegawa (Japan) devises the strategic board game Othello, one of the most popular board games in Japan

1979 Chris and John Haney, Scott Abbott and Ed Werner (all Canada) devise the general knowledge quiz board game Trivial Pursuit, first test-marketed in Canada in 1980, the United States in 1982 and mass-produced by Selchow & Righter from 1983

1991 The first World Scrabble Championships take place, in London, England

bracelet as counters. Darrow produced the first 5,000 sets privately before Parker Brothers (U.S.A.) began mass-producing Monopoly in 1935. Darrow is often said to have developed Monopoly from a rent-and-sale game devised by Elizabeth Phillips in 1924, but it seems that there is an even earlier version of Monopoly in the anticapitalist Landlord's Game patented by the radical Lizzie Margie in 1904 (granted 1905).

Puzzles

The first jigsaw puzzles were made in England and France, initially as educational tools, during the 1760s. John Spilsbury (England) is described in a 1763 directory as an "Engraver and Map Dissector in Wood, in order to facilitate the Teaching of Geography." M. Dumas (France) was selling "dissected maps" in France at about the same time.

Compiled by Arthur Wynne (England) and based on a Victorian parlor game, the world's first crossword puzzle, billed as "word-cross," appeared in *New York World* in 1913. Twelve years later, in 1925, the world's first *cryptic* crossword appeared in the *Saturday Westminster* (England), devised by a compiler known by the alias Torquemada.

DID YOU KNOW?

● The expression "checkmate" in chess derives from the Arabic *al shah mat*, meaning "the king is dead"

● In 1892, Lady Emily Lytton wrote to the Rev. Whitwell Elwin, describing a game of Tiddlywinks at great length and calling it: "the most exciting game that ever was invented … everyone begins to scream at the top of their voices and to accuse everyone else of cheating. Even I forgot my shyness and howled with excitement … I assure you no words can picture either the intense excitement or the noise. I almost scream in describing it"

● At the turn of the millennium, Monopoly was the world's best-selling board game with more than 150 million sets sold in 80 countries in 26 languages and set in cities including Athens, Madrid, Paris, Moscow and Tokyo

● Yachtzee, originally called the Yacht Club, was created by a Canadian couple in the 1800s. In the 1920s they sold the rights of the game to Edwin Lowe of BINGO fame

Above Scrabble
Below Monopoly
Opposite Subbuteo

Arts & Entertainment

VIDEO GAMES

Today millions of dollars are spent on research and development of the latest video games, but the first one was a simple game of screen table tennis, devised by U.S. physicist Willy Higinbotham in just two weeks in 1958 for a laboratory open day.

Above Game Boy
Below "If it can't test your nerve and skills with the most challenging range of new hit games, it's not Atari"
Opposite "Do not underestimate the power of PlayStation"

Willy Higinbotham (U.S.A.) wanted to make physics look more interesting for visitors to the 1958 open day at the Brookhaven National Laboratory so he decided to liven up the usual round of exhibits by devising a game using an oscilloscope linked to a television screen. He came up with a form of screen table tennis in which two players would use handheld controls to hit a ball back and forth over the net. Being a government employee, Higinbotham expected no royalties and therefore did not patent his idea, but it was to prove the precursor of a multimillion dollar industry.

Three years later, Steve Russell (U.S.A.), a computer programmer at the Massachusetts Institute of Technology, had the privilege of using one of the first computers to have a screen and keyboard instead of punched cards or paper tape. Instead of using it for research, Russell devised the first computer video game, called Spacewar, in which two players could fire torpedoes at each other from their "spaceships." Spacewar was played on a $4-million computer, so it was restricted to universities and research establishments, but, a decade later, the advent of microprocessors meant

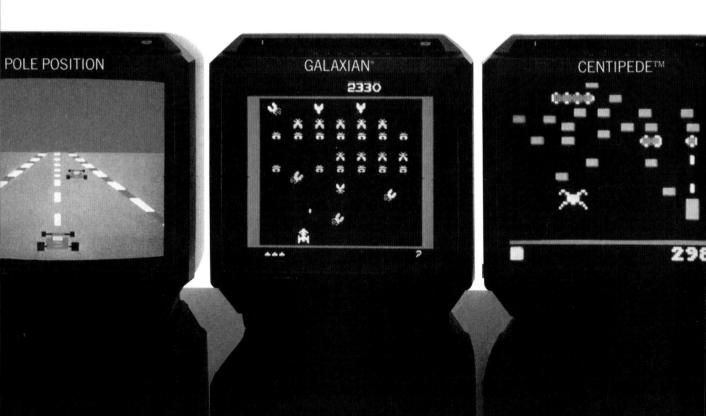

POLE POSITION

GALAXIAN
2330

CENTIPEDE™

298

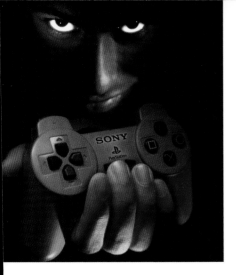

DID YOU KNOW?

• The Nintendo company (Japan) began life in 1889 as a manufacturer of playing cards

• The American company Atari takes its name from a Japanese gaming word similar in meaning to "check" in chess

TIMELINE

1958 Willy Higinbotham (U.S.A.) produces the first video game

1961–62 Steve Russell (U.S.A.) devises Spacewar, the first computer video game

1971 Nutting Associates (U.S.A.) builds Computer Space, the first arcade computer video game, written by Nolan Bushnell (U.S.A.) and based on Spacewar

1972 Bushnell founds his own company, Atari, and produces a screen-tennis game called Pong, the first commercially successful arcade computer video game. The first Pong is installed in Andy Capp's Tavern in Sunnyvale, California

1974 Atari launches Home Pong, the first home video game

1978 Taito Corporation (Japan) launches Space Invaders

1989 Nintendo (Japan) launches Game Boy, the first handheld computer games console

1994 Sony (Japan) launches PlayStation

that an arcade game was feasible. Nolan Bushnell (U.S.A.) had played Spacewar at the University of Utah, and he had also worked in an amusement arcade, and he realized that computer games could become as popular as pinball. In 1971, together with arcade game manufacturer Nutting Associates, Bushnell devised Computer Space, the first arcade computer video game. It did not catch on but, the following year, Bushnell founded his own company, Atari, and produced a screen table tennis game called Pong. Atari installed the first console in Andy Capp's Tavern in Sunnyvale, California, and Pong went on to become the first commercially successful arcade computer video game.

Although at first Pong spawned a number of copycat games, Atari was later squeezed out of the market by ever more sophisticated games, handheld consoles such as Nintendo Game Boy, and multigame home consoles such as Sony PlayStation, but not before pioneering another first—in 1974, Atari launched the first home video game, which was a huge success despite going by the unlikely name of Home Pong.

THE BEST OF THE REST...

The circus

During the late 1770s the equestrian shows organized by Philip Astley (England) in Lambeth, London, developed into the first circus. By 1777 Astley was employing a strongman, and by 1780 he had been joined by two clowns and several acrobats. The first circus in continental Europe was established in 1780 by Juan Porte (Spain) in Vienna, Austria; the first in North America was Rickett's Circus in Philadelphia, established 1792, and the first in Australia was the Australian Olympic Circus, opened in Sydney in 1842. The first circus to be televised was the Bertram Mills Circus, broadcast from Olympia, London, in 1938

Astley's Amphitheatre, Westminster Bridge Road, 1808. Loved by Charles Dickens, this was also the scene of clowns, such as Grimaldi, and popular melodrama

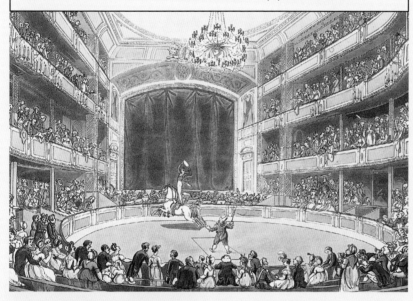

Pinball

The first coin-operated pinball game, known as Baffle Ball, was developed in 1930 by David Gottlieb (U.S.A.) from the 19th-century game of bagatelle. The game became known as pinball because a ring of nails, or pins, surrounded the scoring holes. The following year, Raymond Maloney (U.S.A.), one of Gottlieb's distributors, founded the Bally company to market Ballyhoo, his variation of Baffle Ball, and in 1934 Henry Williams (U.S.A.) introduced the first tilt mechanism for pinball games. Bumpers were introduced in 1936 and flippers in 1947

The Ferris wheel

The first Ferris wheel was designed by George Washington Gale Ferris Jr. (U.S.A.) and erected in Chicago in 1893. The original Ferris wheel was 76 m (228 ft.) in diameter, compared with 135 m (405 ft.) for the London Eye in England, currently the world's largest observation wheel, which opened in 2000

Opposite London Eye Millennium Wheel

The rollercoaster

The first rollercoaster, or switchback, was built at Coney Island, NY, in 1884 by L.A. Thompson (U.S.A.)

The opera

The first opera was *Dafne*, composed by Jacopo Peri and Jacopo Corsi with libretto by Ottavio Rinuccini (all Italy), first performed at the Palazzo Corsi in Florence, Italy, in 1597. The first opera to be televised was Bizet's *Carmen*, broadcast by the BBC in 1934

Wendy

The first girl to be named Wendy was Wendy Darling, a central character in J.M. Barrie's 1904 play *Peter Pan*. In 1911 the story was published in book form as *Peter and Wendy*

Chapter Seven

Medical Achievement

Sight and sound are often taken for granted by those with perfect vision and hearing. Fortunately there are devices to help those with impaired senses—the first glasses were invented in Italy in the 1280s, and the first electric hearing aid in North America in 1901.

SEEING AND HEARING

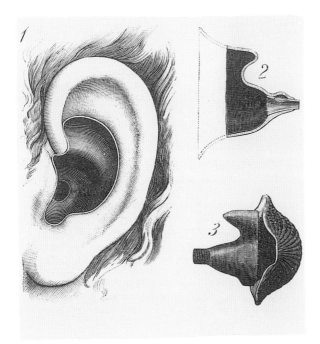

Opposite above
The oldest known representation of glasses, *The Cardinal Hugo of Provence*, Tomaso da Modena, fresco, Treviso (1352)
Opposite below
An optician using a photopter; it contains a range of lenses, to determine the ideal prescription for the patient (c.1895)
Right Dr. F.M. Blodgett's Micro-Audiphone; *Scientific American* (January 30, 1886)

Glasses

Humans have tried to aid their natural senses of hearing and sight since people first cupped a hand round an ear to hear better or narrowed their eyes to focus. The Roman emperor Nero is said to have watched gladiator fights through an emerald, but the first time glass lenses were used to assist vision (other than in the form of a magnifying glass) was in Italy during the 1280s.

The exact date is uncertain, but one early reference to glasses appears in a manuscript by Sandro di Popozo, dated 1289, in which he writes of "glasses known as spectacles, lately invented for the benefit of elderly people whose sight has become weak," and in 1305 Giordano da Rivalto wrote that "it is not yet twenty years since the art of making spectacles, one of the most useful arts on earth, was discovered."

The first glasses had convex lenses, and were used for long-sightedness. The first recorded use of glasses for short-sightedness occurred more than 200 years later in the form of a painting by Raphael that shows Pope Leo X using glasses with concave lenses. Most early glasses were held up to the face or clamped over the nose, and the first modern glasses, with side arms, were not invented until the early 18th century. Later in the same century Benjamin Franklin (U.S.A.) created the first bifocal glasses by placing two lenses together in the same frame, but it wasn't until 1910 that Carl Zeiss Co. (Germany) produced the first one-piece bifocal lens.

Hearing aids

The first electric hearing aid was patented by Miller Reese Hutchinson in 1901. It was a heavy, unwieldy device but it was the first move toward the miniaturized hearing aids of today—and it was successful enough to earn its inventor a medal from one of its first users, Princess Alexandra of Denmark, who used one during the coronation of her husband, Edward VII, when he became king of England in 1902.

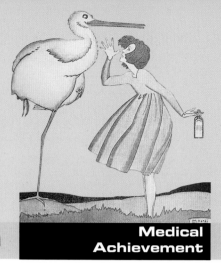

Medical Achievement

CONTRACEPTION

The first method of contraception was *coitus interruptus*, which is referred to in Genesis, the first book of the Bible, as a sin committed by Onan. Since then all methods of contraception have provoked moral arguments, none more so than the Pill, first made commercially available in 1960.

Sheaths

It is thought that the first sheaths, made from animal gut, were worn as long as 3,000 years ago by the ancient Egyptians. The first modern reference to what is now known as a condom comes in *De Morbo Gallico Liber Absolutissimus*, an account by Gabriele Falloppius (Italy, a.k.a. Gabriello Fallopio) of his research into the use of the sheath to prevent syphilis (published in 1564). Falloppius wrote that he had designed a linen sheath and had tested it on 1,100 men; but, despite the introduction of linen, condoms made from animal intestines were still common 200 years later. Casanova (Italy) referred to them in his *Memoirs* as "English overcoats," and described how they were tied at the base with a ribbon. However, toward the end of the 19th century rubber eventually replaced intestines.

The sheath advocated by Falloppius was intended primarily for protection against disease rather than for contraception, but the effect of early condoms as protection against anything at all was open to question. In 1671 the French lady of letters Madame Marie de Sévigné described the sheath as "an armor against enjoyment and a spider-web against danger."

The contraceptive pill

For a while the contraceptive pill, first introduced in 1960, seemed to provide the ideal alternative to this "armor against enjoyment," although the uncertainty regarding its long-term side effects, and the possibility of contracting AIDS, led to a condom revival (whose prophylactic qualities had been improved since the 17th century) in the 1980s.

During the 1940s Margaret Sanger of the Planned Parenthood Movement was looking for a contraceptive that would be "harmless, entirely reliable, simple, practical, universally applicable and acceptable to both husband and wife." In response to this, Gregory Pincus and John Rock (both

Above "Thanks to *Eutrofina*, an Italian girl can thumb her nose at the stork." Advertisement in *L'illustrazione Italiana* (1925)
Opposite left Contraceptive pills (2000)
Opposite right Condom made of animal caecum, manufactured by John Bell & Croyden Ltd. (early 20th century)

Biblical *Coitus interruptus* is referred to in the book of Genesis as a sin committed by Onan	**1564** Gabriele Falloppius (Italy) provides the first written reference to a (linen) condom, in a work published two years after his death	**1881** The first birth control clinic opens, in Holland. The use of the diaphragm is encouraged, giving rise to the name Dutch cap	**1916** Margaret Sanger (U.S.A.) opens a birth control clinic in New York, for which she is imprisoned	**1928** Ernst Grafenberg (Germany) develops the first contraceptive coil (though various forms of IUD [intrauterine device] have been used since antiquity)

TIMELINE

U.S.A.) developed the first contraceptive pill, first marketed commercially in 1960 by the G.D. Searle Drug Company. Medical risks have since come to light, but the Pill set the tone for the "swinging sixties" and immediately became a hugely popular form of contraception. The biggest problems were the ethical ones, illustrated by British writer and broadcaster Irene Thomas's quip: "Protestant women may take the pill. Roman Catholic women must keep taking The Tablet."

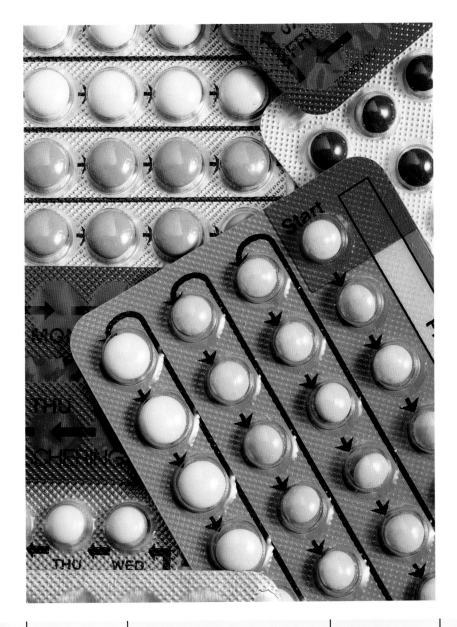

| **1957** The London Rubber Co. (England), manufacturer of Durex, introduces the first lubricated condom | **1960** Enovid 10, the first approved contraceptive pill, becomes commercially available in the United States. (Developed by Gregory Pincus and John Rock [both U.S.A.] using a method of synthesizing progesterone patented by Frank Colton [Poland–U.S.A.] in 1953) | **1969** The Pill was introduced in Canada in 1961, but doctors were not legally permitted to prescribe it for eight years | **1986** Norplant®, the first contraceptive hormonal implant, is licensed for use in the United States |

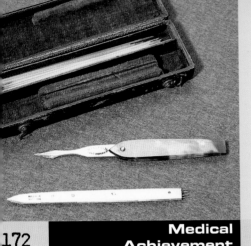

It is often said that prevention is better than cure. While many doctors have helped to cure diseases, two are notable for their efforts to prevent it. In 1796 Edward Jenner pioneered vaccination, and in 1847 Ignaz Semmelweis insisted on the first use of antiseptics in hospitals.

**Medical
Achievement**

DISEASE
PREVENTION

Above Vaccination set used by Edward Jenner (c.1800)
Below "A vaccination party" in Philadelphia, PA. Illustration from *The Day's Doings* (December 16, 1871)

Vaccination

One of the first ways of preventing disease was to infect people with a weak strain of a disease (often smallpox) to immunize them against catching a stronger, possibly deadly strain. Known as inoculation, or variolation, this idea was practiced in the Middle and Far East long before it was introduced to western Europe from Turkey in the early 18th century.

Dr. Edward Jenner (England) is famous for refining this process into a safer form, known as vaccination. Jenner's methods would not be

Carbolic acid solution spray, Paris. A modification by Lucas-Championnière of Lister's invention. French surgeons were some of the first to adopt this method of sterilization (c.1875)

considered ethical today; having infected eight-year-old James Phipps with cowpox to protect him against the deadly smallpox, Jenner later infected him with smallpox to prove that his theory had worked. Jenner was proved right, and his system of vaccination was used to save countless lives, but it appears that he was not in fact the first: there is a record that butcher Robert Fooks was vaccinated by a surgeon called Downe in 1771, but Mr. Downe does not appear to have developed the idea any further.

Antisepsis

Today, cleanliness in hospitals seems a matter of common sense, but at one time medics treated patients immediately after performing post-mortems—without washing in between. The 19th-century obstetrician Ignaz Semmelweiss (Hungary), of the Vienna General Hospital, Austria, noticed that the postnatal death rate from puerperal fever was much higher on the maternity ward visited by surgeons and medical students than on the ward staffed by midwives only.

When his friend Dr. Kolletcha died of puerperal sepsis after being grazed during a postmortem, Semmelweiss realized that disease was being carried onto the wards by the medics themselves, and began to insist on a rigorous program of washing hands, clothes and instruments in chlorinated lime between autopsies and the examination of patients. It was the first systematic use of antiseptics and the results were dramatic, but Semmelweiss was ridiculed for his ideas, as was Joseph Lister (England), who pioneered the first use of antiseptics in surgery. It was only after Lister's ideas were adopted in Germany, and Robert Koch (Germany) demonstrated the existence of bacteria, that Lister and Semmelweiss were proved right.

TIMELINE

1771 British surgeon Mr. Downe makes what is thought to be the world's first vaccination

1796 Edward Jenner (England) makes his first vaccination, the beginning of the first detailed investigation of the practice

1847 Ignaz Semmelweis (Hungary) pioneers the first use of antiseptics

1865 Inspired by the work of Semmelweis, Joseph Lister (England) introduces antiseptics to surgery. Known as "the father of antiseptic surgery," Lister becomes the first medic to be made a peer

The 20th century saw many important cures for disease. Insulin was first synthesized in 1921, the first antibiotic was discovered in 1928, and a seemingly trivial but hugely important drug was first marketed on the eve of the century in 1899—aspirin.

PILLS AND POTIONS

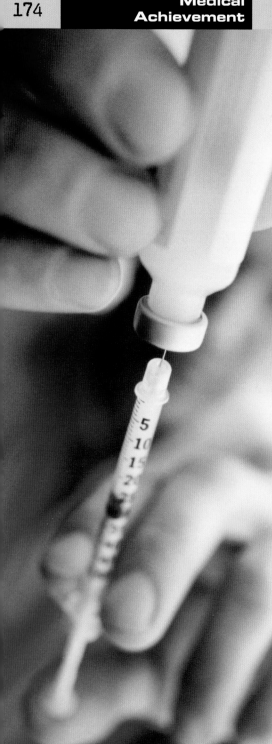

Aspirin

Human beings have always sought ways to ease pain and cure disease. One early remedy for fevers and gout, used by Hippocrates in the 5th century b.c., was an infusion of willow bark. The active ingredient, salicyclic acid, was first synthesized in 1853 by Charles Gerhardt (France). Gerhardt did not realize the importance of the compound, and in 1898 Felix Hoffman (Germany) of Bayer patented a method of synthesizing acetylsalicyclic acid, first marketed commercially the following year as aspirin.

Aspirin has proved to be something of a wonder drug, being used as an anti-inflammatory, a painkiller and an anticoagulant for sufferers of strokes and heart attacks, and is thought to be a preventative against nerve disorders and certain cancers. It has also helped millions through bouts of the common cold and flu, and led to the development of Alka-Seltzer, which was based on a homemade curative made from aspirin and bicarbonate of soda.

Insulin

Insulin is a hormone produced in the pancreas, and it is vital for the control of blood sugar levels. People suffering from *diabetes mellitus* cannot produce sufficient insulin, and the discovery of a means of synthesizing this hormone has normalized the lives of millions of diabetics. In 1921 Frederick Grant Banting and Charles Best (both Canada) isolated insulin for the first time, and on January 11, 1922 14-year-old Leonard Thompson became the first human to be treated with insulin. Banting was awarded the 1923 Nobel Prize for Physiology or Medicine, and shared the prize money with Best.

Penicillin

In 1928 Alexander Fleming (Scotland), working at St. Mary's Hospital in London, was annoyed to find mold growing on a petri dish in which he was growing bacteria. Fortunately, rather than simply throwing the dish away, he noticed that the mold had killed the bacteria. The mold was *penicillium notatum*, and Fleming called the substance that had killed the bacteria penicillin. Just over a decade later, Howard Florey (Australia) and Ernst Chain (Germany–Britain) succeeded in isolating penicillin, using it to manufacture the first antibiotic, for which they shared the 1945 Nobel Prize for Physiology or Medicine with Fleming.

Opposite top Soluble aspirin powder
manufactured by F. Bayer & Co.
Above Stained glass window in St. James's
Church, London, depicting Sir Alexander

Fleming in his laboratory. Fleming was
working at St. Mary's Hospital at the time of
his discovery of penicillin in 1928

TIMELINE

1853 Charles Gerhardt (France) is the
first person to synthesize acetylsalicylic
acid but makes no practical use of it

1898 Felix Hoffman (Germany) takes
out the first patent for acetylsalicylic
acid (aspirin)

1899 Bayer (Germany) markets aspirin
for the first time

1905 Aspirin first becomes available in
Britain

1921 Frederick Grant Banting and
Charles Best (both Canada) of the
University of Toronto Medical School
produce the first synthetic insulin

1922 Leonard Thompson (Canada) is the
first human to be treated with insulin

1928 Alexander Fleming (Scotland)
discovers the effects of *penicillium
notatum* on bacteria, paving the way
for the first antibiotics

1931 Miles Laboratories (U.S.A.)
markets Alka-Seltzer for the first time

1933–35 Dr. Hagedorn (Denmark)
develops the first protamine insulin,
allowing a day's supply to be
administered in a single injection

1939 Howard Florey (Australia) and
Ernst Chain (Germany–Britain) succeed
in isolating penicillin, the first antibiotic

1972 Bryan Molloy and Klaus
Schmiegel (both U.S.A.) develop
Fluoxetine, the active ingredient of
Prozac, which is approved as an
antidepressant in 1986 and first made
available in Belgium that year. Prozac
becomes available in the United States
in 1988 and Canada in 1989

1981 Artificially produced insulin
becomes the first genetically
engineered protein used to treat a
human disease

1994 Nicholas Terrett and Peter Ellis
(both Britain) of Pfizer Ltd. receive a
patent for Viagra as a treatment for
impotence (based on sildenafil citrate,
patented in 1990 by Terrett and
others as a treatment for heart
disease and hypertension)

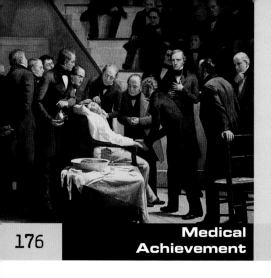

The first operation to be carried out using an anesthetic was performed by Dr. Crawford Long in 1842. But instead of hailing this medical breakthrough, the citizens of Jefferson, Georgia, accused Long of sorcery and threatened him with a lynch mob.

Medical Achievement

ANESTHETICS

Above First public demonstration of an operation under anesthetic, on October 16, 1846, in Massachusetts General Hospital. Painting by Robert Hinckley (1882)
Below Lampoon by Gilray depicting Sir Humphrey Davy operating hydraulic bellows filled with laughing gas at his Royal Institution demonstrations (1802)

Early attempts to diminish the pain of surgery included hypnotism or administering drugs such as opium or a mixture of alcohol and gunpowder. At the beginning of the 19th century, Sir Humphrey Davy (England) discovered that nitrous oxide was more effective in dulling pain than opiates or alcohol, but Davy's discovery led to more "laughing gas" parties than painless operations. The first surgical operation to be performed using anesthetic did not take place until nearly half a century later, in March 1842, when Dr. Crawford Long (U.S.A.) used a preparation of ether to render James Venable unconscious while he removed a cyst from Venable's neck. Long performed a further nine operations using ether, including the amputation of a boy's finger, but he gave up using anesthetic after the local community threatened to lynch him for sorcery.

c.1800 Sir Humphrey Davy (England) discovers that nitrous oxide, or "laughing gas," can be used to dull the sensation of pain	**1842** Crawford Williamson Long (U.S.A.) performs the first operation to use ether as a general anesthetic. Because of threats, he does not reveal his discovery until after ether anesthesia is patented in 1846	**1846** Dentist William Morton (U.S.A.) administers ether in the first public demonstration of anesthesia	**1847** James Simpson (Scotland) becomes the first surgeon to use chloroform as a general anesthetic in preference to ether (chloroform was first synthesized by Justus von Liebig [Germany] in 1831)	**1884** Cocaine is used as the first local anesthetic, in an eye operation performed by Josef Brettauer (Italy), after its painkilling properties are discovered by Karl Koller (Austria)	**1902** Emil Fischer (Germany) synthesizes Veronal, which is used as the first intravenous general anesthetic

▌TIMELINE

Meanwhile, in 1844 dentist Horace Wells (U.S.A.) used nitrous oxide as an anesthetic for the extraction of teeth. His public demonstration was a failure (possibly because of a badly prepared compound), and chemist Charles T. Jackson suggested to Wells's colleague William Morton (U.S.A.) that ether would be more effective. In 1846 Morton successfully used ether for a tooth extraction. This was reported in the *Boston Daily Journal*, as a result of which Morton was invited by Henry J. Bigelow, a Boston surgeon, to administer ether in the first public demonstration of surgery under anesthesia. The operation was performed by surgeon John Warren at the Massachusetts General Hospital and was a success. Subsequently the principle of anesthesia was patented in the names of Morton and Jackson, although the patent was later revoked when a court ruled that anesthesia was a discovery rather than an invention, and therefore not patentable.

The doctors and surgeons who observed Warren's operation were astounded to witness surgery performed without the patient thrashing about in agony. A plaque in the operating theater commemorates the historic moment: "The patient declared that he felt no pain ... Knowledge of this discovery spread from this room throughout the civilized world and a new era for surgery began."

A chloroform inhaler dating from the 1850s. The mask was made of lead and molded to the patient's features

DID YOU KNOW?

● William Morton wanted to call his discovery "letheon," after the mythical River Lethe, but the poet and physician Oliver Wendell Holmes Sr. (U.S.A.) suggested that "the state should I think be called anaesthesia ... the adjective will be anesthetic"

● Crawford Long was not the only one to encounter objections to anesthesia. Scottish surgeon Sir James Young Simpson, the first to use chloroform, had to convince Calvinists that anesthesia was not against the teachings of the church. Ecclesiastics accepted that it was no sin for men, because God had put Adam in a deep sleep to remove his rib, but they were not convinced about women, particularly in childbirth, because of the edict in the Book of Genesis that: "In sorrow shalt thou bring forth children." Simpson's methods were finally accepted after chloroform was used to assist Queen Victoria in the birth of her eighth child, Prince Leopold, in 1853

Medieval tooth extraction was a barbaric business and the first professional dental qualification was not established until 1699, by the French College of Surgeons, allowing members who passed the examination to describe themselves as *Experts pour les Dents*.

Medical Achievement

DENTISTRY

Pierre Fauchard (France) is generally considered to be the father of dentistry. He was the first man to ensure that dentistry was taken seriously within the medical profession, and he set up a dental practice in Angers, France, in 1696. Three years later the first professional dental qualifications were established by the French College of Surgeons, following an edict issued by King Louis XIV. In 1728 Fauchard published *Le Chirurgien-Dentiste* (The Surgeon-Dentist), which described the tools and practice of dentistry. His book led to a huge expansion in dental practice across Europe, but it was to be more than 100 years before the foundation of the first school in the world to specialize exclusively in dentistry: the Baltimore College of Dental Surgery in Baltimore, MD.

The dreaded dental drill was first used by the Roman surgeon Archigenes c.a.d. 100. Drills became less painful as they became faster; one significant improvement was the foot treadle engine drill (1872), and things took a turn for the better in 1957 with the introduction of the first air-turbine drill, which used compressed air to reach speeds of up to 200,000 rpm.

The dental chair is the scene of many nightmares but it is an improvement on the early days, when the patient had to sit between the dentist's knees. The first specialist dental chair, designed by James Snell (England), appeared in 1832, and the first electrically operated dental chair was built in 1950.

Toothbrush and toothpaste

Frayed sticks have been used as toothbrushes since antiquity but the toothbrush as we know it, with the bristles at right angles to the handle, is first mentioned in a 17th-century Chinese encyclopedia as an invention of 1498. Toothpaste, first used by the Romans, did not appear in tubes until 1892, when the idea was adapted from the paint tubes used by artists—a great boon unless you were U.S. presidential aide H.R. Haldeman who, after being disgraced in the Watergate scandal, said: "Once the toothpaste is out of the tube, it is awfully hard to get it back in."

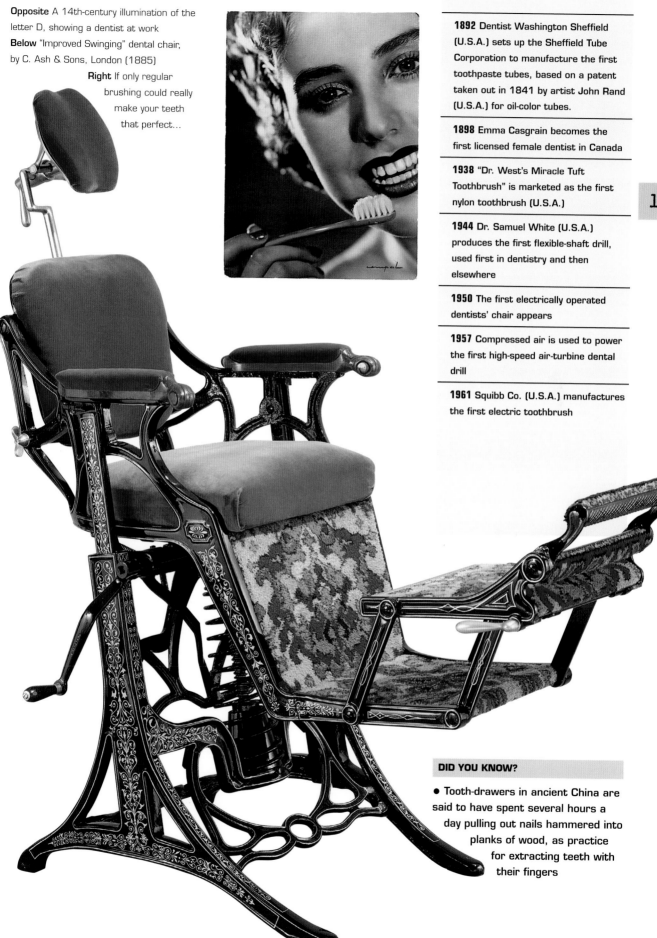

Opposite A 14th-century illumination of the letter D, showing a dentist at work

Below "Improved Swinging" dental chair, by C. Ash & Sons, London (1885)

Right If only regular brushing could really make your teeth that perfect…

1892 Dentist Washington Sheffield (U.S.A.) sets up the Sheffield Tube Corporation to manufacture the first toothpaste tubes, based on a patent taken out in 1841 by artist John Rand (U.S.A.) for oil-color tubes.

1898 Emma Casgrain becomes the first licensed female dentist in Canada

1938 "Dr. West's Miracle Tuft Toothbrush" is marketed as the first nylon toothbrush (U.S.A.)

1944 Dr. Samuel White (U.S.A.) produces the first flexible-shaft drill, used first in dentistry and then elsewhere

1950 The first electrically operated dentists' chair appears

1957 Compressed air is used to power the first high-speed air-turbine dental drill

1961 Squibb Co. (U.S.A.) manufactures the first electric toothbrush

DID YOU KNOW?

● Tooth-drawers in ancient China are said to have spent several hours a day pulling out nails hammered into planks of wood, as practice for extracting teeth with their fingers

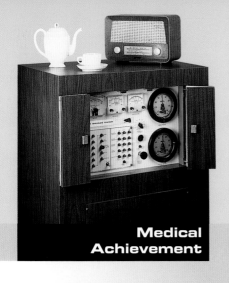
If disease or injury cannot be prevented or cured, the only answer is to replace the affected part—important in the case of limbs and vital in the case of organs. The first artificial limbs were used in the ancient world, but the first organ transplants did not take place until the 20th century.

PROSTHESES AND TRANSPLANTS

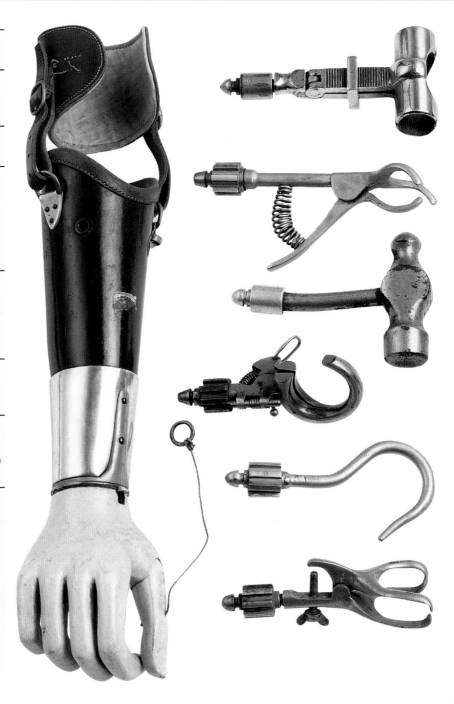

Prostheses

The Greek historian Herodotus provides the first written record of an artificial limb, describing a man named Hegesistratus who was condemned to death in 484 b.c., cut off his foot in order to escape, and later made himself a wooden foot. His efforts were in vain because he was recaptured and put to death. There are also accounts of artificial limbs being made for Roman warriors, but the first physician to make systematic use of prosthetic limbs was Ambroise Paré (France), after he became an army surgeon in 1537.

Paré is often referred to as the father of modern surgery for his advances in surgical techniques, particularly the use of ligatures after amputation instead of cauterization with boiling oil or red hot irons. Paré also attempted to replace lost limbs with mechanical ones; these included hands with jointed fingers and, by 1561, the first artificial legs to have movable ankle and knee joints. He was the pioneer in a field that now produces myoelectric prostheses that can be controlled by nerve impulses from the brain.

Transplants

Irretrievably damaged organs can be replaced either by machines or by transplants. The first artificial respirator (iron lung) was built in 1927 by Philip Drinker (U.S.A.), using a sealed box with the air pressure controlled by a vacuum cleaner. A more sophisticated version was tested at Boston Hospital in 1928, and the iron lung was produced for general use from 1931.

The first mechanical organ replacement was the kidney dialysis machine, invented in 1943 by Willem Kolff (Netherlands), to remove blood from the patient, filter it as the kidney would do, and return it to the body. Such machines have saved the lives of countless patients, but transplants are even more effective. The kidney was the first of the vital organs to be transplanted, the first successful operation taking place in 1954. The first liver and lung transplants both took place in 1963, followed four years later by the holy grail of organ transplants, the human heart (see p. 183).

Opposite top Kidney machine used for home dialysis, c.1966. Manufactured by Milton Roy (U.S.A.), this machine was used by Moreen Lewis, one of the first patients to have a dialysis machine at home
Opposite Artificial right arm with attachments, c.1925, made for use in heavy-duty work. Attachments include a carpenter's tool-holder with a square clamp, a brace and chisel holder and a hammer

Aimee Mullins' legs were amputated when she was just one year old, but with the help of the most advanced artificial legs she has set world records in running the 100-meter, 200-meter dash and the long jump at the Paralympics (1998)

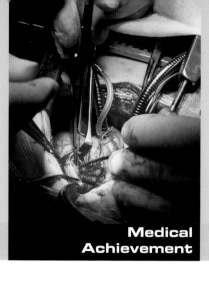
Progress in heart surgery has been rapid. The first pacemaker, developed in 1952, was the size of a television, but the first to be implanted beneath the skin appeared just six years later. Less than a decade later, in 1967, Christian Barnard carried out the first human heart transplant.

HEART SURGERY

Above A surgeon performs coronary by-pass surgery on an infant
Below Dr. Christian N. Barnard (South Africa [left]} speaks with Dr. Michael de Bakey and Dr. Adirn Kantrowitz, prior to their appearance on the television program *Face The Nation* to discuss their accomplishments in performing the first successful human heart transplants (December 24, 1967)

Pacemakers

The first cardiac pacemaker was invented by Paul Zoll (U.S.A.) in 1952. It was a large, heavy piece of equipment that worked by sending electric shocks through the chest, often resulting in burns. Six years later Ake Senning and Rune Elmquist (both Sweden) developed the first pacemaker that could be implanted in the body. However, it was still not portable because it required an external power source, which entailed passing wires through the skin. The real breakthrough came in 1960, when Wilson Greatbatch (U.S.A.) perfected the first self-contained (battery-powered) pacemaker, implanted near the surface of the skin so that the batteries could be changed. The first Greatbatch pacemaker was implanted in the chest of 77-year-old Henry Hennafeld at the Millard Fillmore Hospital in Buffalo, NY, in 1960.

An artificial heart, 2000. Hundreds of people die every year because there are not enough human hearts available for transplantation. A human body would not reject an artificial heart because the immune system will not recognize any of its materials

Heart transplants

The first human to receive a transplanted heart was 58-year-old Boyd Rush, operated on in the United States in 1964. The intended donor, dying of brain damage, was still alive when Rush's heart failed, so instead Rush was given the heart of a chimpanzee by surgeon James D. Hardy (U.S.A.). This is not as absurd as it may sound (the heart valves of pigs have since been successfully used to replace those of humans), but the heart was too small and Rush survived for only a few hours. Three years later, Christian Barnard (South Africa) performed the first human heart transplant, at Groote Schurr Hospital in Cape Town. He transplanted the heart of Denise Ann Darvall into 55-year-old Louis Washkansky, who died 18 days later of pneumonia.

The life expectancy of heart transplant recipients has increased dramatically since the pioneering operations, some patients leading a normal life for as long as 20 years and many of them ultimately dying of causes unrelated to the heart.

TIMELINE

1952 Paul Zoll (U.S.A.) invents the first cardiac pacemaker, but he does not patent it

1958 Ake Senning and Rune Elmquist (Sweden) invent the first implantable pacemaker

1960 Wilson Greatbatch (U.S.A.) patents the first self-contained implantable pacemaker. Henry Hennafeld is the first recipient

1961 The first artificial heart valves are inserted in a human heart by Albert Starr (U.S.A.)

1964 Boyd Rush becomes the first human to receive a transplanted heart

1967 Christian Barnard (South Africa) performs the first successful human heart transplant; the recipient is Louis Washkansky

1982 The Jarvik-7 becomes the first artificial heart to permanently replace a human heart. Designed by Robert K. Jarvik (U.S.A.), it is implanted in 61-year-old dentist Dr. Barney Clark (U.S.A.) by surgeon William de Vries at the University of Utah Medical Center

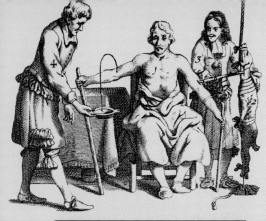

The two most important names in the story of blood are William Harvey, the first person to describe circulation, but ridiculed for his ideas until they were proved correct shortly after his death, and Karl Landsteiner, who in 1900 discovered blood groups, making safe transfusions possible.

Medical Achievement BLOOD

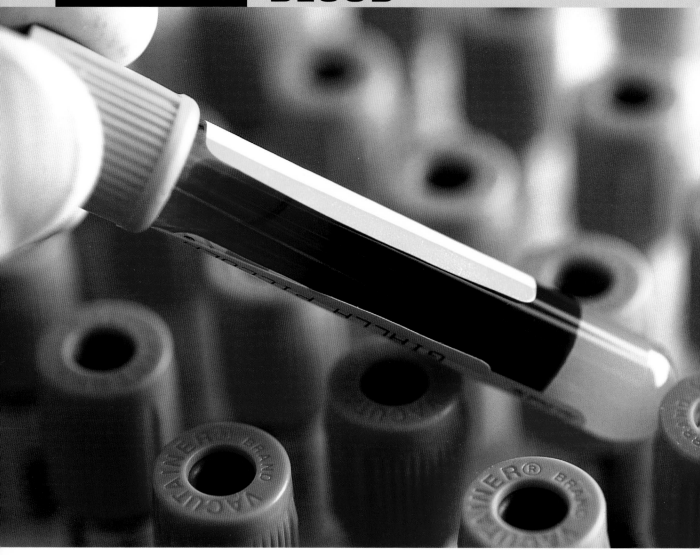

1628 William Harvey (England) is the first person to describe the circulation of blood in mammals

■TIMELINE

1652 Francis Potter (Britain) devises the first syringe by attaching an animal bladder to a sharpened goose quill

1667 Jean-Baptiste Dénis (France) injects a patient with a liter of lamb's blood, the first blood transfusion involving a human being

1818 James Blundell (England) performs the first transfusion of human blood

1896 The sphygmomanometer, for measuring blood pressure, reaches its recognizably modern form with the addition of the inflatable cuff by Scipio Riva-Rocci (Italy)

1900 Karl Landsteiner (Austria–U.S.A.) discovers the four major blood groups. In 1940 he discovers the Rhesus factor

ike pioneers in many fields, William Harvey (England) was ridiculed for his theories, which were published in *Exercitatio Anatomica de Motu Cordis et Sanguinis* (An Anatomical Exercise on the Motion of the Heart and Blood in Animals) in 1628. Harvey's suggestion that blood circulated around the human body, and that the heart was a muscle that acted as a pump, seemed preposterous. His critics latched onto the fact that he could not show how the blood passed from the arteries, carrying blood away from the heart, to the veins, which returned it to the heart. Harvey concluded that the link between the two systems must be too small to see and was further ridiculed. Then, in 1661, just four years after Harvey's death, Marcello Malpighi (Italy) used a microscope to prove the existence of capillaries linking the arterial and venous systems, completely vindicating Harvey's theories.

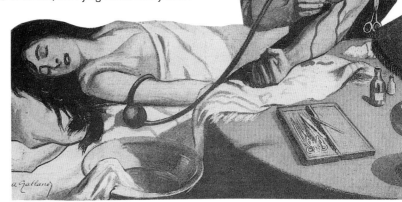

Various experiments were subsequently made in transfusing the blood of animals and humans, but there was a high failure rate for reasons that were not understood until Karl Landsteiner (Austria–U.S.A.) established, in 1900, the existence of the major blood groups. He subsequently discovered two further groups in 1927, and was awarded the 1930 Nobel Prize for Physiology or Medicine for his discoveries.

The discovery of anticlotting agents by A. Hustin (Belgium) and storage techniques pioneered by Oswald Robertson (U.S.A.) meant that during World War One blood could be held in readiness for transfusion. These discoveries enabled Dr. Percy Oliver (England) to establish the first voluntary blood donation service in 1921, and Professor Sergei Yudin (U.S.S.R.) to establish the first blood bank in 1931.

The first transfusion of artificial blood was carried out by Ryochi Naito (Japan) in 1979. Naito injected himself with 200 ml of fluosol DA, which was later used at the Fukushima Medical Center, Japan, to save the life of a man whose blood group was so rare that no human blood was available for transfusion.

Opposite top Engraving of an early experimental blood transfusion between a dog and a man. Engraving by Johann Scultetus, Amsterdam (1671)

Opposite below Vacutainer containing blood. A vacutainer removes blood using a partial vacuum. The colored caps on the tubes indicate which test is to be carried out on them

Above "L'heroïsme d'un Médicin" (The Heroism of a Doctor). In order to save a dying woman, the surgeon injects her with his own blood. Illustration by Andre Galland in *Le Petit Journal* (February 6, 1921)

| **1921** Dr. Percy Oliver (England) establishes the London Blood Transfusion Service as the world's first voluntary blood donor service | **1931** Sergei Yudin (U.S.S.R.) sets up the world's first blood bank, at the Sklifosovsky Institute in Moscow | **1937** The first blood bank in the United States opens in Chicago | **1947–51** Arthur Voorhees (U.S.A.) develops the first artificial blood vessels, using parachute silk. The first human implant takes place in 1952 | **1964** Andreas Grünzig (Switzerland) performs the first angioplasty (clearing an arterial blockage using an inflatable balloon) | **1979** Ryochi Naito (Japan) performs the first transfusion of artificial blood |

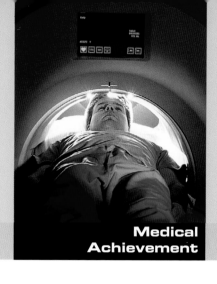

Medical Achievement

X-RAYS AND SCANS

The earliest means of diagnosing what was going on inside the body were manipulation ("tell me where it hurts"), auscultation (listening to the chest) and percussion (tapping the body). The discovery of X-rays and the invention of the ECG, CAT and MRI have made diagnosis a little more precise.

DID YOU KNOW?

● Leopold Auenbrugger, the first physician to use percussion (1761), was the son of an innkeeper. He would tap wine barrels to determine the level of fluid, and later applied the method to the internal organs of his patients, diagnosing the health of an organ by the sound it made when tapped. He also wrote the libretto for an opera by the Italian composer Antonio Salieri

Above A CAT scanner in operation
Below An early X-ray photograph (1896)
Opposite A colored MRI scan of the brain of a 10-year-old girl suffering from multiple sclerosis

X-rays are so-named because the man who discovered them did not know what they were. X is the scientific symbol for an unknown factor. In November 1895 Wilhelm Konrad von Roentgen (Germany) discovered a new form of electromagnetic radiation. The following month he produced the first ever X-ray photograph, clearly showing the bones of his wife's hand, creating a revolution for medical diagnosis and earning its discoverer the first Nobel Prize for Physics, awarded in 1901.

The first effective electrocardiogram (ECG) was built in 1903 by Willem Einthoven (Netherlands). ECG uses electrical impulses to record a pictorial image of the pattern of the heartbeat, a tool of such importance in heart diagnosis that Einthoven was awarded the 1924 Nobel Prize for Physiology or Medicine.

Computerized tomography (CT), also known as computer-aided tomography (CAT), was patented by Sir Godfrey Hounsfield (England) in 1968, and the first working scanner was built by EMI in 1971. The principle involves taking a number of X-ray images from different angles (tomography), which are then assembled by a computer to produce three-dimensional images of the area under investigation. At first, CAT was used for scanning the brain but has since come to be used for the entire body. It was another invention of Nobel Prize-winning worth: Hounsfield shared the 1979 Nobel Prize for Physiology or Medicine with Allan MacLeod Cormack (South Africa–U.S.A.), who had been carrying out theoretical research in the same field.

A year after the first CAT scanner was built, Raymond Damadian (U.S.A.) filed a patent for the first magnetic resonance imaging (MRI) scanner, a machine that could provide highly accurate images of soft as well as hard tissue. Following the work of Felix Bloch (Switzerland–U.S.A.) in nuclear magnetic resonance, Damadian decided to apply the principle to the human body. He realized that if the body is exposed to a magnetic field, differing types of cell will take differing amounts of time to return to their normal state. A computer then analyzes these "recovery times" and produces a visual image of the results.

| **1761** Leopold Auenbrugger (Austria) publishes *Inventum Novum* (New Invention) describing the art of percussion | **1895** Wilhelm Konrad von Roentgen (Germany) discovers electromagnetic rays that he calls X-rays, sometimes referred to as Roentgen rays | **1901** Roentgen is awarded the first Nobel Prize for Physics, for the discovery of X-rays | **1903** Willem Einthoven (Netherlands) produces the first effective electrocardiogram (ECG) | **1971** EMI builds the first CAT scanner, patented by Sir Godfrey Hounsfield (England) in 1968 | **1972** Raymond Damadian (U.S.A.) files a patent for the first MRI scanner (granted 1974) | **1977** Damadian produces the first MRI of a human body, that of his colleague Lawrence Minkoff |

▌TIMELINE

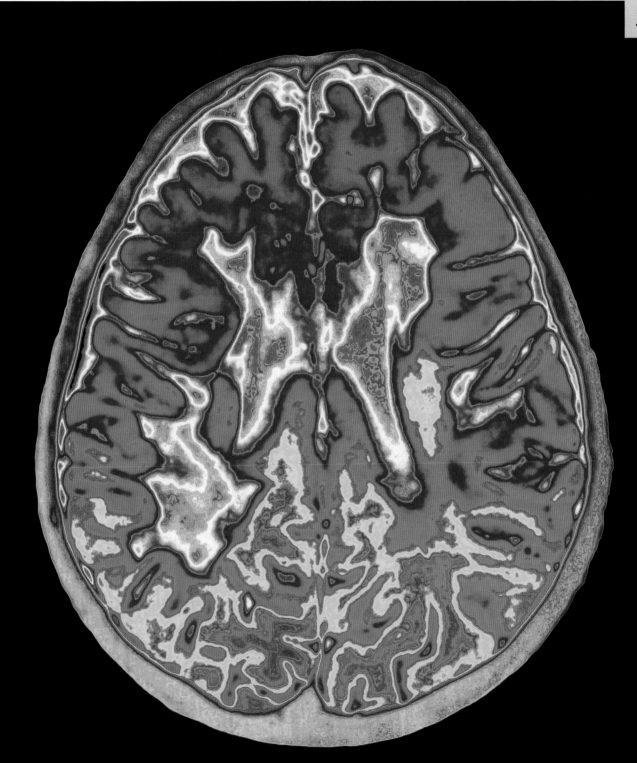

THE BEST OF THE REST...

Cloning

The first cloned mammals were Morag and Megan, two Welsh mountain ewes, born in 1995 as a result of work by the Roslin Institute, Edinburgh, Scotland. The following year, lamb number 6LL3, a.k.a. Dolly the sheep, was the first mammal to be cloned from adult cells, the result of work by Keith Campbell and Ian Wilmut (both Britain) at the Roslin Institute. In 1993 Jerry Hall and Robert Stillman (both U.S.A.) cloned the first human embryos, but even the most successful died at the 32-cell stage

Left Dolly the sheep, 1996–2003

Test-tube baby

The world's first test-tube baby was Louise Brown, born in Oldham General Hospital, England, on July 25, 1978. Her birth was a triumph not just for her parents, Lesley and John, but also for Patrick Steptoe and Robert Edwards (both Britain), who had pioneered the technique of in vitro fertilization (IVF). IVF is a treament for women with blocked Fallopian tubes—the egg is removed from the body and fertilized in a test tube (in vitro literally means "in glass"). Louise was transferred to her mother's womb in November 1977 as a bundle of just eight cells, and developed normally until Mrs. Brown suffered from toxaemia in July 1978. As a result Louise was delivered by Caesarian section

Sex-change operation

In 1952 American soldier George Jorgensen became Christine Jorgensen after the world's first sex-change operation, performed at the Serum Institute, Copenhagen, Denmark, by Dr. Christian Hamburger (Denmark)

Plaster casts

Precursors of the plaster cast for fractured limbs go back to ancient Egypt, where bands soaked in mud, which hardened as the mud dried, were used to immobilize broken bones. Military physician Dr. Anthonius Mathi (Netherlands) was the first to use the modern method of bandages soaked in plaster, in 1850. Then American company 3M developed a lightweight, breathable, waterproof, fiberglass cast in 1982, under the brand name of Scotchcast

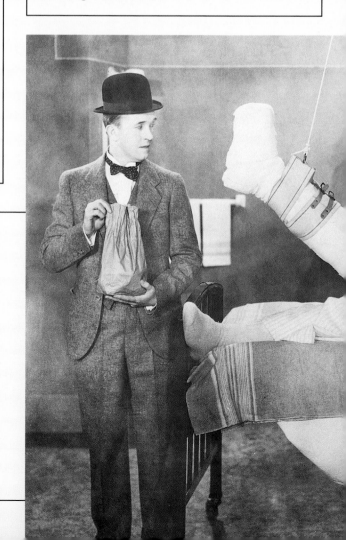

Right Laurel and Hardy in *County Hospital* (1932)

Woman doctor

The first woman to qualify as a doctor was Elizabeth Blackwell (England–U.S.A.), who graduated from the Geneva Medical Institute, New York, in 1849 (her sister Emily qualified as a doctor shortly afterward). In 1865 Elizabeth Garrett Anderson became the first British woman to qualify as a doctor (Blackwell became a U.S. citizen in 1832), and was also awarded a medical degree by the University of Paris in 1870. Anderson became England's first female mayor when she was elected Mayor of Aldeburgh in 1908

Folding wheelchair

The first folding wheelchair was invented in 1932 by Harry Jennings for his friend Herbert Everest (both U.S.A.), who was injured in a mining accident

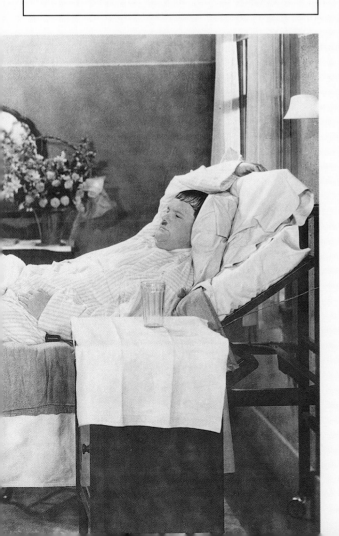

Ambulance

The first purpose-built ambulance was designed by French military surgeon Dominique Jean Larrey in 1792. It was a properly sprung horse-drawn cart used to move wounded men from the battlefield to mobile field hospitals, which were another recent innovation. The first motor ambulance went into service with the French Army in 1900, and the first civilian motor ambulance went into service in Alençon, France, the same year. The first civilian ambulances in North America were put into service by the Bellevue Hospital, New York City, in 1869. Australia's first ambulance service was inaugurated in 1897 by the Queensland Ambulance Transport Brigade, horses being replaced by motorized ambulances in 1908

Above Military ambulance carrying Russian wounded during the Russo–Turkish War (1877)

Stethoscope

The stethoscope was invented in 1816 by French physician René Théophile Hyacinthe Laënnec, while working at l'Hôpital Necker in Paris. Laënnec's stethoscope was a simple wooden tube; the first binaural stethoscope was devised in 1852 by George P. Cammann (U.S.A.)

Chapter Eight

Government, Law & Order

In the modern world it is taken for granted that heads of state and government will embrace new technology, but in the past the first time a monarch or president bought a car, traveled by rail or broadcast on radio or television it was a matter of great excitement.

HEADS OF STATE AND GOVERNMENT

Heads of state may not be the first people to adopt new technology but when they do it is usually a matter of note. In 1896 Queen Victoria became the first British monarch to be filmed, noting in her diary for October 3: "At twelve … we were photographed by Downey by the new cinematographic process." The following year politicians caught up with royalty, when Grover Cleveland became the first serving U.S. president to be filmed, at the inauguration ceremony of his successor, William McKinley, who thereby became the second U.S. president to be filmed. In the same year Lord Salisbury became the first British prime minister to be filmed.

In 1922 Billy Hughes (Australia) became the first prime minister of any nation to make a radio broadcast, and in 1924 George V of Great Britain became the first reigning monarch to make a radio broadcast; eight years later he became the first British monarch to make a Christmas Day (radio) broadcast, saying: "Through one of the marvels of modern science, I am enabled, this Christmas Day, to speak to all my peoples throughout the empire."

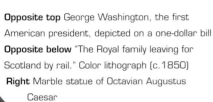

Opposite top George Washington, the first American president, depicted on a one-dollar bill
Opposite below "The Royal family leaving for Scotland by rail." Color lithograph (c.1850)
Right Marble statue of Octavian Augustus Caesar

DID YOU KNOW?

• U.S. President Harry S Truman did not have a middle name. He was christened Harry S because both his grandfathers had names beginning with "S" (Anderson Shippe Truman and Solomon Young) and his parents did not want to offend either side of the family

• The expression "Bob's your uncle" is said to have derived from British Prime Minister Robert ("Bob") Gascoyne-Cecil, 3rd Marquess of Salisbury, who appointed his nephew Arthur Balfour to several important government posts. It was said of Balfour that preferment came easily if "Bob's your uncle"

• The tune of the British national anthem, *God Save the Queen* (or *King*), has been used by several other countries for their national anthems, including Denmark, Sweden, Russia, Liechtenstein, Germany and Switzerland. After the Declaration of Independence Americans sang *God Save George Washington* to the same tune, followed by other variations of the words, before the official adoption of *The Star-Spangled Banner* as the U.S. national anthem in 1931. Although Canada's national anthem, *O Canada*, was written in 1880, it did not gain official status until 1980

1829 Arthur Wellesley, 1st Duke of Wellington, becomes the first British prime minister to fight a duel while in office

1833 Andrew Jackson becomes the first U.S. president to travel by rail

1841 William Henry Harrison is the first U.S. president to die in office

1842 Queen Victoria becomes the first British monarch to travel by rail

1865 Abraham Lincoln is the first U.S. president to be assassinated

1867 Sir John A. MacDonald (Scotland–Canada) becomes the first prime minister of Canada

1888 The Sultan of Turkey becomes the first monarch to drive a car (an electric car built in England)

1896 Queen Victoria becomes the first British monarch to be filmed

1897 Grover Cleveland becomes the first serving U.S. president to be filmed. Lord Salisbury becomes the first British prime minister to be filmed

1901 Sir Edmund Barton becomes the first prime minister of Australia

1903 The first exchange of greetings by radio between heads of state takes place between U.S. President Theodore Roosevelt, and British King Edward VII

1906 Theodore Roosevelt becomes the first U.S. president to visit a foreign country while in office, and the first American to receive a Nobel Peace prize

1910 Louis Botha becomes the first premier of the Union of South Africa

1911 George V lands at Gibraltar to become the first reigning British monarch to visit a Commonwealth country

1919 Philipp Scheidemann becomes the first Chancellor of the Republic of Germany

1922 Billy Hughes (Australia) becomes the first prime minister of any nation to make a radio broadcast. Arthur Griffith becomes the first premier of the Irish Free State

Television followed radio and in 1930 the first television set to be installed at No.10 Downing Street was given to Prime Minister Ramsay MacDonald by fellow Scot John Logie Baird. MacDonald told Baird: "You have put something in my room which will never let me forget how strange this world is and how unknown." On May 12, 1937, his coronation day, British King George VI became the first monarch to be televised; a year later Neville Chamberlain became the first British prime minister to be televised, and a year after that Franklin D. Roosevelt became the first U.S. president to be televised, when he opened the New York World's Fair. In 1957 Queen Elizabeth II became the first British monarch to make a Christmas Day television broadcast to the people of the Commonwealth.

Opposite *La Marseillaise,* national anthem of France, words and music by Rouget de l'Isle (late 19th-century sheet music cover)
Top "Mr. Perceval assassinated in the Lobby of the House of Commons by John Bellingham, May 11th 1812."

Above The National Broadcasting Company inaugurated the first regular television service to the American public with a telecast of the ceremonies in the Court of Peace at which President Franklin D. Roosevelt officially opened the New York World's Fair (April 30, 1939)

1930 The first television set to be installed at No. 10 Downing Street is given to Prime Minister Ramsay MacDonald by John Logie Baird

1931 U.S. Congress officially adopts *The Star-Spangled Banner* as the nation's anthem

1932 George V becomes the first British monarch to make a Christmas Day (radio) broadcast

1937 On May 12, his coronation day, British King George VI becomes the first monarch to be televised

1938 Neville Chamberlain becomes the first British prime minister to be televised

1939 Franklin D. Roosevelt becomes the first U.S. president to be televised. George VI makes the first visit by a reigning British monarch to Canada and to the United States

1954 Queen Elizabeth II makes the first visit by a reigning British monarch to New Zealand and Australia

In 1893 New Zealand became the first country to grant women the right to vote. Two years later, the government of the colony of South Australia serendipitously became the first to allow women to run for parliament, and in 1907 Finland became the first country to elect female MPs.

WOMEN IN POLITICS

The vote for women

The first woman to vote in a parliamentary election was Mrs. Lily Maxwell of Manchester, England, in 1867, though this was due to a legal loophole rather than forward-thinking government. Because Mrs. Maxwell was a ratepayer she had been placed on the electoral register by mistake, which meant that she was able to cast her vote in the Manchester by-election. By the time of the election the following year the loophole had been closed and women's suffrage declared illegal.

In 1880 the House of Keys (the parliament of the Isle of Man) became the first government to sanction women's suffrage, though with restrictions: widows or spinsters owning a certain value of real estate were allowed to vote, and took part in the election of 1881. In 1893 New Zealand became the first country to grant women, without restriction, the right to vote; when Britain finally caught up in 1918 only women over the age of 30 were allowed to vote, and it was 1928 before British women had the same voting rights as men.

Female politicians

The first government to allow women to run for parliament did so by accident in 1895, when the colony of South Australia followed New Zealand's lead by tabling a women's suffrage bill. Agnes Macphail was the first woman to be elected as a member of parliament in Canada, in 1921. It would be more than 30 years before a Canadian woman became a federal cabinet minister when Ellen Fairclough was appointed secretary of state in 1957. In 1993 Kim Campbell became the first female prime minister of Canada. In the United States, Jeanette Rankin became the first woman elected to Congress, in 1916. In 1922 Nellie Tayloe Ross became the first female governor and Rebecca Ann Latimer Felton became the first female member of the U.S. Senate in 1925 at the age of 87. The world's first female MPs were elected in Finland in 1907, the year after Finland became the first European country to allow votes for women.

The first female minister of state was Aleksandra Kollontai (Russia), who became People's Commissar for Social Welfare in 1917, and in 1924 became the first female ambassador. The world's first female prime minister was Sirimavo Bandaranaike (Ceylon, now Sri Lanka), who succeeded her husband in 1960 after he was assassinated in 1959. She held office from 1960–65 and again from 1970–77.

Opposite top Miss Dorothy Newell (U.S.A.) makes an elegant but forceful appeal for "Votes for Women" during the first decade of the 20th century

Opposite below Campaigners for women's suffrage on the march in England (1913)

Right English suffragettes Emmeline Pankhurst and her daughter Christabel, in prison dress (undated)

TIMELINE

1848 Elizabeth Candy Stanton and Lucretia Coffin Mott (both U.S.A.) organize the first Women's Rights Convention

1867 Mrs. Lily Maxwell (England) becomes the first woman to vote in a parliamentary election

1869 Stanton and Susan B. Anthony (both U.S.A.) found the National Woman Suffrage Movement (in 1979 Anthony becomes the first woman to appear on a U.S. coin)

1893 New Zealand becomes the first country to grant all its women the right to vote

1895 The colony of South Australia becomes the first country to grant women the right to run for parliament

1906 Finland becomes the first European country to grant women the right to vote

1907 Finland becomes the first country to elect female MPs

1916 Jeannette Rankin becomes the first woman elected to the U.S. Congress

1917 Aleksandra Kollontai (Russia) becomes the first female minister of state when she is made People's Commissar for Social Welfare (in 1924 she becomes the world's first female ambassador)

1921 Agnes Macphail becomes the first elected female member of parliament in Canada

1925 Nellie Tayloe Ross becomes the first female governor in the Unites States

1960 Sirimavo Bandaranaike (Ceylon, now Sri Lanka) becomes the first female prime minister of any nation

1993 Kim Campbell becomes the first female prime minister of Canada

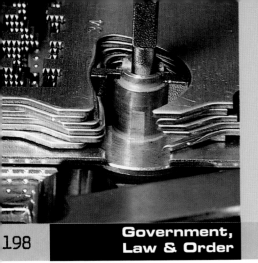

Key-operated locks date back to ancient Egypt and padlocks to ancient Rome, but it was 2,500 years later before the appearance of the first tumbler lock and another century after that before Linus Yale patented his famous pin-tumbler cylinder lock in 1861.

LOCKS AND KEYS

Above Lock with the casing cut away to show the components inside it

Below Faroe Islands lock, c.1821. These locks closely resemble locks made in ancient Egypt thousands of years earlier

Opposite Lynn Redgrave as the Queen and Woody Allen as the Fool in *Everything You Always Wanted to Know About Sex, But Were Afraid to Ask* (1972)

Early doors were held closed with sliding wooden latches. The first lock was developed by the Egyptians c.2000 b.c., and had a set of wooden pins that dropped into notches cut in the latch to stop it from sliding. The wooden key was carved in such a way that it would lift the pins out of the notches, allowing the latch to be opened. It was an intricate system, but its security value was limited because any suitably shaped stick could be used to raise the pins. The Romans took things a step further. Not only did they make the first metal locks (iron, with bronze keys) and invent the first padlocks, but they also invented the "ward." This was an outer guard that only allowed keys of the right profile to enter the lock, thus making it more secure.

It was another two and a half centuries before anyone made any significant improvements on this design. In 1778 Robert Barron (England) invented the first tumbler lock; this had a number of levers, or tumblers, but with the added security that they had to be raised to exactly the right height. Barron was the first, but he was not the most successful, and he has been overshadowed by the high-security locks of Joseph Bramah (England) and the detector locks of Jeremiah Chubb (England). Detector locks incorporated a mechanism to jam the lock if any of the pins was raised to the wrong position by a lock-picker or a false key, preventing the break-in and alerting the owner to the fact that someone had tampered with the lock.

In 1861 Linus Yale Jr. (U.S.A.) patented the first mass-produced pin-tumbler cylinder lock, operated by the characteristic flat latchkey. Yale formed the Yale & Towne Lock Co. with father and son John Henry Towne and Henry Robinson Towne, but died three months later. In his memory, Henry Towne decided to stamp Yale's name on every lock and key made by the company, and as a result "Yale" has now become a by-word for this type of lock.

c.2000 b.c. The earliest surviving key-operated locks are made by ancient Egyptians	c.750 b.c. The Romans produce the first metal locks, the first padlocks and the first ward locks	1778 Robert Barron (England) invents the first tumbler lock	1784 Joseph Bramah (England) invents the first high-security tumbler lock	1818 Jeremiah Chubb (England) invents the first detector lock	1861 Linus Yale Jr. (U.S.A.) patents the first mass-produced pin-tumbler cylinder lock	1872 James Sargent (U.S.A.) devises the first modern time lock (patent granted 1873)	1970s The first card-access electronic locks appear

TIMELINE

Locks and Keys

199

The first assassin to be caught on film was Leon Czolgosz when he murdered U.S. President William McKinley in 1901. For criminals not filmed in the act, two effective methods of proving guilt have been fingerprinting (1892) and DNA evidence, patented by Alec John Jeffreys in 1984.

Above Dick Tracy, a detail from the cover of *Dick Tracy Monthly* (undated)

Below DNA autoradiographs showing banded DNA sequences or genetic fingerprints. The unique patterns formed by autoradiographs can be analyzed and compared for similarity to other DNA samples

Opposite "Zangara, assassin of Mr. Cermak, mayor of Chicago, and would-be assassin of President Franklin Roosevelt, goes to the electric chair," *Police Magazine* (March 1933)

The first use of fingerprint evidence to solve a crime was in *The Story of a Thumb-Mark*. The story was published in *Chambers' Journal* in 1881, more than a decade before fingerprints were used to solve a real crime and only a year after fingerprinting had first been suggested as a means of solving crime by Henry Faulds (Scotland) in a letter to *Nature* magazine.

Fingerprints had been used as early as 1858, by William Herschel (England) as a form of unforgeable signature, but Faulds was the first to suggest using them for detecting criminals. In 1884 English scientist Sir Francis Galton devised a system of classifying fingerprints, but it was 1892 before the first nonfictional criminal conviction was secured using fingerprint evidence. Juan Vucetich (Argentina) adopted the Galton system in 1891, setting up the world's first fingerprint bureau the following year. Four months later, Francesca Rojas (Argentina) accused her neighbor, Signor Velasquez, of murdering her two children. Vucetich used fingerprint evidence to show that

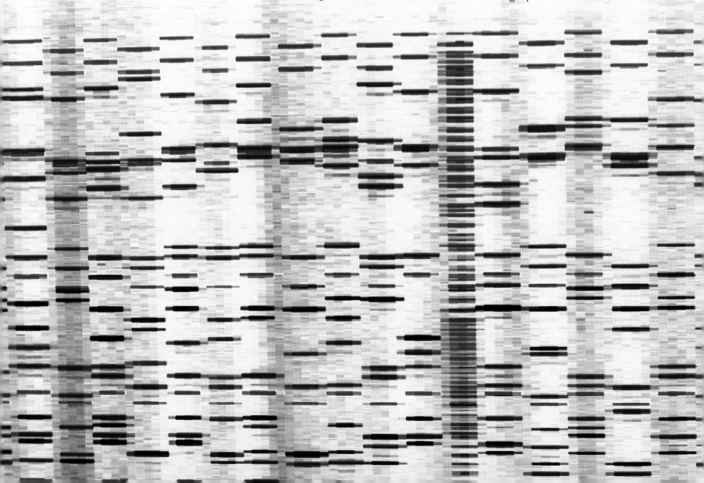

N° 122 - 26 Mars 1933. 1 fr. Tous les Dimanches.

POLICE MAGAZINE

ZANGARA A ÉTÉ EXÉCUTÉ

Zangara, qui voulut tuer le président Roosevelt et qui assassina le maire de Chicago, M. Cermak, a été exécuté peu après sa condamnation à mort. Ci-dessus : le meurtrier, la cellule dans laquelle il passa ses dernières heures. A droite : la chaise électrique qui a servi à l'exécution.

in fact Rojas herself was the murderer and, faced with this evidence, she confessed to the crime.

In 1984 Alec John Jeffreys (England) patented a system that provided even more incontrovertible evidence than conventional fingerprinting: the use of DNA to identify an individual. Jeffreys's patent covered a method of producing "an individual-specific 'fingerprint' of general use for genetic identification purposes, paternity and maternity testing, forensic medicine and the diagnosis of genetic diseases and cancer." In November 1987, at Bristol Crown Court, Robert Melias (England) became the first criminal to be convicted using DNA evidence.

Melias was the first to be convicted but not the first to be identified using DNA: earlier in 1987 Jeffreys's method had been used to identify Colin Pitchfork as the murderer of two schoolgirls, and he was convicted on that evidence the following year. Samples of blood and saliva had been requested from 5,000 local men; Pitchfork bribed a colleague to provide samples on his behalf and, when the colleague later confessed to the concealment, Pitchfork was DNA-tested, convicted and sentenced to life imprisonment.

TIMELINE

1611 Mary Frith, a.k.a. Moll Cutpurse (England), becomes the first woman to be arrested for wearing men's clothes

c.1650 Transportation is devised in England as a punishment for convicted criminals. The first convicts are exiled to the American Colonies

1787 British convicts are transported to Australia for the first time. Austria becomes the first country to abolish capital punishment

1788 Convicts are landed at Sydney Cove, Port Jackson, Australia; Sydney becomes Australia's first penal colony

1890 William Kemmler (U.S.A.) becomes the first person to be executed using the electric chair

1892 Francesca Rojas (Argentina) becomes the first criminal to be convicted using fingerprint evidence

1901 Leon Czolgosz (U.S.A.) becomes the first assassin to be caught on film, while murdering U.S. President McKinley

1910 Dr. Crippen (U.S.A.) becomes the first murderer to be caught by wireless telegraphy, when he flees England aboard a cruise liner and arouses the suspicions of the captain, who liaises with police by radio in Quebec City

1959 Sheriff Peter Pitchess (U.S.A.) makes the first use of an identikit image of a suspect (Identikit is the brainchild of Hugh C. McDonald of the Los Angeles Identification Bureau)

1962 Arthur Lucas and Robert Turpin are the last criminals to be executed in Canada

1976 Canada abolishes capital punishment

1982 Charlie Brooks Jr. is the first person to be executed by lethal injection, at Fort Worth, Texas

1984 Alec John Jeffreys (England) files a patent for the use of DNA to identify individuals (granted 1986)

1987 Robert Melias (England) becomes the first criminal to be convicted using DNA evidence

In many countries the introduction of police forces was seen as an infringement of personal liberty, but eventually the curbing of crime was seen to be more important. In 1667 Paris became the first city to have a police force that was independent of the judiciary.

POLICE

Above Jack Lemmon as the naive gendarme and Shirley MacLaine as a Parisian prostitute in *Irma La Douce*
Below A rural gendarme (1850)

The formation of the Paris police force in 1667 from what had been part of the Royal Watch separated the dispensation of justice and the enforcement of the law for the first time. The police continued to operate from Le Petit Châtelet (the little castle) near Pont-au-Change until 1698, when they moved to new headquarters close to Pont Neuf, effectively the world's first police station. In 1829 the Paris police became the world's first uniformed force, adopting uniforms just nine months before the formation of Sir Robert Peel's Metropolitan Police in England later that year.

In the ordinance announcing the adoption of uniforms, Paris Prefect Louis-Marie Debelleyme wrote: "The purpose of this uniform will be to constantly keep in the public's mind the presence of policemen at points where they will be of service; at the same time to compel them to intervene and restore order instead of vanishing into the crowd for fear of being noticed as often happens."

The world's first police detective was Eugène François Vidocq (France). Vidocq stole from his father, was imprisoned while still a schoolboy, then worked as an acrobat and a soldier before being sentenced to eight years as a galley slave for forgery. He escaped from the galleys, joined a band of highwaymen, betrayed them to the police, and in 1808 offered his services as a police informer. Four years later the Brigade de Sûreté was set up as the world's first detective branch, with Vidocq as its chief.

The new Sûreté was highly efficient and saw an immediate increase in rates of detection and a reduction in crime. There are differing accounts as to whether this was due to "the scientific methods of detection that Vedocq pioneered" or whether "Vedocq himself carried out many of the burglaries he showed such skill in detecting." His *Memoires*, published in 1828, are considered to be an unreliable source of information, being those of a convicted forger.

1667 The Paris police force is formed as the first police force to be independent of the judiciary	**1698** The Paris police force moves into the world's first police station	**1800** The Thames River Police Act officially establishes the Marine Police Force (formed 1798 as a private venture) as Britain's first statutory police force	**1812** Acrobat and ex-convict Eugène François Vidocq (France) becomes the first head of the newly established Brigade de Sûreté and the world's first police detective	**1829** MARCH, the Paris police adopt uniforms to become the first uniformed police force. SEPTEMBER, Sir Robert Peel's Metropolitan Police Force (London) becomes Britain's first uniformed statutory police force

■ TIMELINE

Larry Wilcox and Erik Estrada in the popular 1970s and 1980s television series *Chips*

DID YOU KNOW?

● Britain's first uniformed statutory police force was formed by Sir Robert Peel. The nickname Peelers has long gone out of use but Bobbies (from Robert) is still in use 170 years later

| **1873** The Royal Canadian Mounted Police (RCMP) (originally named the North-West Mounted Police [NWMP]) is created by an act of parliament | **1899** Ghent police in (Belgium) are the first to officially adopt the use of police dogs | **1903** The Boston Police Department acquires the first police car in regular service | **1905** The New York City Police Department establishes the first police motorcycle patrol | **1910** Alice Stebbins Wells (U.S.A.) joins the Los Angeles Police Department as the first uniformed policewoman with full powers of arrest | **1921** Two cars used by London's Metropolitan Police Flying Squad are adapted to become the first police cars equipped with radio. The Detroit Police Dept installs experimental radios in its cars the same year |

The first organized fire fighting service dates from Roman times, but the idea was subsequently forgotten and not revived until the 17th century, when the idea of specialist fire brigades reemerged due to the commercial interests of fire insurance companies.

FIRE FIGHTING

c.27 b.c. Augustus Caesar forms a corps of *Vigiles* as the first fire brigade	**1518** Anthony Blatner (Germany) builds the first recorded fire engine (for the city of Augsburg)	**1591** The first mutual fire insurance society is founded, in Hamburg, Germany	**1672** Jan van der Heijden (Netherlands) invents the first flexible fire hose	**1676** Hamburg's fire insurance society is reorganized as the Hamburger General-Feur-Cassa, the world's first fire insurance company	**1679** Boston establishes the first paid fire department in the American Colonies	**1763** Montreal establishes the Fire Club as the first (volunteer) fire department in Canada

like many great ideas pioneered by the Romans, the concept of a public fire fighting service was forgotten after the decline of the empire and not reinvented until centuries later. The Roman fire brigade, known as *Vigiles* (who also acted as the police force) were equipped with sophisticated bronze *siphos*, or water pumps.

Handheld water pumps reappeared in medieval Europe, where they were known as squirts. Early fire engines were simply enlarged squirts or force pumps mounted on wheels; the first was built in 1518 by Anthony Blatner (Germany) for the city of Augsburg. Fire engines often had to be placed dangerously close to the fire in order for the pump to reach the flames, a problem solved in 1672 when Jan van der Heijden (Netherlands) invented the first flexible fire hose.

Usually a parish or town would appoint an engine-keeper who would enlist the help of passersby in fighting fires; the idea of a specialist fire brigade grew out of the commercial interests of fire insurance companies. The first known fire insurance company was a mutual society of property-owners formed in Hamburg, Germany, in 1591 in which members would each pay a contribution to any other member who suffered a loss by fire. This society was replaced in 1676 by the Hamburger General-Feur-Cassa, which became the first fire insurance company to issue individual policies at agreed premiums in the modern way.

As the idea of fire insurance spread, the companies realized that it would be in their own interests to put out fires in order to limit damage, and therefore the amount of compensation paid. Each company enlisted a brigade of men to put out fires in properties carrying a "fire mark" to show that they were insured by that company—fires in other properties would be left to burn unless they were endangering a property insured by the brigade's company. These private fire brigades later began to work together and eventually came under the control of local authorities rather than private companies.

Opposite top Advertisement for Minimax fire extinguishers (1922)
Opposite below 20th-century fire engine rushing to an emergency
Right 19th-century fire engine

| **1816** George Manby (England) invents the first pressurized-cylinder fire extinguisher | **1833** Ten fire insurance company brigades are amalgamated to form the London Fire Engine Establishment, Britain's first full-time fire brigade (reorganized under public control as the Metropolitan Fire Brigade in 1866) | **1866** François Carlier (France) invents a chemical-based fire extinguisher | **1937** The "999" emergency telephone service is introduced to Britain for the first time, in London | **1959** The "999" emergency telephone number is introduced in Canada, in Winnipeg | **1968** The United States adopts the "911" emergency telephone number. Canada adopts "911" four years later |

WEAPONRY

Since the invention of explosives, mankind has developed ever more efficient means of killing their fellow man. The 14th-century cannon developed through the centuries to the assault rifle (1944), while the V-2 rockets of World War Two developed into the ICBMs of the Cold War.

Firearms

Modern firearms developed from the medieval cannon (1326), which was in essence just an iron tube—gunpowder and a ball were put in the open end and the powder was lit through a touchhole cut in the barrel near the closed end. Early guns operated on the same principle. Matchlocks (1411) were so-called because the powder was lit with a flame (usually a smoldering cord); wheel locks (1500s) used iron pyrites and a serrated wheel to produce a spark; flintlocks (c.1620) used a cheaper and more reliable method, a flint and strikeplate.

The real breakthrough for efficient firearms came in 1807 when the Rev. Alexander Forsyth (Scotland) patented the first use of explosive mixtures in guns. These mixtures explode when hit, dispensing the need for a spark. Forsyth used a loose mixture, but his innovation led directly to the invention of the percussion cap (c.1820) and then to self-contained cartridges, which developed separately in several countries in the mid-19th century.

The percussion cap paved the way for the first successful revolver, patented by Samuel Colt (U.S.A.) in 1835, and cartridges allowed the manufacture of the first successful repeating rifles (Henry, 1860) and machine guns (Gatling, 1862). The Henry rifle was patented as a "magazine fire arm" and was referred to by Confederate soldiers as "the damned Yankee rifle you could load on Sunday and shoot all week."

The Gatling gun was a multibarrelled machine gun that was operated by cranking a handle. Fed by a belt of ammunition and using the recoil to load the next cartridge, the first automatic machine gun was patented in 1883 by Hiram Stevens Maxim (U.S.A.–England). Heavy automatic machine guns were followed by submachine guns, which were light enough to be fired on the move by one person, and these were soon superseded by the assault rifle, which could discharge single shots or bursts of fire. Maxim would have approved—he had reputedly been advised that if he wanted to make money he should "invent something that will enable these Europeans to cut each other's throats with greater facility."

Air power

In March 1794 the Company of Aérostiers was formed under Captain Coutelle (France) as part of the French Artillery Service to carry out reconnaissance from balloons, making it effectively the world's first air force. The first use of an aircraft in war came on June 26 in that year at the Battle

1912 Gunter Burstyn (Austria) files the first patent for an armored vehicle with caterpillar tracks	
1915 Walter Wilson and William Tritton (both England) build the first tank, known as Little Willie	
1916 Tanks are first used in battle	
1918 The German Bergman MP18 is the first submachine gun	
1920 The first submachine gun to be so-called is the Tommy Gun, designed by and named after John Thompson (U.S.A.)	
1942 The first V-1 flying bomb is launched, in Germany. The first V-2 rocket (a.k.a. A-4) is tested in Germany	
1944 The V-2 is first used, against Paris, France. The Sturmgewehr Stg. 44 (Germany) becomes the first mass-produced assault rifle	
1945 The first atomic bomb is dropped (on Hiroshima, Japan, by the U.S.)	
1952 The first hydrogen bomb (U.S.A.) is tested in the western Pacific	
1957 The first intercontinental ballistic missile (ICBM) is launched by the U.S.S.R. (to place a space satellite in orbit)	

of Fleurus, Belgium, when the Aérostiers went aloft in their reconnaissance balloon *L'Entreprenant* to observe the enemy. The first use of aircraft to deliver bombs took place, ineffectively, in Austria in 1849, and the first regular balloon corps was the American Army Balloon Corps, formed in 1861 under the command of Chief Aeronaut Thaddeus Lowe. The first air force to be equipped with an airplane rather than balloons was the Aeronautical Division of the U.S. Army Signal Corps, which was formed in 1907 under the command of Captain Charles de Forest Chandler.

Opposite Medieval cannons and handguns in use at The Battle of Avray, 1364
Above A U.S. B-52 Stratofortress releasing a Tomahawk air-launched cruise missile. In 1957 three B-52s completed the world's first nonstop round-the-world flight by jet aircraft
Right A British soldier explains the workings of a tommy gun to Prime Minister Winston Churchill (August 1940)

The Tank

Richard Edgeworth (England) filed the first patent for what are now known as caterpillar tracks as early as 1770, but it was to be more than 200 years before anyone built a vehicle that could run on them. The first patent for an armored vehicle with caterpillar tracks was filed in Germany in 1912 by Gunter Burstyn (Austria). The Germans were slow to adopt Burstyn's idea and the first tank, known as Little Willie, was British. It was built in 1915 to the designs of Walter Wilson and William Tritton (both England) at the instigation of Winston Churchill, then First Lord of the Admiralty. An improved version, known variously as Big Willie, the Wilson Machine or Mother, went into service with the British army the same year.

Tanks were first used in battle during World War One, at Delville Wood, near Flers, France, on September 15, 1916, where they caused panic among the German infantry but proved vulnerable to artillery fire. The first major tank battle took place at the Battle of Cambrai, France, on November 20, 1917, when some 400 tanks helped to make what has been estimated to be the Allies greatest single day's advance of the entire war.

Below Parade of Chinese ground-to-air missiles, considered to be amongst the most modern in the world, during the 50th anniversary of communist China (1999)
Right First battle of the Somme. British tanks are used in action for the first time, causing panic amongst the German troops (September 15, 1916)

THE BEST OF THE REST...

Refuse collection

France's first municipal refuse collection service was initiated by Eugene Poubelle, a 19th-century Prefect of Police in Paris, who was also the inventor, in 1883, of the first dustbin—his name is still used as the French name for garbage

Right Refuse collector in Paris (1907)

Racial equality

On October 16, 1901 former slave Booker T. Washington, a leading campaigner for racial equality, became the first African-American to dine at the White House. Later the same month 34 people were killed in riots protesting the historic visit

Old-age pensions

The first old-age pensions were introduced in Germany by Prince Otto
Edward Leopold von Bismarck in 1889 and first paid in 1891. His
scheme paid pensions below subsistence level and was intended as a
supplement to income (those incapable of work received an infirmity
pension). The first subsistence level old-age pension plan was introduced
in New Zealand in 1898, first paid in 1899. Australia's old-age pensions
were first paid in 1901, Britain's in 1909, the first U.S. Federal Old-Age
Pensions in 1935, and the first old-age pensions in Canada in 1937

Crematorium

The first purpose-built
incinerator for cremation was
designed by Dr. L. Brunetti
(Italy) and first used in 1869.
The first crematoria were
opened in Milan, Italy, by
Dr. Pini and in Washington,
Pennsylvania by Julius le
Moyne, both in 1876. Britain's
first crematorium was built in
Woking, Surrey, in 1879, but
could not be used until 1885,
after a change in the law the
previous year. Australia's first
crematorium opened in
Adelaide in 1903

Boy Scouts

The Boy Scout movement was founded by Sir Robert Stephenson Smyth
Baden-Powell, 1st Baron Baden-Powell of Gilwell (England), in 1908,
after an experimental camp the previous year. Scouting began in Canada
in 1908, and the first Australian scout troop was the 1st Mosman
Kangaroos, also formed in 1908. By 1910 there were so many female
scouts that a separate Girl Guide movement was founded early that year
by Baden-Powell and his sister, Agnes; the first registered Canadian
Guide Company was formed the same year by Mrs. A.H. Malcolmson in
St. Catharines, Ontario. William D. Boyce founded the Boy Scouts of
America in 1910 after being given help by a British boy scout in London
the previous year, and in 1912 Juliette Gordon Low founded the Girl
Scouts of the United States in Savannah, Georgia

Left Boy Scouts of Troop 446, Chicago (1942)

Chapter Nine

Communication

Pencils were invented in the 16th century and the first practical typewriter in 1808—long before Lewis Waterman managed to make the first successful fountain pen, in 1883. Then the fountain pen faced a serious challenge from the ballpoint, developed from 1938–43 by Laszlo Biró.

WRITING IMPLEMENTS

Pencils

The first written reference to a lead pencil appears in the writings of Swiss naturalist Conrad Gesner, dated 1565. The previous year an unusually solid and workable form of graphite had been found in Cumbria, England, and the first pencils were made by inserting thin strips of this graphite into wooden holders. (Later, leads were manufactured by firing a mixture of crushed graphite and clay.)

Typewriters

In 1714 Queen Anne granted Henry Mill (England) a patent for "a machine capable of replacing handwriting by the printing of letters similar to those used in print shops." The machine was never built and the first practical typewriter did not appear until 1808, made by Pellegrino Turri (Italy). The first mass-produced typewriter was the Danish *skrivekugle* (writing ball, 1865), and the first to use a QWERTY keyboard, the precursor of all modern typewriters and computer keyboards, was patented by Christopher Sholes (U.S.A.) in 1871 and built by the Remington Co. from 1874, achieving fame as the Remington No.1.

Fountain pens

For centuries, ink was transferred to the page by continually dipping a nib into an inkwell. The first fountain pen, containing its own supply of ink, was mentioned as early as 1656, and more than 400 patents for fountain pens were filed during the 19th century. The flow of ink was

Right "The Mackinnon Pen or Fluid Pen," an early form of fountain pen. Illustration in *Scientific American* (1880)
Opposite "Underwood 'electrifies' the Business World"; advertisement for the new all-electric Underwood typewriter (1947)

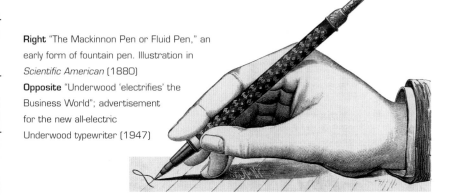

• The first author to use a Scholes/Remington typewriter was Mark Twain (U.S.A.), who wrote to the manufacturers: "Please do not use my name in any way. Please do not even divulge that I own a machine." The reason was that whenever he sent a typewritten letter to anyone, they wanted to know all about the new machine, which Twain called "this curiosity-breeding little joker." He signed the letter with his real name, Samuel Langhorne Clemens

• The Sharp Corporation, now well known for its electronic products, started life in 1912 as a Tokyo metal works. In 1915 the company produced a metal propelling pencil, called the Ever-Sharp, from which the corporation took its name

• The typists' correction fluid Liquid Paper was invented by Bette Nesmith Graham (U.S.A.), mother of Michael Nesmith, a former member of pop band The Monkees

1938 Laszlo Biró (Hungary) patents a prototype ballpoint pen

1943 Biró (now working in Argentina) patents the first practical ballpoint pen and sells the British rights to Henry Martin (England)

1944 The Miles-Martin Pen Co. manufactures Britain's first ballpoint pens, for the RAF (first sold to the public Christmas 1945)

1945 Biró's Eterpen Co. produces the first commercially available ballpoint pens (in Buenos Aires, Argentina). Businessman Milton Reynolds (U.S.A.) employs William Huenergardt to copy Biró's idea. The result is the Reynolds Rocket, the United States's first ballpoint pen, patented in 1945 and first sold by Gimbel's of New York the same year

1953 Marcel Bich (France) acquires the rights to Biró's patent and manufactures the first disposable ballpoint pen

1978 Gillette (U.S.A.) invents the first erasable ballpoint pen, known as the Eraser Mate

notoriously unreliable until insurance salesman Lewis Waterman (U.S.A.) made the first successful fountain pen in 1883, having realized that air must flow into the reservoir to equalize the pressure as the ink flowed out; he called his pen the Waterman Regular.

Ballpoint pens

Laszlo Biró (Hungary) developed the first practical ballpoint pen from 1938–43. He had been searching for a means of using printers' ink in pens because it was quick-drying and did not blot. The ink was too thick to be used in a fountain pen so Biró replaced the nib with a metal ball; the idea of using a ball as the delivery mechanism for liquid later inspired the first roll-on deodorant.

Communication

PRINTING AND COPYING

Johannes Gutenburg built the first successful moveable-type printing press c.1450. Today we take books and newspapers for granted, but Gutenberg's press marked the beginning of a process that meant information could be reproduced in unlimited quantities and made available to everyone.

Top Engraving entitled "Death Amongst the Printers" taken from *Danse Macabre* (Lyons, 1499), showing one of the earliest known illustrations of a printing press
Above The Gutenberg Bible: Prologue to Proverbs and Proverbs Chapter One (c.1455)
Opposite The *New-York Tribune*, which in 1886 became the first newspaper to use the Linotype process

Although both block and moveable-type printing were known in China (c.500 and 1041 respectively), neither was widely used and Johannes Gensfleisch Gutenburg (Germany) is generally acknowledged to be the father of printing. Gutenberg experimented with moveable type during the 1430s but abandoned his experiments after his patron died. He then returned to his birthplace of Mainz, Germany, where Johann Fust (Germany) lent him money to continue his work. Gutenberg built a printing press, but ran out of money before he could print anything. Fust lent him more money with which he began to print a Bible, but before it was completed Fust called in his debts and sued for Gutenberg's printing press and business.

Fust then set up his own printing business with his son-in-law, Peter Schöffer, employing Gutenberg to complete the famous Bible that is now known as the Gutenberg Bible. Fust's timing in calling in his debts was almost certainly a cynical attempt to take advantage of Gutenberg's invention, but Schöffer went even further: after the deaths of Gutenberg and Fust, Schöffer claimed to have invented the printing press himself.

Braille

Valentin Haüy (France) devised the first embossed typeface for the blind in 1784. Haüy's complex system was used at the Institution Des Jeunes Aveugles (Institution for Young Blind People) where Louis Braille was a pupil from the age of 11, having been blinded at the age of 3 in an accident at his father's workbench. While Braille was a pupil at the Institute, an artillery officer named Charles Barbier visited to demonstrate a "night writing" code that he had devised for use on the battlefield. It had not been a success, but Braille understood the potential of a system that could be read with one hand and spent several years simplifying and perfecting it. In 1854, two years after Braille's death, the Institution where he had been both a pupil and a teacher officially adopted his system, improving the lives of countless blind people.

1650 *Einkommenden Zeitungen* is published in Leipzig, Germany, as the first daily newspaper

1784 Valentin Haüy (France) devises the first embossed typeface for the blind

c.1796 Aloys Senefelder (Germany, b. Czechoslovakia) invents the process of lithographic printing

1829 Louis Braille (France) develops the first internationally successful embossed typeface for the blind

1884 Ottmar Mergenthaler (Germany–U.S.A.) patents the first Linotype machine (which composes and casts lines of type using a keyboard)

1886 The *New-York Tribune* becomes the first newspaper to use the Linotype process

1892 The *Weekly Summary* (England) is the first newspaper to be printed in Braille

1903 George C. Beidler (U.S.A.) invents the first (wet chemical) photocopier, known as the Rectigraph (patent granted 1906, marketed 1907), but it is not a success

1938 Chester F. Carlson (U.S.A.) invents a process that he patents as electron photography (later electrophotography and then xerography)

1959 Haloid Corp (later Xerox Corp., U.S.A.) produces the first successful photocopier, based on Carlson's patent

DID YOU KNOW?

• Italic type takes its name from Italy, being characteristic of the typefaces used by early Italian presses such as the Aldine Press of Venice

• The first photocopier literally photographed documents—a slow, complicated process involving wet chemicals. Not surprisingly, it did not catch on. Modern photocopiers (1938) use dry, untreated paper in a process that became known as xerography from the Greek *xeros* (dry) and *graphein* (to write)

In the 4th century b.c. Greek historian Herodotus wrote of the Persian postal service that: "Neither snow, nor rain, nor heat, nor gloom of night stays these couriers from the swift completion of their appointed rounds." Modern postal services have a lot to live up to.

POSTAL SERVICE

The great empires of the ancient world had well-organized postal systems, usually working on a relay system with messengers or couriers stationed at intervals along major routes. The efficiency of such systems led to high praise from Greek historian Herodotus, but the idea went out of use after the collapse of the Roman Empire. Private postal systems began to reemerge in medieval Europe to serve the needs of merchants, guilds, universities and the Church, and these were followed by official government postal services such as those established by Louis XI (France, 1477) and Henry VIII (England, 1512).

By the 17th century most European countries had official public mail services as well as a number of private concerns often serving particular cities. One of the privately run services was the *Petite Poste* (small post), established by Jean-Jacques Renouard de Villayer (France) in Paris in 1653. De Villayer initiated the first system of prepaid postage, consisting of a ribbon or paper band around the letter; until then it had been the norm for the recipient to pay for postage. William Dockwra (England) introduced Britain's first system of prepayment in 1680 with the London Penny Post, using a hand-stamp to indicate postage paid.

Capt Bedlow carrying letters to Forraigne Parts.

Dockwra's standard charge proved very effective for local post, but mail sent between cities was still charged according to the distance it traveled. In 1837 Rowland Hill (England) published *Post-office Reform*, pointing out that the cost of sorting letters was greater than the cost of transporting them, so the extra administration in working out the fee for distance was uneconomical. He proposed a system similar to Dockwra's, with a standard charge for postage regardless of

Top "Just in time to catch the post." Undated drawing by Lance Thackeray
Left "Capt. Bedlow carrying letters to Forraigne Parts." Design for playing card by W. Faithorne (1684)
Opposite Penny Black (c.1840)

• The world's most valuable stamp is the 1857 *Treskilling Yellow* (Sweden), which was sold at auction for U.S. $22 million in 1996, becoming the world's most expensive item by weight. The three-shilling stamp should have been green but turned out yellow because of a printing error, and it is the only one in existence

• Australia's first postmaster (1809) was Isaac Nichols, who had been transported to the penal colony for stealing a donkey

• The first rule of the UPU (1874) was that all postage stamps must bear the name of the issuing country except those of Britain, in recognition of the fact that Britain was the first country to issue stamps

1842 New York City issues postage stamps for local delivery, the first postage stamps in the United States

1847 The United States's first national postage stamps are issued, a 5-cent Benjamin Franklin and a 10-cent George Washington

1849 The world's first postal pillar boxes appear in Belgium

1850 New South Wales and Victoria, Australia, issue the world's first pictorial stamps (all previous stamps bore portraits or simply the value)

1854 The British General Post Office issues the Penny Red as the first stamp with perforated edges (made using a machine invented in 1847)

1861 John P. Charlton (U.S.A.) invents the first postcard and sells the rights to stationer Hyman Lipman (U.S.A.)

1869 The Austrian Post Office issues the *Correspondenz-Karte*, the first prepaid postcard (suggested by Emmanuel Herrman the previous year)

1872 J.H. Locher (Switzerland) produces the first picture postcard, engraved by Franz Rorich (Zurich views)

1874 The Universal Postal Union is set up as the first international postal organization

1898 The Canadian Post Office issues the first Christmas stamp (2 cents, showing a map of the world)

1903 The first postal franking machine, invented by Karl Uchermann (Norway), is made by Krag Maskinfabrik but the system only lasts 18 months

1904 The New Zealand Post Office introduces the first permanent franking service

1928 Airmail postal service is introduced in Canada

1944 The first postcodes are introduced, in Germany

1988 Austria issues the first holographic postage stamp

destination. Hill proposed that the charge should be prepaid either by post-paid envelopes (which he favored) or by adhesive stamps, which had been suggested by James Chalmers (Scotland) in 1834; Chalmers had even printed the world's first adhesive postage stamps as samples. In 1840 the General Post Office (Britain) acted on Hill's proposals and issued the world's first official adhesive postage stamp, the Penny Black (the Twopenny Blue was issued two days later).

In the age of the information superhighway it is difficult to imagine the impact made by the invention of the electric telegraph. For the first time, instantaneous communication was possible across great distances—a concept as revolutionary then as that of the Internet in the 1990s.

TELEGRAPHY AND FAX MACHINES

TIMELINE

1791 Claude Chappe (France) invents the first mechanical telegraph

1793 Chappe invents the first semaphore, later adapted for use with hand flags and widely used at sea

1837 William Cooke and Charles Wheatstone (both England) are granted the first patent for an electric telegraph. Samuel Finley Breese Morse (U.S.A.) files a caveat for a superior telegraph system, employing his Morse alphabet

1843 Alexander Bain (Scotland) patents the first facsimile (fax) machine, but does not make a transmission. The world's first paid telegrams are sent via the Great Western Railway's Paddington–Slough telegraph line (England)

1851 Frederick Bakewell (England) makes the first public demonstration of a fax machine

1861 Giovanni Caselli (Italy) is granted a patent for his pantelegraph, the first truly practical fax machine, leading to the first commercial fax service in 1865

Telegraphy

Telegraphy literally means "writing from afar." Primitive methods included smoke signals and drum beats, but until the invention of the mechanical semaphore by Claude Chappe (France) the only reliable form of long-distance communication was by messenger. Chappe's first attempt (1791) was a series of towers that passed a signal from one to the next by means of a dial with a number of symbols; a pointer swept round the dial and a drum was beaten when the pointer reached the symbol to be transmitted. This, the first telegraph, was limited by the distance from which the drumbeat could be heard, but in 1793 Chappe devised a semaphore system, replacing the dial with wooden beams whose relative positions indicated letters of the alphabet.

Scientists and inventors then began experimenting with electric signaling systems. Baron Schilling (Russia), Francis Ronalds (England) and Carl Gauss and Wilhelm Weber (both Germany) all devised systems before William Cooke and Charles Wheatstone (both England) obtained the first patent for an electric telegraph in 1837. This telegraph used electric current to deflect needles that would

Top The world's first mechanical telegraph system in action

Left Five-needle telegraph, invented by Cooke and Wheatstone in 1837

indicate letters of the alphabet. The same year, Samuel Morse (U.S.A.) filed a caveat (a means of registering an idea in progress pending a full patent application) for a simpler and more effective system employing his Morse alphabet (patent filed 1838, granted 1840). The Morse telegraph was developed with the largely unacknowledged assistance of Joseph Henry and Alfred Vail (both U.S.A.) and tested in 1844 with the famous transmission "What hath God wrought?"

Fax

The facsimile (fax) machine is now closely associated with the telephone, but in fact it was invented 33 years earlier than the telephone and the first faxes were transmitted by telegraph. Alexander Bain (Scotland) patented the first fax machine in 1843, outlining the principle that is still used in modern fax machines—the transmission of a signal to indicate whether a given part of the document is black or white. Bain did not make a transmission, but an improved version of his machine was used by Frederick Bakewell (England) to make the first fax transmission in 1851.

Samuel Morse (1791–1872). Unknown artist (c. 1850)

Communication

TELEPHONES

The invention of the electric telegraph meant that people could send signals along a wire. It also inspired inventors to strive for even more exciting developments, one of which was the quest to send not just a signal but the human voice along the wire—the telephone.

Below Batman is put on hold
Opposite Kiosk No.6, popularly known as the Jubilee, designed in 1935 for what was then the General Post Office (U.K.) by architect Sir Giles Gilbert Scott to celebrate the silver jubilee of King George V. Some 2,400 of these telephone call boxes, said to be the world's most universally recognized item of street furniture, are now listed buildings. Illustration by Andrew Johnston (1936)

The first telephone to be demonstrated in public was made by German schoolteacher Johann Philipp Reis in 1860, using the principle of intermittent current, an idea that had been outlined by Charles Bourseul (France) in 1854. Sound caused a diaphragm to move in the transmitter, sending an intermittent current to the receiver where another diaphragm moved to reproduce an indistinct but intelligible version of the original sound—the first time that sounds had been transmitted electrically. (The telegraph used electricity to create tones at the receiver rather than transmitting the sounds themselves.)

The breakthrough for commercially practical telephones came when Alexander Graham Bell (Scotland–Canada, U.S. citizen from 1882) realized that variations in an unbroken current (what he calledundulatory currents) would give a much clearer signal than an intermittent current. On February 14, 1876 Bell filed his patent application. It was the fifth entry in the patent office register for that day. Within hours, his rival Elisha Gray (U.S.A.) filed a caveat for the same invention (a caveat is a means of registering an idea in progress pending a full patent application—an option not open to Bell as a British subject). Gray's caveat was the day's 39th entry, and those few places in the queue were crucial.

Bell's patent was granted on March 7. The first use of a telephone was on August 3, 1876 when Bell—in a Dominion Telegraph Company office in Mount Pleasant, Ontario—heard his Uncle David—3 km (2 miles) away in a telegraph office in Brantford, Ontario—speak the Shakespeare line "To be or not to be…"

Bell's first priority was his work as a vocal physiologist for the deaf and speech-impaired. He maintained that he did not fully understand the electrical principles behind his

| **1860** Johann Philipp Reis (Germany) builds *das telephon*, the first (experimental) telephone to be publicly demonstrated | **1871** Antonio Meucci (Italy) files a caveat for a telephone that he claims to have built in 1849, though it is not demonstrated and is never patented | **1876** Alexander Graham Bell (Scotland–Canada) files a patent for the telephone. Hours later, Elisha Gray (U.S.A.) files a caveat for the telephone. The U.S. patent office grants Bell the patent | **1880** The Connecticut Telephone Co. (U.S.A.) opens the first public call box | **1889** Almon Strowager (U.S.A.) files a patent for the first automatic telephone exchange (granted 1891). William Gray (U.S.A.) is granted the first patent for a coin-operated telephone. The first payphone is installed, in the Hartford Bank, in Hartford, CT |

TIMELINE

1896 The first dial telephones go into use, in Milwaukee, WI

1898 Valdemar Poulsen (Denmark) files a patent for the Telegraphone, the world's first magnetic recorder, designed as a telephone answering machine (U.S. patent filed 1899)

1906 The first directory enquiry service is inaugurated, in New York

1927 AT&T demonstrates the first videophone, developed by Bell Laboratories (U.S.A.)

1933 The French Ministry of Posts & Telecommunications inaugurates the *horloge parlante*, the first speaking clock, using the voice of popular broadcaster Marcel Laporte

invention, only that it worked, and once wrote to his wife: "I think I can be of far more use as a teacher of the deaf than I can ever be as an electrician."

Exchanges, telephone booths and cell phones

The first telephone exchanges were manually operated, a job that entailed plugging in tielines to connect one telephone to another. Callers would contact the exchange and speak to the operator, who would then connect the call to the required telephone—or not, if the suspicions of undertaker Almon Strowager (U.S.A.) were correct. He thought that the operators had been bribed by his rivals to reroute his business calls, so to circumvent the problem he devised the first automatic telephone exchange, filing a patent in 1889 (granted 1891)—the first automatic exchange went into operation in Indiana, in 1892. To make a call using Strowager's system, users had to press one of three keys (for 100s, 10s and units) the correct number of times to make up the required number, a system superseded in 1896 by the first dial telephones.

The first telephone booth was a cubicle in the offices of the Connecticut Telephone Co., which was opened to the public in 1880. Nine years later the coin-operated telephone was invented by William Gray (U.S.A.) and the world's first payphone was installed in the Hartford Bank, in Hartford, CT. The world's most familiar call box is the British K6, designed by architect Sir Giles Gilbert Scott to celebrate the silver jubilee of King George V in 1935.

The ancestor of the modern cell phone is the radiotelephone. Radiotelephones were being used as early as 1900 by the pioneers of radio, but it was nearly half a century later before the first commercial mobile radiotelephone service was inaugurated, by AT&T and Southwestern Bell in St. Louis, MO. The first commercial radiotelephones were fitted in the cars of Henry L. Perkinson (U.S.A.) and the Monsanto Chemical Co. More than 30 years later, in 1978, Illinois Bell inaugurated the first cellular mobile telephone service, in Chicago.

The increasing popularity of cell telephones means that one day the thought of telephoning a building in the hopes that the person is inside (as happens with landlines) will seem a very quaint idea.

Above French switchboard girls are instructed as to the insults they may legitimately use to customers. Insults include "old pear," "turkey," "mussel" and "tart." Luc Leguey in *Le Pele-Mele* (1905)

Opposite left Size matters, and in the case of cell phones small is beautiful. In 1990 some cell phones were almost the size of a house brick

Opposite right "Beam me up, Scotty"

1935 The first K6 telephone box (Britain) is installed, designed by architect Sir Giles Gilbert Scott to celebrate the silver jubilee of King George V

1937 The 999 emergency telephone service is first introduced in London, England. The first call is made by a Mrs. Beard, as a result of which Thomas Duffy is arrested for attempted burglary. The *Daily Sketch* reports the incident under the headline "She is the first to dial 999"

1946 AT&T and Southwestern Bell (U.S.A.) inaugurate the first commercial mobile radio-telephone service

1949 Joseph L. Zimmerman (U.S.A.) builds the first practical telephone answering machine (Poulsen's, 1898, was never used for that purpose)

1978 Illinois Bell inaugurates the first cellular mobile telephone system, in Chicago (based on a concept devised by Bell Laboratories in 1947)

DID YOU KNOW?

● In 1972 Mogens Glistrup, founder of Denmark's Progressive Party, suggested that his country's ministry of defense should be replaced with a telephone answering machine carrying the message *Miy Sdavaemsya*—"We Surrender" in Russian

● The first speaking clock (1933) was invented because its designer, Monsieur Esclangon, Director of the Paris Observatory, was fed up with the number of calls to the observatory by members of the public wanting to know the exact time

● At the turn of the millennium Finland was the country with the greatest number of cell phones per capita, with more than 65% of the population owning at least one cell phone

1981 The Nordic Mobile Telephone System becomes the first international cellular mobile telephone system, serving Sweden, Finland, Denmark and Norway

1988 Integrated Services Digital Network (ISDN) begins operating for the first time

When Heinrich Hertz proved the existence of radio waves, he said, "I don't see any useful purpose for this mysterious, invisible electromagnetic energy." Guglielmo Marconi could, however, and in 1896 he patented "a system of telegraphy using Hertzian waves"—radio was born.

RADIO

Below Eddie Robinson, Donald Shingler and Harry Oakes (l–r) recording an episode of the world's longest-running radio soap opera, *The Archers*, at the BBC Studios (November 29, 1954)

Opposite Colored X-ray of a portable radio showing its electronic components. The circular object upper center is the loudspeaker (the batteries have been removed)

Most people associate Guglielmo Marconi (Italy) with the invention of radio, but in fact U.S. dentist Mahlon Loomis was the first person to make a radio transmission. In 1866, 30 years before Marconi's patent, Loomis flew kites from two mountains 14 miles (23 km) apart, using wires instead of strings, and showed that discharging the static electricity in the wire of one kite deflected the needle of a galvanometer attached to the other. Loomis cannot have known how or why his experiment worked, because the scientific basis of radio waves was not proved until 1887, the year after his death.

The first person to describe the existence of radio waves was James Clerk Maxwell (Scotland), who published *A Dynamical Theory of the Electromagnetic Field* in 1865, the year before Loomis's experiment. Many scientists rejected Maxwell's theory until Heinrich Hertz (Germany) proved it in 1887 by making sparks jump across the gap in a wire loop sited away from the source of a discharge and not connected to it. Hertz was the first person to scientifically generate radio waves; the next step was to find a more practical means of detecting them. Between 1835 and 1866 several scientists had noticed that the conductivity of a tube of metal filings would alter if a spark discharged nearby. In 1890 Edouard Branly (France) used such a tube to detect Hertzian waves, making it the first radio receiver. The Branly tube was later named a coherer.

It was now possible to transmit signals by radio, but the range of the transmitter-coherer arrangement was severely limited. The answer was the addition of antennae (aerials) to the transmitter and receiver, an idea that occurred to two men at the same time: Alexander Stepanovitch Popov (Russia), who transmitted the first intelligible message in 1896, and Guglielmo Marconi, who was quicker to patent and exploit his discovery. When the Italian government showed no interest in his invention, Marconi

1865 James Clerk Maxwell (Scotland) theorizes that electricity can create a remote effect through electromagnetic propagation (radio waves)	**1866** Mahlon Loomis (U.S.A.) makes the world's first radio transmission	**1872** Loomis patents a means of "establishing an electrical current for telegraphic or other purposes without the aid of wires, batteries or cables," the first patent for wireless telegraphy	**1887** Heinrich Hertz (Germany) proves Maxwell's theory (Hertz's findings are published the following year in *Annalen der Physik*)	**1890** Edouard Branly (France) creates the first radio receiver, later named the coherer tube by Oliver Lodge (England)	**1895** Alexander Stepanovitch Popov (Russia) and Guglielmo Marconi (Italy) independently invent the first radio antennae (aerials)

TIMELINE

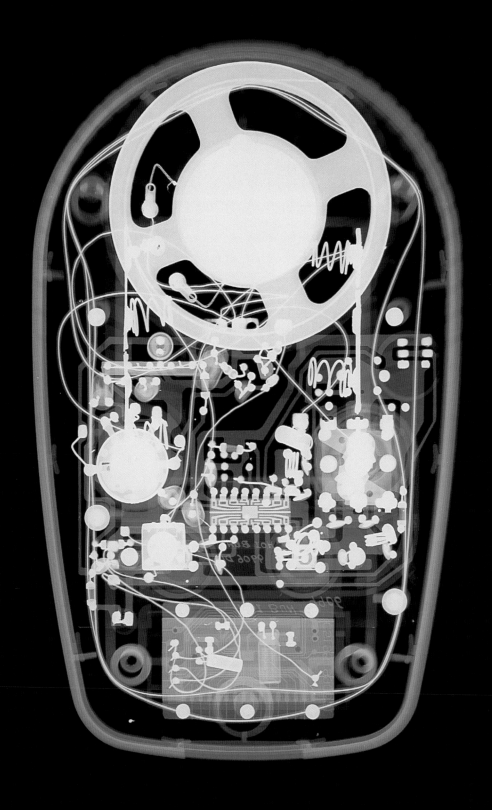

1896 Popov makes the first intelligible radio transmission: the words "Heinrich Hertz" in Morse code. Marconi is granted a GB patent for "a system of telegraphy using Hertzian waves" (U.S. patent granted 1897)

1898 Oliver Lodge patents the first adjustable radio tuning coils

1900 Reginald Aubrey Fessenden (U.S.A., b. Canada) makes the first radio voice transmission

1901 Three dots for the letter S are sent from Cornwall, England, to Marconi in Newfoundland, in the first transatlantic radio transmission

1906 Fessenden makes the first radio broadcast. Lee De Forest (U.S.A.) invents the first triode valve (patent filed 1906, granted 1907)

1913 Edwin Howard Armstrong (U.S.A.) invents the first regenerative (or feedback) circuit, hugely increasing radio sensitivity (patented 1914)

traveled to Britain and filed the first patent for a practical system of radio communication, earning him the title father of radio.

By being the first to the patent office, Marconi staked his claim as the inventor of radio despite the fact that he could not have achieved this without the prior work of Hertz and Branly. But if Marconi is famous as the inventor of radio, Edwin Howard Armstrong (U.S.A.) is the unsung hero of its development.

Lee De Forest (U.S.A.) invented the triode valve in 1906, the first device capable of amplifying a weak electric signal. It was an important step forward but it was nothing compared with the regenerative or feedback circuit invented by Armstrong in 1913, which increased the sensitivity of receivers up to a thousand-fold and is still used in modern radios. (Armstrong filed a separate patent for a regenerative transmitter as well as his revolutionary receiver, but after a long court battle the patent for the transmitter was awarded to

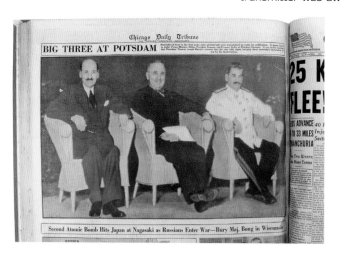

Left The back page of the *Chicago Daily Tribune* showing the first color news photograph ever transmitted by radio for publication (August 9, 1945)
Right Sex sells, 50s-style. At the Radio Show in Earl's Court, London, Rosamund Leslie demonstrates that the Mighty Midget transistor radio makes the ideal stocking filler (August 28, 1957)

| **1917** Armstrong invents the first superheterodyne circuit, making variable frequency receivers feasible (patent filed 1919, granted 1920) | **1919** XWA Montreal becomes North America's first licensed radio station | **1920** Station 8MK Detroit makes the first broadcast news bulletins | **1921** The first vocal weather forecast is broadcast by the University of Wisconsin radio station (previously weather forecasts were broadcast in Morse code) | **1930** Armstrong files a patent for the first frequency modulation (FM) system (granted 1933) | **1932** NBC's *Betty and Bob* and *One Man's Family* (USA) are broadcast as the first soap operas. *One Man's Family* was adapted for television in 1949 with a new cast, leaving the original cast to continue on radio |

De Forest.) Four years later, while serving in the U.S. Army Signal Corps during World War One, Armstrong developed the first superheterodyne circuit, which enabled precise, variable tuning and formed the basis of amplitude-modulation (AM) radio receivers. In 1921 he improved on the regenerative circuit with the super-regenerative circuit, and in 1930 he filed a patent for the invention that cemented his place in radio history—the first frequency modulation (FM) system.

In 1947 William Shockley, John Bardeen and Walter Brattain (all U.S.A.) produced the first transistor, an invention of such overwhelming importance for all electronic equipment (from radios and mobile phones to computers, robots and satellites) that the three of them shared the 1956 Nobel Prize for Physics for this and subsequent work on transistors. The first commercial products to use transistors were hearing aids, which went on sale in 1953, and the first transistor radio, the TR-1, was marketed by Regency Electronics (U.S.A.) in 1955.

Clockwork radio in action in Tananarive, Madagascar

| **1941** Broadcasts of CBC National News Service begin in Canada | **1947** William Shockley, John Bardeen and Walter Brattain (all U.S.A.) invent the first transistor (patent filed by Bardeen & Brattain 1948, granted 1950) | **1951** Radio's longest-running soap opera, BBC's *The Archers* (Britain), is first broadcast (following a one-week pilot the previous May) | **1955** Regency Electronics (U.S.A.) markets the TR-1, the first transistor radio | **1991** Trevor Baylis (England) files a patent for the clockwork radio. Manufacture of the first commercially produced clockwork radio begins in 1994 in Cape Town, South Africa, but the discovery of earlier patents (including one from 1923) causes Baylis to withdraw his patent application in 1996 |

The Internet has grown from a military communications exchange of just four host computers, set up in 1969, into a global network of networks connecting millions of users. The biggest boon for private users was the establishment in 1989 of the World Wide Web by Tim Berners-Lee.

THE INTERNET

| **1960s** Donald Davies (England) and Paul Baran (U.S.A.) independently develop packet switching, making computer networks possible | **1969** ARPAnet, the precursor of the Internet, is established by the U.S. Department of Defense. The first e-mails are sent using **ARPAnet** | **1970s** ARPAnet introduces communication protocols (TCP/IP) and internetworking, giving rise to the Internet | **1985** Symbolics.com becomes the first registered domain name | **1989** Tim Berners-Lee (England) proposes a global hypertext project to be known as the World Wide Web | **1990** Berners-Lee creates the first web browser. The first web server is nxoc01.cern.ch (later changed to info.cern.ch). The first web page is http://nxoc01.cern.ch/hypertext/WWW/TheProject.html |

TIMELINE

At one time, a computer could only be connected to one other computer, via a hard wire or a telephone line. That began to change in the 1960s when Donald Davies (England) and Paul Baran (U.S.A.), working independently of each other, developed the concept of "packet switching." This entailed converting data into discrete units (packets) that could be sent to a central location to be collected by the recipient, allowing data to be transferred between any number of connected computers via a router; computer networks were born.

One such network was the Advanced Research Projects Agency Network (ARPAnet), set up in 1969 by the U.S. Department of Defense and later merged with the National Science Foundation network. These networks were initially intended as a means of allowing remote access to specialist computers, but they came to be used as a means of direct communication between users, through electronic mail (e-mail) and newsgroups. During the next decade a number of subnetworks developed and protocols (Transmission Control Protocol/Internet Protocol or TCP/IP) were set up to enable the different networks to communicate with each other; the resulting interconnected network of networks became known as the Internet.

Until 1989 it was extremely difficult to access the vast amount of information available on the Internet without knowing exactly what to look for and where to look for it. Then Tim Berners-Lee (England), working at CERN (Conseil Européen pour la Recherche Nucléaire, a.k.a. the European Particle Physics Laboratory), devised a method of organizing all this information for the use of CERN; he called it the World Wide Web (WWW). He wrote the first web browser in 1990 and the following year CERN opened up the web to the public. Browsing became known as surfing, and within a decade users of the web had grown from a small band of academics and scientists into a massive community of over 150 million people.

DID YOU KNOW?

● Tim Berners-Lee, who wrote HTML, the language used on the Internet, did not patent his work, since he wanted to encourage its use

● A village in Wales has long been famous for having the longest name of any railway station. Now it also has the world's longest URL (website address)—http://llanfairpwllgwyngyllgogerychwyrndrobwllllantysiliogogogoch.co.uk

● Verbally, WWW does not work as an abbreviation—it has three times as many syllables as "World Wide Web"

Opposite Hindu temple and Cyber Prince Internet café, Bangalore, India (2001)
Above right The world's first web cam, set up by computer engineers at Cambridge University, England, so that they could check whether there was coffee in the pot before making the long trek to the kitchen

1991 CERN makes the World Wide Web available to the public

1993 Daniel Gordon and Martyn Johnson of Cambridge University, England, connect a camera (trained on the departmental coffee pot) to the World Wide Web, making it the first web cam

1994 The first international WWW conference is so over-subscribed it becomes known as the "Woodstock of the Web"

1995 James Gosling (Canada) invents Java, the Internet language used to view animation, stock market tickers and games, regardless of the type of computer being used

1996 Leslie Rogge becomes the first criminal on the FBI's most wanted list to be caught by using the Internet, after a netsurfer in Guatemala sees Rogge's picture on the FBI homepage and reports his whereabouts

The word navigate derives from the Latin *navis*, meaning "ship," but the word now applies equally to sea, air and land. The first navigational instrument was the astrolabe and the most recent is GPS (1970s). The first road map was published in 1901, by the Belgian Automobile Club.

Communication

NAVIGATION

Above Sixteenth-century compass
Below "Leaning on their new Austin 8, a couple of motorists check their position on a road map" (1949)
Opposite GPS computer in the dashboard of a Lexus

FYF 80

c.2000 b.c. First known map is drawn, on a clay tablet in Babylonia (now Iraq)

c.575 b.c. Anaximander (Asia Minor) is thought to have drawn the first map of the world

6th century a.d. John Philoponos (Egypt) provides the first written record of an astrolabe

12th century Mariners in China and Europe independently discover that a magnet will align itself with the North Star, which leads to the development of the first magnetic compass c.1190

1569 Gerardus Mercator (Flanders, originally Gerhard Kramer) publishes the first map to use the Mercator projection (projecting the globe onto a flat surface)

1585 Mercator is the first person to describe a book of maps as an atlas

1757 John Campbell (Britain) devises the first sextant by adapting the 1731 octant of John Hadley (England)

1759 John Harrison (England) completes H4, the first timepiece accurate enough to solve the problem of calculating longitude at sea

1852 Jean Bernard Léon Foucault (France) constructs the first gyroscope

1901 The Automobile Club Belgique publishes the first road map (of Belgium)

1908 Dr. Anschutz (Germany) builds the first successful gyroscopic compass

1950 Bill Bloggs of the Ordnance Survey (Britain) invents the first tilt-finder (used to make accurate maps from aerial photographs); it is known as the Bloggoscope

1970s The U.S. military begins developing the first GPS (global positioning system)

1978 The first GPS satellite is launched

1989 Magellan Corp. (U.S.A.) launches the first handheld GPS receiver

1990 The first commercially manufactured in-car satellite navigation system is marketed by Pioneer (Japan)

The first known map was drawn on a clay tablet in Babylonia (now Iraq) c.2000 b.c., showing settlements, waterways and mountains, while the first known map of the world was drawn some 1500 years later in Asia Minor, probably by the philosopher Anaximander. But maps, however accurate, are of little use unless the map reader knows where he or she is.

The first instrument to be used for determining location was the astrolabe, which could measure the angle of elevation of the sun or the stars in order to calculate latitude. The next important navigational instrument was much simpler—the compass. Mariners had long used the North Star to determine their direction of travel and during the 12th century a.d. sailors in China and Europe discovered that a magnet will align itself with the North Star, leading to the development of the first magnetic compass c.1190.

Knowledge of latitude and direction were very useful, but for centuries there was no reliable way of calculating longitude at sea. The answer lay in knowing the time at a given place; by comparing midday at the ship's position (measured by the height of the sun) with midday at a fixed point, navigators could tell how far east or west they were. Knowing the time at the nominated point simply meant carrying a clock—but the first timepiece accurate enough to tell the correct time after months at sea was not built until 1759, when John Harrison (England) completed his famous chronometer, H4.

Modern mariners, explorers, hikers and even car drivers can keep constant track of their position using the Global Positioning System (GPS), which uses satellites called Navstars, communicating with computerized radio receivers, to give an exact location based on the position of the receiver relative to the satellites. Differential GPS is accurate to within 10 meters, while "carrier phase" GPS can determine location anywhere on the earth's surface to within 1 centimeter.

DID YOU KNOW?

● The Greek god Atlas was condemned by Zeus to stand on earth and support the heavens on his shoulders. The god was depicted in a 16th-century book of maps by Gerardus Mercator (1585) and the name Atlas has been used for books of maps ever since

● Ordnance is the word for heavy guns or artillery. The reason Britain's Ordnance Survey maps are named as such is that the OS was originally set up to provide precise maps for the military so that troops moving heavy cannon knew which routes were suitable to use

The first timepieces measured the apparent movement of the sun, caused by the rotation of the earth. But highly accurate atomic clocks, first built in 1948, have proved that the earth's rotation is not only irregular, it is also slowing down, making the planet an inaccurate timekeeper.

234 **Communication** # CLOCKS

Above "Hang on a minute!" Harold Lloyd in *Safety Last!* (1923)
Below The 15th-century astronomical clock on the Old Town Hall in Prague, Czech Republic. It shows the time and the season, as well as plotting the movement of the sun, moon and stars
Opposite Customs agent Ken Stroud destroys 17,000 fake designer watches seized during Operation Stopwatch in 1985

The first method of measuring time was the sundial, which used a shadow to indicate the sun's progress through the sky (or, more scientifically, the earth's rotation about its axis). The astrolabe could be used to tell the time by measuring the position of the sun or stars, and other ancient methods included the water clock, the sandglass and the candle clock, all of which measured the passage of time by an artificial method—the flow of a measured amount of water or sand, or the rate of burning of a candle marked with the hours.

The first recorded mechanical clock was built in China c.1088, and had a water-powered driving wheel with an escapement to regulate the mechanism. Early clocks had an hour hand only, partly because they were not accurate enough to warrant a minute hand; the first clock known to have had a minute hand was built c.1577 by Jost Bürgi (Switzerland) for the Danish astronomer Tycho Brahe. Clocks did not become really accurate until 1657, when Christiaan Huygens (Netherlands) built the first successful pendulum clock, which made practical use of the fact noted by Galileo that a pendulum will always take the same amount of time to complete its cycle regardless of the extent of the swing. (In 1675 Huygens used a spiral spring to achieve similar accuracy in watches and smaller clocks.)

It was the constant frequency of a pendulum that made it such an accurate timekeeper, but in the 1920s Warren Alvin Marrison (U.S.A. b. Canada) found something with an even greater constancy: the resonance of a quartz crystal, which he used to build the first quartz clock in 1929. Then, in 1948, Harold Lyons (U.S.A.) built the first atomic clock, based on the vibrations of the atoms of an ammonia molecule. Later atomic clocks used cesium atoms, making them so accurate that the definition of a second was altered at an international conference in 1967. Instead of being 1/86,400th of the time taken for the earth to rotate, a second is now defined as the time taken for a cesium atom to vibrate 9,192,631,770 times.

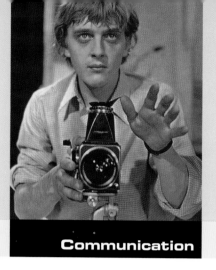

The pioneers of photography were Niepce, Daguerre and Talbot, but it was George Eastman who brought photography to the masses with the No. 1 Kodak camera. It was the first roll-film camera, introduced in 1888 under the slogan "You press the button—we do the rest."

PHOTOGRAPHY

The world's first photograph was taken by Joseph Nicéphore Niepce (France) in 1826 or 1827. He exploited the principle of the *camera obscura* (dark chamber), which had been known for centuries—that a beam of light entering a darkened room or box through a small aperture produces an inverted image of the scene outside. In 1822 Niepce had attempted to capture such an image by allowing it to fall on a plate coated with a light-sensitive compound, but the picture soon faded and so could not be described as the first true photograph. Then, in 1826/7, he found a way of fixing the image and took the world's first photograph (now preserved at the University of Texas).

Niepce's work was continued by Louis Daguerre (France), who, in 1837, discovered a method that vastly reduced the 8-hour exposure time. It was the first practicable method of photography and became known as the daguerreotype. Daguerre patented his method in 1839, making a claim that encapsulates the very essence of photography: "I have seized the light; I have arrested its flight."

In the meantime, William Fox Talbot (England) had been experimenting with photographic negatives, using paper coated with a compound of silver (which darkens when exposed to light) and in 1835 had made the crucial discovery that the negative could be used to make a positive print of the original image.

Above David Hemmings as Thomas the photographer in Michelangelo Antonioni's *Blow Up* (1966)
Right Daguerrotype camera
Opposite top The world's first photograph, taken by Joseph Niepce from a window of his Le Gras estate at St-Loup-de-Varennes, France

DID YOU KNOW?

- The name Kodak does not actually mean anything. Founder George Eastman said: "I devised the name myself ... The letter K had been a favorite with me—it seems such a strong, incisive sort of letter ... It became a question of trying out a great number of combinations of letters that made words, starting and ending in K"

- The famous Kodak Brownie camera was named not after its designer, Frank Brownell (U.S.A., b. Canada), but after the fairy-like Brownies that featured in the stories of children's writer and illustrator Pamela Cox (Canada)

Daguerreotypes had gained instant popularity, but they were eventually superseded by Talbot's negative-positive process, which remained the basic principle of all modern photography until the advent of the first digital camera in the 1980s.

Photography remained a field for experts, involving complex equipment and specialist knowledge, until George Eastman (U.S.A.) produced the No. 1 Kodak Camera in 1888, which meant that for the first time anyone could take photographs without needing technical know-how—photographers simply clicked away and then sent the entire camera to Kodak. The film was removed and processed, and the camera was returned ready loaded with another film.

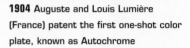

1904 Auguste and Louis Lumière (France) patent the first one-shot color plate, known as Autochrome

1924 Anatol Marco Josepho (Hungary) invents the first photobooth. Lignose, the first color roll film, is introduced in Germany

1932 Leopold D. Mannes and Leopold Godowsky Jr. (both U.S.A.) file a patent for the first commercially practical color film, launched in 1935 as Kodachrome motion picture film and in 1936 as Kodachrome 35 mm stills film (patent granted 1936)

1948 Polaroid Corp. (U.S.A.) launches the Polaroid 95, designed by company founder Edwin H. Land. It is the first instant picture camera, and is first sold at the Jordan Marsh department store in Boston, MA

1959 Jean de Wouters (Belgium) develops the first camera that can be used underwater without a housing

1963 Polaroid introduces Polacolor, the first instant color film. Kodak introduces its first Instamatic camera

THE BEST OF THE REST...

The paper clip

The first patent for a paper clip was filed by Johann
Vaaler (Norway) in 1899 (granted 1900), closely
followed by Cornelius J. Brosnan (U.S.A.), who filed
the first U.S. patent for a paper clip (which he
called the Konaclip) in 1900. The first double oval
slide-on clip, now the standard design, was
patented by Gem Manufacturing Ltd (England) in
1907. In 1989 the world's largest paper clip, 7 m
(23 ft.) long, was unveiled near Oslo, Norway, in
honor of Johann Vaaler

Post-it® Notes

The first Post-it® note was the result of an accidental discovery made in 1970 by Spencer Silver (U.S.A.), a research chemist with 3M Corp. Silver was trying to create the strongest glue on the market, but instead came up with the exact opposite: acrylate copolymer microspheres. This weak glue was reusable and left no residue on the surface it had been stuck to—paradoxically, its weakness was its strength, because it was so weak that it did not even damage paper fibers if stuck to a page and then removed. Silver was convinced there must be a use for his discovery but could not think of one until his colleague Arthur Fry, a member of the church choir, used it to stop the markers in his hymn book from falling out. Post-it® notes were test-marketed in 1977 and officially launched in 1981, since then the concept has been a resounding success: by 2000 the notes were available in 29 colors, 57 shapes and 27 sizes. To celebrate the 20th anniversary, artists created mini-artworks on Post-it® notes that were then auctioned for charity. A work by London-based U.S. artist R.B. Kitaj (medium: charcoal and pastel on a Post-it® note) sold for U.S. $1,000, making it the world's most expensive Post-it® note

Transparent adhesive tape

The first transparent adhesive tape was Scotch Tape, invented by Richard G. Drew (U.S.A.), who was working for the Minnesota Mining and Manufacturing Co. (later 3M Corp.). In 1925 Drew devised a masking tape that had adhesive on the edges only to make it easier to remove. The story goes that one customer told Drew to "take this tape back to your stingy Scotch bosses and tell them to put more adhesive on it," and so the name Scotch Tape was born. When asked to produce a moisture-proof tape, Drew began working on a new self-adhesive tape using cellulose backing based on the recently invented Cellophane. Drew filed a patent for his tape in 1928 (granted 1930), and on September 8, 1930 the first roll of clear Scotch Tape was sent to 3M's client, since then sticky tape has become an indispensable household item. One of Scotch Tape's competitors is Sellotape®, first made in England by Colin Kininmonth and George Gray in 1937, based on a French patent

Chapter Ten

Sporting Milestones

The first recorded Olympic contest took place in Olympia, Greece, in 776 b.c. It was a single event, won by a baker called Koroibos. The first modern Olympics took place in 1896 in Athens, Greece, where James B. Connolly became the first modern Olympic champion.

OLYMPIC GAMES

Above Bowl decorated with images of the pentathlon. Undated watercolor by Peter Connolly

Athletics played an important part in the religious festivals of ancient Greece, and the Olympic Games have their origins in sporting contests dating back to c.1370 b.c. Over time, four important religious festivals emerged: the Isthmian, Nemean, Pythian and Olympic festivals, of which the Olympic was the most important, held in honor of Zeus, King of the Gods. The first recorded Olympic contest took place in 776 b.c., a 192 m (210 yards) running race known as the *stadion*, which was won by a baker called Koroibos (a.k.a. Coroebus). Olympiads were held every four years until they were banned as pagan festivals by the Roman emperor Theodosius I in a.d. 393.

The excavation of Olympia in 1875 by a group of German archaeologists inspired Baron Pierre de Coubertin (France) to propose a modern,

international Olympic Games. His dream was realized in 1896 when the first modern Olympics were held in Athens, Greece. The first of nine events was the hop, step and jump (now known as the triple jump), which was won by James B. Connolly (U.S.A.), making him the first modern Olympic champion.

At the Sydney Olympics in 2000 oarsman Steve Redgrave (England) proved himself to be the supreme Olympian by becoming the first person in modern times to win gold medals in five consecutive Olympics. The fifth was a close finish—journalists described the winning margin as being the width of a cigarette paper—but, when asked whether he thought he would win again, Redgrave answered: "It was never in any doubt after the first 250 meters." It was the answer of a champion, but he may be disappointed to know that he was not the first to achieve this remarkable feat: between 532 and 516 b.c. the ancient Olympic wrestling competition was won five times consecutively by Milon of Kroton.

Left The first modern Olympic Games, April 6–14, 1896. Start of the 100 m race; (from left): Chalkokondylis (Greece), Thomas Burke (U.S.A.), Fritz Hofman (Germany), Alajos Szokolyi (Hungary) and Francis Lane (U.S.A.)

Above Constantine Kondyllis carries the Olympic Torch over the first part of the 3,000-km (1,865-mile) stretch from Olympia to Berlin for the start of the 1936 Olympic Games

TIMELINE

776 b.c. Olympia, Greece. First recorded Olympic contest, won by Koroibos (Greece)

516 b.c. Olympia, Greece. Milon of Kroton becomes the first five-times Olympic champion (wrestling)

1896 Athens, Greece. First modern Olympic Games. James B. Connolly (U.S.A.) becomes the first modern Olympic champion (hop, step and jump)

1900 Paris, France. Women are allowed to compete in the Olympics for the first time. Charlotte Cooper (Britain) becomes the first female Olympic champion (tennis)

1924 Chamonix, France. First Winter Olympics

1928 Amsterdam, Netherlands. Women are allowed to compete in track and field events for the first time. Crown Prince Olav (Norway, later King Olav V) becomes the first royal Olympic gold medalist (yachting crew member)

1932 Lake Placid, NY (Winter Olympics). Edward Eagan (U.S.A.) wins gold with the four-man bobsled team to become the first man to win gold medals in both summer and winter Olympics, having won the light-heavyweight boxing title in 1920 (Antwerp)

1936 Berlin, Germany. First televised Olympics; first relay of Olympic torch from Athens

1960 Rome, Italy. First Paralympics

1976 Montreal. Nadia Comaneci (Romania) becomes the first person to score a perfect 10 in Olympic gymnastics. Örnsköldsvik, Sweden. First Winter Paralympics

1994 Lillehammer, Norway. First Winter Olympics to be held under a new biennial winter–summer schedule

2000 Sydney, Australia. Steve Redgrave (England) becomes the first modern Olympian to win gold medals in five consecutive Olympics (rowing). Birgit Fischer (Germany) becomes the first female Olympian to win gold medals in four consecutive Olympics (canoeing)

MARATHONS

The first marathon race took place in Athens at the first modern Olympic Games (1896) to commemorate Pheidippides, an Ancient Greek messenger who died after running 22 miles to Athens with news of the Athenian victory at the Battle of Marathon in 490 b.c.

Modern marathon runners are lucky that they are not expected to emulate a feat accomplished by Pheidippides shortly before his famous run from Marathon to Athens. When the Persian army landed at Marathon, Pheidippides was sent to Sparta to ask for help in repelling the invaders—he ran 150 miles (240 km) in just two days. By the time the Spartans arrived at Marathon the Athenian army had won the battle without their help, and Pheidippides was sent to Athens with news of the victory. He ran the 22 miles (35 km) without stopping and breathlessly delivered his message: "Rejoice, we conquer." He then collapsed and died, probably from heat exhaustion.

The first organized race commemorating Pheidippides' amazing run was the Greek trial on March 10, 1896 for the first modern Olympic Games, which were to be held in Athens the same year; the course was that run by Pheidippides, from Marathon to Athens. That first trial was won by Charilaos Vasilakos (Greece) and the Olympic event, held a month later on April 10, was won by Spiridon Louis (Greece); Vasilakos came second. Marathons have since become high-profile annual events in a number of cities around the world, attracting an enormous number of competitors and spectators.

The first major city to organize a marathon was Boston, MA, in 1897.

For many years the length of a marathon race varied. The first time the now standard length of 26 miles 385 yards was used was for the 1908 Olympics in London, England—the race began at Windsor Castle and the exact length was set so that the race would end in front of King Edward VII's royal box at the White City Stadium. This odd length was officially adopted in 1924.

Opposite top Lloyd Scott, who raised money for charity by running the 2002 London Marathon in a 59 kg (130 lb) diving suit. He finished in what was then the slowest time ever: 5 days, 8 hrs, 29 mins, 46 secs
Opposite below Painting of Pheidippedes announcing victory. Olivier Merson (1869)
Below Verrazano-Narrows Bridge during the New York Marathon (1985)

GOLF—THE MAJORS

The origins of golf are obscure, but there is no doubt about the dates of sport's most prestigious events. The four Majors are the British Open (first played 1860), the U.S. Open (1895), the U.S. PGA Championship (1916) and the U.S. Masters (1934). The Ryder Cup was inaugurated in 1927.

Opposite below René Russo and Kevin Costner in a still from *Tin Cup*, a film about an underdog who decides to enter the U.S. Open (1996)
Right Miss Kyle tees off at a golf course in Portrush, Northern Ireland (1911)

TIMELINE

1457 A Scottish law banning golf is the first written record of the game

1744 The Honourable Company of Edinburgh Golfers is founded as the world's first golf club

1860 The first Open Championship is held (British Open); won by Willie Park (Scotland) at Prestwick

1873 The Royal Montreal is founded as the first golf club in North America

1892 The Open is played over 4 rounds of 18 holes for the first time

1895 The first U.S. Open is held; won by Horace Rawlins (England) at RI

1916 The first U.S. PGA Championship is held; won by James M. Barnes (Britain) at Siwanoy, NY

1927 The first Ryder Cup (U.S.A. v. Britain) is held; won by the United States at Worcester, MA

1934 The first U.S. Masters is held; won by Horton Smith (U.S.A.) at the Augusta National, Georgia

1946 The first U.S. Women's Open is held; won by Patricia (Patty) Berg (U.S.A.) at Spokane (changed to strokeplay in 1947)

1953 The first World Cup of Golf is held (known as the Canada Cup until 1966); won by Argentina in Montreal

1955 The first Ladies' PGA Championship is held; won by B. Hanson at Orchard Ridge, IN

1958 The U.S. PGA Championship becomes a stroke-play event for the first time

1976 The first Women's British Open is held; won by J. Lee Smith at Fulford

1979 The Ryder Cup becomes U.S.A. v. Europe for the first time

1990 The first Solheim Cup (Europe v. U.S.A. professional ladies' tournament) is held; won by the United States at Lake Nona, FL

2003 Mike Weir becomes the first Canadian to win a Major when he captures the green jacket at the U.S. Masters in Augusta

The origins of golf date back at least to Roman times, to a game called *paganica*, which is thought to have reached Britain by 400 a.d. (although the Chinese also lay claim to having invented the game c.2500 b.c.). Golf developed toward its modern form in Scotland, where the first written reference comes in a decree of 1457 banning the game: "futeball and golf be utterly cryit doune [cried down] and not usit [not used/played]." The name of the sport is thought to derive either from the Dutch *kolf* or *colf*, meaning "club," or from the Old Scots *gowff*, meaning "cuff" or "strike hard" (although the Scots verb may have come from the game rather than the other way round).

The first golf club was the Honourable Company of Edinburgh Golfers, founded in 1744. The Edinburgh Golfers instituted the first golf trophy the same year, known as the Silver Cup, and the competition was held on Leith Links in Edinburgh, Scotland. Golf is thought to have been played at St. Andrews since the 12th century, but the Society of St. Andrews Golfers was not founded until 1754, a decade after the Edinburgh club. In 1834 the St. Andrews club became known as the Royal & Ancient Golf Club (by decree of King William IV), and from 1897 was recognized as the arbiter of golfing rules worldwide except in the United States and Mexico.

The first set of rules for lawn tennis was drawn up by the Marylebone Cricket Club (MCC) at Lord's cricket ground in 1875. Then, in 1877, the All England Croquet Club, based in Wimbledon, altered the rules and instituted the first Lawn Tennis Championship.

TENNIS

Lawn tennis evolved from the 11th-century French game *jeu de paume* (game of the palm), which was later introduced to England where it developed into the indoor game of Real or Royal tennis—the name tennis is said to come from the French practice of shouting *tenez* (hold *or* attention) before serving the ball. Major Walter Clopton Wingfield (England) is often credited with inventing an outdoor version of the game in 1873, but in fact *Sporting Magazine* referred to "field tennis" as early as 1793, and Major Harry Gem (England) founded the Leamington Club in 1872 as the first club for outdoor tennis, which by then was known as Pelota or Lawn Racquets.

Wingfield was, however, the first to popularize lawn tennis. In 1874 he patented a game called *Sphairistiké* (from the Greek *sphaira*, a ball), began advertising it in the newspapers, and published a pamphlet entitled *The Game of Sphairistiké: or, Lawn Tennis*, having first played it at Nantclwyd, Wales, in December 1873. In 1875 Mary Ewing Outerbridge saw British army officers playing Wingfield's game in Bermuda and introduced it to the United States, where it was first played at the Staten Island Cricket and Baseball Club, of which her brother was secretary.

The first set of rules for lawn tennis was drawn up by a subcommittee of the MCC at Lord's in 1875. The game was also being played by members of the All England Croquet Club in Wimbledon, and in 1877 the club changed its

name to the All England Croquet and Lawn Tennis Club, refined the rules, and instituted the first Lawn Tennis Championship. (The club's name has been changed twice since to arrive at the current All England Lawn Tennis and Croquet Club.) Wimbledon has remained the spiritual home of the game ever since, where the championships are now famous for strawberries and cream as well as tennis—according to the All England Club, spectators at the championships consume 27,000 kg (60,000 lbs) of strawberries and 7,000 litres (1,850 gallons) of cream during the two weeks of the event.

Opposite top A ball boy at Wimbledon Tennis Championships 2001, day two (June 26)

Opposite below Detail from an advertisement for F.H. Ayres, Manufacturer of Sports and Games, 111 Aldersgate St., London (undated)

Above Björn Borg (Sweden) goes down on his knees in celebration of his victory over John McEnroe (U.S.A.) at the Wimbledon Tennis Championships, winning the men's singles title for the fifth successive year (July 5, 1980)

1900 The Davis Cup is inaugurated as the first international lawn tennis competition; first won by the United States. (U.S.A.–Britain only until 1903)

1905 The first Australasian Tennis Championship is held (renamed Australian Championships 1927, becomes Australian Open 1969)

1913 The International Lawn Tennis Federation is established

1923 The Wightman Cup is inaugurated as the first international lawn tennis competition for women (restricted to Britain–U.S.A.); first won by the United States

1938 Don Budge (U.S.A.) becomes the first person to win the Grand Slam (British, U.S., French and Australian Open titles)

1953 Maureen Connolly (U.S.A., a.k.a. Little Mo) becomes the first woman to win the Grand Slam

1963 The Federation Cup is inaugurated as the first international lawn tennis competition to include women from outside Britain or the United States; first won by the United States

1969 Rod Laver (Australia) becomes the first person to win the Grand Slam twice (1962 and 1969)

1980 Björn Borg (Sweden) becomes the first player to win five consecutive Wimbledon singles championships

1987 Martina Navratilova (U.S.A.) becomes the first woman to win six consecutive Wimbledon singles championships

1990 Navratilova becomes the first woman to win the Wimbledon singles championship a total of nine times

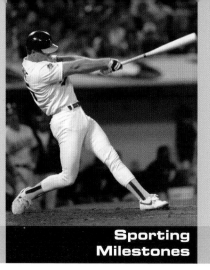

Sporting Milestones

BASEBALL

According to a 1907 commission into the origins of baseball, the game was invented by American Abner Doubleday in 1839. However, it has since been shown that the game developed from rounders, and that the father of organized baseball was Alexander Cartwright Jr.

"Whoever wants to know the heart and mind of America had better learn baseball." This comment from philosopher and educator Jacques Martin Barzun (France–U.S.A.) encapsulates the importance of baseball to the American way of life—indeed, baseball is so universal that it is known as "the national pastime." The man who did more than any other to shape the modern game was Alexander Cartwright Jr. (U.S.A.) but baseball did not begin with him—it developed from the English game of rounders, which had been played from the 17th century.

North American colonists brought rounders to New England, where it was known by several names including town ball, baseball and the Massachusetts game. It was played informally according to various local rules until Cartwright formalized the rules in 1845 and began to organize the game into a sport. He founded the Knickerbocker Base Ball Club of New York in 1845 as the first club purely for baseball, and the first game played under the Cartwright Rules took place at Hoboken, New Jersey, the following year, when the New York Nine beat the Knickerbocker Club 23–1 in four innings.

Other clubs were soon founded and the game began to spread. New rules were introduced (one of the most significant being overhand pitching, in 1884), but the basic shape of the game remained that envisaged by Cartwright. In 1869 the Cincinnati Red Stockings decided to pay all its players, thus becoming the first professional baseball team. Others followed suit, leading to the formation of the National League in 1876 as the first Major League. The

rival American League was formed in 1900 and began a second Major League competition in 1901. In 1903 the winners of the two leagues met to play a seven-game series to decide the overall champions—the Boston Red Sox (AL) defeated the Pittsburgh Pirates (NL) to win the first World Series.

Top Oakland's Mark McGwire hits a home run in the bottom of the ninth inning to win the third game of the World Series against the Los Angeles Dodgers (October 18, 1988)
Left The legendary Babe Ruth in action (1927)
Opposite California Angels pitcher Nolan Ryan

DID YOU KNOW?

- In 1962 the U.S.S.R. claimed to have invented the American national pastime. An article appeared in *Nedelya*, the weekly supplement to the Soviet newspaper *Izvestiya*, claiming that "Beizbol" was an old Russian game

- In July 1931 Joe Sprinz of the Cleveland Indians caught a baseball dropped 244 m (800 ft.) from an airship, breaking his jaw in the process

- At the turn of the millennium Cuba had won the baseball World Cup a record 21 times, more than any other nation

- English novelist Jane Austen refers to "base ball" in her 1798 novel *Northanger Abbey*

1904 The first international baseball event takes place—an exhibition game in the Olympic Games, St. Louis, MO

1926 Herman "Babe" Ruth (New York Yankees) becomes the first player to hit three home runs in a World Series. He achieves the feat again in 1928, after which it is not repeated until 1977 (by Reggie Jackson, also of the New York Yankees)

1927 Babe Ruth becomes the first player to hit 60 home runs in a season (before Babe Ruth no player had hit more than 24 in a season)

1938 The first baseball World Cup is held, in London, England, between the United States and Great Britain; Great Britain win the championship. The International Baseball Federation is founded

1953 The New York Yankees becomes the first team to win five consecutive World Series titles

1956 The first perfect game (no hits and no runs) in a World Series is pitched by Don Larsen (for the New York Yankees against the Brooklyn Dodgers)

1986 Roger "Rocket" Clemens (Boston Red Sox) becomes the first player to pitch 20 strikeouts in a single game (against Seattle Mariners)

1991 Nolan Ryan (Houston Astros) becomes the first player to pitch seven no-hit games in major league baseball (having been the first to pitch five in 1981 and the first to six in 1990)

1992 The Toronto Blue Jays (Canada) become the first non-U.S.A. team in the World Series, beating the Atlanta Braves four games to two

1998 Mark McGwire (St. Louis Cardinals) becomes the first player to hit 70 home runs in a season

2001 Barry Bonds (San Francisco Giants) becomes the first player to hit 73 home runs in a season

The longest-ever cricket Test match (in Durban, South Africa) lasted for 11 days—no wonder Lord Mancroft described cricket as "a game which the English, not being a spiritual people, have invented in order to give themselves some conception of eternity."

Sporting Milestones

CRICKET

c.1550 First written reference to cricket (at Guildford, England)

1744 The first agreed rules of cricket are formulated, in England

1788 The Marylebone Cricket Club (MCC) issues revised rules and takes over the administration of the game

1803 Cricket is played in Australia for the first time

1820 W. Ward (England) scores the first recorded double century in first-class cricket (278 for the MCC against Norfolk)

1826 The Military Club and the Australian Club are founded in Sydney as Australia's first cricket clubs

1858 Frederick Lillywhite and John Wisden (both England) patent a bowling machine for batsmen to practise against

1864 *Wisden's Cricketers' Almanack* is first published. Overarm bowling is introduced for the first time

1874 W.G. Grace (England) becomes the first cricketer to score 1,000 runs and take 100 wickets in a season

1876 W.G. Grace scores the first two triple centuries by any player (344 and 318 not out within 10 days of each other)

1877 The first Test Match is played, between England and a combined NSW–Victoria team, in Melbourne, Australia

The origins of cricket are obscure, but the first written reference is to a game at Guildford, England, c.1550. There are records of an 11-a-side cricket match as early as 1697 and a county match as early as 1709, although the first agreed rules of cricket were not published until 1744, by the Hambledon Club in Hampshire; these rules included 22-yard pitches, 4-ball overs, stumping and no-balls. In 1788 the Marylebone Cricket Club (MCC) took over the administration of the rules from its new ground, Lord's, which had been opened by Yorkshireman Thomas Lord the previous year. Without doubt the most important rule change was in 1864 with the introduction of overarm bowling for the first time.

The first Test match took place between England and Australia at Melbourne in 1877. The England–Australia Test Series has since become known as the Ashes because, early in 1882, Australia won a one-game Test

Opposite "W.G. Grace leaves the pavilion" The painting was used for a mustard advertisement, with the slogan "Colman's Mustard—Like Grace—Heads the Field" (undated)
Below A view from the Members' pavilion at Worcester County Cricket Club, England
Bottom The Ashes

1880 W.G. Grace scores the first century by any player in a Test match, with 152 against Australia at the Oval, England

1882–83 The England–Australia Test Series becomes known as the Ashes for the first time

1887 The six-ball over is introduced in Australia (the rule is adopted in England in 1900)

1888 The first England–South Africa Test Match is held

1895 W.G. Grace becomes the first batsman to score 100 first-class centuries

1900 Bernard James Tindal Bosanquet (England) bowls the first googly (for Middlesex against Leicestershire at Lord's, England). In Australia the technique is known as a Bosie, after its inventor

1928 The West Indies' matches are accorded Test status for the first time (against England)

1932 India's matches are accorded Test status for the first time (against England)

1934 The first women's Test matches are held (England v. Australia and England v. New Zealand)

1952 Pakistan's matches are accorded Test status for the first time (against India)

1968 Gary Sobers (Barbados, properly Garfield St. Auburn Sobers) becomes the first batsman to hit six sixes off a six-ball over (for Nottinghamshire against Glamorgan at Swansea)

1973 The first women's cricket World Cup is held; England beat Australia in the final

1975 The first men's cricket World Cup is held; West Indies beat Australia at Lord's in the final

at the Oval, England, as a result of which a mock obituary appeared in the *Sporting Times*, saying that "the body [of English cricket] will be cremated and the ashes taken to Australia." England won the 1882–83 tour of Australia and, continuing the joke, an Australian lady presented England captain Ivo Bligh with an urn containing the ashes of a bail used in the Third Test. Bligh bequeathed the Ashes to the MCC in 1927 and they are now kept in the Memorial Gallery at Lord's, where they remain regardless of who wins the series.

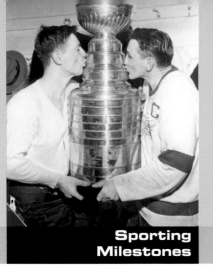

HOCKEY

Hockey is thought to date from ancient Egypt c.2000 b.c., and the first evidence of the game being played on ice is a 17th-century Dutch illustration. Ice hockey reached North America in the 1850s; some 20 years later the first formal rules were drawn up, by university students in Montreal.

Above Goalie Terry Sawchuk and Captain Sid Abel of the Detroit Red Wings kiss the Stanley Cup, won in 4 straight games against the Montreal Canadiens in Detroit (April 17, 1952)

Two Canadian cities—Kingston, Ontario and Halifax, Nova Scotia—claim to have been the scene of the first game of hockey in North America c.1855, but the rules were not formalized until the 1870s, by students at McGill University, in Montreal.

Ice hockey's most prestigious trophy, the Stanley Cup, was donated in 1892 by Lord Stanley, then Governor-General of Canada, and was first awarded in 1893, to the champions of the Amateur Hockey Association of Canada, the Montreal Amateur Athletic Association. The cup is now contested by the two teams winning the eastern and western conferences of the National Hockey League (NHL), which was founded in Canada in 1917.

The International Ice Hockey Federation (IIHF) was founded in 1908 and in 1920 ice hockey was introduced as an Olympic sport in the

17th century	**1870s**	**1892**	**1893**	**1904**	**1908**
First evidence of hockey being played on the ice (Netherlands)	The first formal rules of ice hockey are drawn up, at McGill University, in Montreal	The Stanley Cup is donated to the sport	Montreal AAA becomes the first Stanley Cup champions	The International Pro Hockey League is founded in the United States as the first professional ice hockey league	The International Ice Hockey Federation is founded

| TIMELINE

Ice hockey at Font-Romeu in the Eastern Pyrénèes. Railway travel poster by Tony-George Roux, 1923

summer games (won by Canada), and from 1924 onwards it became part of the winter games. The Ice Hockey World Championships were first held in 1920 (for amateurs) in conjunction with the Olympic Games, and an open World Championship has been held since 1976. The first women's World Championship was contested in 1990, and women's ice hockey first became an Olympic sport at the 1998 Winter Olympics, when the United States beat Canada to become the first women's Olympic champions.

DID YOU KNOW?

● The highest score to date in a World Championship game is Australia 58, New Zealand 0 in a match played in Perth, Australia, on March 15, 1987

● Sports historians believe that hockey took its name from the French word *hoquet*, meaning "shepherd's crook" or "bent stick"

1920 Ice hockey is first introduced as an Olympic sport at the Antwerp summer games; won by Canada. The first Ice Hockey World Championships (for amateurs) are held in conjunction with the Olympic Games	**1924** Boston Bruins becomes the first U.S. team to join the NHL. Ice hockey is transferred from the summer to the winter Olympics	**1960** The Montreal Canadiens become the first team to win the Stanley Cup five consecutive times	**1982** Wayne Gretzky (Edmonton Oilers) sets a new record for goals scored in a season, with 92	**1998** Women's ice hockey is introduced to the Winter Olympics for the first time; won by the United States

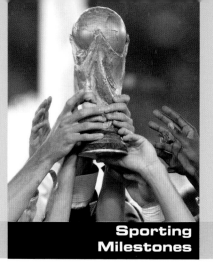

SOCCER

Football originated in ancient China but the first set of rules for a recognizably modern game of soccer was drawn up at Cambridge University, England, in 1848. The Football Association was formed in 1863 and soccer was born, its name a contraction of the more formal "association football."

TIMELINE

c.350 b.c. *Tsu chu* (kick ball) is played in ancient China

12th century A primitive form of football is played in Britain for the first time

1848 The first set of common rules are drawn up, at Cambridge University, for what later becomes known as association football (soccer)

1863 The Football Association is formed in London, England; the first standardized rules of association football are drawn up

1872 The first FA Cup is held; the Wanderers beat Royal Engineers 1–0. The first international soccer match is played; England and Scotland draw 0–0

1888 The Football League (England) is formed as the world's first professional league competition

1889 Preston North End become the first league champions and the first club to achieve an FA Cup and League Championship double

1904 The Fédération Internationale des Football Associations (FIFA) is founded

1930 The first FIFA World Cup final is held, in Montevideo, Uruguay; Uruguay beat Argentina 4–2

1954 The Union des Associations Européennes de Football (UEFA) is founded. The Asian Football Confederation is founded

1956 The first European Champions' Cup (European Cup) is held; the first five competitions are won by Real Madrid (Spain). The African Football Confederation is founded

Association football, like all other codes of football, has its roots in the ancient Chinese game of *tsu chu* (kick ball). Football was being played in Britain by the 12th century, and often involved entire villages competing against each other to propel a ball to one or other village from a point somewhere between the two. During the 19th century the game evolved in public schools and universities into a more formal sport between matched teams, and the first record of an 11-a-side match is at Eton College in 1841. The rules varied from place to place until students at Cambridge University made the first attempt to standardize them in 1848. The Cambridge Rules were adopted by some clubs, but they were not fully standardized until the formation of the Football Association at the Freemasons' Tavern in London, in 1863.

In 1872 the Football Association (FA) inaugurated the first FA Cup competition. The final was played at the Oval cricket ground in Kennington, London, where the Wanderers beat the Royal Engineers 1–0 in front of a crowd of 2,000. In 1888 the Football League was formed as the world's first professional league competition, won in its first two years by Preston North End, who also became the first club to achieve a league and cup double.

International soccer began in 1872 with a 0–0 draw between England and Scotland at Partick. The Fédération Internationale de Football Associations (FIFA) was formed in Paris, France, in 1904, and in 1930 instituted the first World Cup, largely due to the efforts of French football administrator Jules Rimet, who also provided the famous trophy and whose name is still the official title of the world cup title. The final was played in Uruguay, where the host nation beat Argentina 4–2 to become the first World Champions.

Opposite Football World Cup final Brazil v. Germany, in Yokohama, Japan; the Brazilian team hold the World Cup aloft (2002) **Below** Cameroon players celebrate Milla's goal; Cameroon v. Colombia, World Cup (1990)

DID YOU KNOW?

● Edson Arantes do Nascimento (Brazil) got his more famous nickname from his skill at a game of street football that he played as a child. The game—*pelada*: the nickname—Pelé

1957 The first Africa Cup of Nations is held; won by Egypt

1958 The first European Nations' Cup (later European Football Championship) begins, taking two years to complete; won by U.S.S.R. in 1960

1960–61 The first European Cup Winners' Cup is held; won by Fiorentina (Italy)

1961 The Confederación Norte-Centroamericana y del Caribe de Fútbol (CONCACAF) is founded

1966 The Oceania Football Confederation is founded

1968 Hungary becomes the first country to win the Olympic amateur football title three times

1984 The first women's European Championship is held; Sweden beat England on penalties

1991 The first FIFA-sponsored women's World Soccer Championship is held; won by the United States

1994 Brazil becomes the first country to win the World Cup four times

RUGBY

Contrary to popular belief, rugby did not develop from soccer. Both sports derive from an earlier game known as football, and developed separately after disagreements over the rules. The Rugby Football Union was formed in 1871 and in 1895 another disagreement led to the development of Rugby League.

A plaque at Rugby School commemorates an event that supposedly occurred in 1823, when schoolboy William Webb Ellis, "with a fine disregard for the rules of football as played in his time, first took the ball in his arms and ran with it, thus originating the distinctive feature of Rugby game." There is considerable doubt about this tradition, but it is known that football was an amorphous game played under various local rules (including handling the ball), and that during the 1820s–30s the idea of *running* with the ball, rather than merely handling it, was incorporated in the rules of football at Rugby School. Old Rugbeians popularized their game in their universities and home towns, and eventually the need was felt to form a governing body. In 1871 representatives of several football clubs wanting to formalize the handling code met at the Pall Mall Restaurant in London, England, and established the Rugby Football Union.

Working-class players in the north of England could not afford time off to play rugby and so northern clubs began making "broken time" payments to reimburse players for their loss of earnings. The RFU outlawed such payments as a breach of amateurism and, in the face of a continued lack of sympathy toward their predicament, a group of clubs met on August 29,

DID YOU KNOW?

- The Twickenham stadium is known as the "cabbage patch" because when it was bought by the RFU it was being used as a market garden

- At one time no points were scored for a try. Touching the ball down was called a "run in" and simply allowed the team to "try" to convert the touchdown into a goal. From 1875 the number of tries was counted if the goals were equal, and eventually tries counted toward the points total; from 1884 unconverted tries were worth one point and goals three

- The only rugby league teams to maintain a continuous presence in the top flight since the reintroduction of two divisions in 1973–74 are Castleford, Leeds, St. Helens and Warrington

1895 at the George Hotel in Huddersfield, England, where they formed the breakaway Northern Union. Because the NU relied on gate receipts, the rules were altered to produce a faster game that would attract more spectators; in 1922 the resulting new sport gained its own identity when the NU adopted the title Rugby Football League.

For 100 years bigotry and hypocrisy surrounded the split between League and Union until, in 1995, the RFU bowed to the inevitable and openly accepted professionalism. In 1996 the previously unthinkable happened—the top club from each code met to play two exhibition matches: Wigan beat Bath 82–6 at Rugby League, and Bath beat Wigan 44–19 at Rugby Union. Wigan were also invited to compete in Rugby Union's Middlesex Sevens at Twickenham, where they beat all comers to win the tournament.

Opposite top In the Wigan v. Bath Crosscode Challenge Jason Robinson shows why he is nicknamed Billy Whizz

Opposite below Boys at Rugby School play rugby football in the school grounds

Below Scrum down

RUGBY UNION TIMELINE

1823 According to tradition, William Webb Ellis invents Rugby Football

1846 Rugby School publishes the first *Laws of Football as Played at Rugby School*, drawn up by senior pupils

1871 The Rugby Football Union is formed; the first international is held (Scotland beat England in Edinburgh)

1873 The Scottish Football Union is formed (becomes Scottish RFU in 1924)

1874 The Irish Football Union is formed (becomes Irish RFU in 1879). Number of players reduced from 20 to 15 per side. The Southern RFU is formed (becomes NSW RFU in 1892; incorporated into Australian RFU 1949

1881 The Welsh RFU is formed as the successor to earlier organizations

1883 The first sevens tournament is held, organized by Melrose RFC

1889 The South African Rugby Football Board is formed

1892 The New Zealand RFU is formed

1909 The first match is held at Twickenham (Harlequins beat Richmond)

1920 The Fédération Française de Rugby is officially founded after an application the previous year

1926 The first Middlesex Sevens is held

1943 The first intercode match is held; Northern Command Rugby League XV beats Northern Command Rugby Union XV (both Army) 18–11 at Headingley, Leeds, England, under R.U. rules

1971–72 The first national knock-out cup competition is held; won by Gloucester (inaugurated as John Player Cup, later sponsored by Pilkington, Tetley's Bitter and Powergen)

1976 First Hong Kong Sevens is held

1987 The first World Cup (the Webb Ellis Trophy) is held; New Zealand beat France in the final

1991 The first women's World Cup is held; U.S.A. beat England in the final

1997 The first Women's Hong Kong Sevens is held; won by New Zealand

American Football was first played in 1874 after a variant of Rugby Football was introduced to Harvard University from England via Canada by McGill University in Montreal. The first professional league began in 1920 and the first Super Bowl was played in 1967 and won by the Green Bay Packers.

AMERICAN FOOTBALL

Above Green Bay Packers' Bart Starr (15), Jim Taylor (31) and Paul Hornung (5) take time out at the 1967 Super Bowl
Below Ronald Reagan in *Knute Rockne, All American* (1940)
Opposite Washington Redskins' linebacker LaVar Arrington prepares to eat Houston Texans' rookie David Carr for breakfast

America's first intercollegiate football game was played on November 6, 1869, when Rutgers defeated the College of New Jersey (now Princeton University) 6–4 in a round-ball game resembling soccer. In 1873 representatives of Rutgers, Columbia, Princeton and Yale universities formulated a set of rules for the round-ball game and it seemed that American Football would develop along the lines of Association Football. Then, in 1874, a football team from McGill University, in Montreal, visited Harvard University; the Canadians wanted to play Rugby Football but Harvard wanted to play the American game. In the end they played two matches, the first under Harvard rules and the second under McGill rules. The Americans liked McGill's rugby game so much that Harvard introduced the sport to other Eastern colleges, and so rugby became the starting point for modern American Football.

The first rules were codified at Harvard in 1874, but the game soon began to change. One of its greatest architects, often referred to as the father of American Football, was Yale University's Walter Camp (U.S.A.), who gave the sport the basic form it has today. Among other things, Camp reduced the team size from 15 to 11, introduced the concepts of downs and yards to gain, and helped develop the scoring system.

The first professional league was organized in 1920 by the newly formed American Professional Football Association, which changed its name to the National Football League (NFL) in 1922. The rival American Football League was established in 1960, but just six years later it was incorporated into the NFL. The new NFL was then divided into the National Football Conference and the American Football Conference, with the winners of the two conferences meeting at the end of each season to compete for the ultimate prize: in 1967 the Green Bay Packers defeated the Kansas City Chiefs 35–10 to win the first Super Bowl.

| **1874** The first rules of American Football are codified at Harvard University | **1880s** Walter Camp (U.S.A.) of Yale University develops new rules and shapes the game of American Football | **1892** Walter "Pudge" Heffelfinger (U.S.A.) is paid $500 to play for the Allegheny Athletic Association against Pittsburgh Athletic Club, thus becoming the first recorded professional American Football player | **1906** The forward pass is introduced to the rules. The first forward pass is believed to have been made by Wesleyan University in a game against Yale |

|TIMELINE|

1913 Gus Dorais (U.S.A.) and Knute Rockne (Norway– U.S.A.) popularize the forward pass, using it to gain a victory for Notre Dame University against the U.S. Army

1920 The American Professional Football Association is founded as the first professional league, changing its name to National Football League (NFL) in 1922

1936 The league holds its first draft of college players

1967 The first Super Bowl is played. The Green Bay Packers defeat the Kansas City Chiefs 35–10

1991 The World League of American Football (WLAF) is formed as an international professional league with three European, one Canadian and six U.S. teams

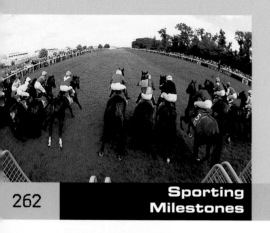

The first known horse races were held by the Hittites of Anatolia (Turkey) c.1500 b.c., and the ancient Greeks introduced horse racing to the Olympics in 648 b.c. The Romans later introduced the sport to Britain, where the first recorded race took place in a.d. 210.

HORSE RACING

Above The start of the 1992 Epsom Derby
Below "Horse Racing at Epsom." Théodore Géricault (1821)

Modern horse racing consists of two types of race: flat-racing and jumping "over the sticks," which is also known as steeplechasing because it developed out of cross-country races from one village to another, where the church steeple usually marked the end of the race. The first steeplechase to be held on a course with artificial fences took place in England at the Newmarket Craven meeting in 1794.

England's most prestigious horse races are the Grand National (first run in 1839), and the English Classics: the St. Leger Stakes (first run in 1776),

DID YOU KNOW?

● The reason American horse races are run counter-clockwise is due to the patriotism of William Whitley of Kentucky. In 1780 he built the first circular racecourse in the United States. To show support for the American Revolution, he insisted that horses run in the direction opposite that run by horses in England

● North America's oldest continuously held horse race is the Queen's Plate, inaugurated on June 27, 1860 at the Carleton Track in Toronto

the Oaks Stakes (1779), the Derby (1780), the 2,000 Guineas (1809) and the 1,000 Guineas (1814). The most successful jockey in the English classics is Lester Pigott, who in 1992 won the 2,000 Guineas at Newmarket to become the first jockey to win 30 English Classics.

The most prestigious races in the United States are known collectively as the U.S. Triple Crown: the Belmont Stakes (first run in 1867), the Preakness Stakes (1873) and the Kentucky Derby (1875). The first horse to win the U.S. Triple Crown was *Sir Barton* in 1919.

TIMELINE

c.1500 b.c. The Hittites (Anatolia) hold the first known horse races

648 b.c. Horse racing first becomes part of the ancient Olympic Games

1711 Queen Anne (England) attends the first Royal Ascot race meeting, at Ascot Heath, near Windsor

1750 Jockey Club founded, in England

1776 First St Leger Stakes is held, the first of the English Classics

1779 First Oaks Stakes (England)

1780 First Epsom Derby (Epsom Downs, Surrey, England)

1809 First 2,000 Guineas (England)

1814 First 1,000 Guineas (England)

1839 First Grand National Steeplechase (Aintree, Liverpool, England), under the title Grand Liverpool Steeplechase

1853 *West Australian* becomes the first horse to win the British Triple Crown

1860 First Queen's Plate (Canada)

1861 First Melbourne Cup (Australia)

1863 First Grand Prix de Paris (France)

1866 First Irish Sweeps Derby (Ireland)

1867 First Belmont Stakes (U.S.A.)

1873 First Preakness Stakes (U.S.A.)

1875 First Kentucky Derby (U.S.A.)

1894 American Jockey Club founded

1919 *Sir Barton* becomes the first horse to win the U.S. Triple Crown

1924 First Cheltenham Gold Cup (England)

1964 *Northern Dancer* becomes the first Canadian horse to win the Kentucky Derby

1971 Stan Mellor (Britain) becomes first National Hunt jockey to reach 1,000 wins

1992 Lester Piggot (England) becomes first jockey to win 30 English Classics

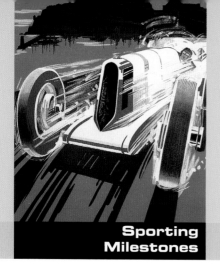

AUTO RACING

Auto racing has given rise to legendary events such as the Isle of Man TT (1907), the Indianapolis 500 (1911) and the Le Mans 24-hour race (1923). Top of the tree is the Formula One Grand Prix, which developed from the first international auto racing event, the Gordon Bennett Trophy (1900).

TIMELINE

1887 The first automobile race is organized by the editor of *Vélocipède* magazine, but attracts only one competitor, Georges Bouton (France) on a steam quadricycle

1894 The Paris–Rouen–Paris Concours des Voitures sans Chevaux is initiated as a reliability test, but becomes the first automobile race

1895 A Paris–Bordeaux–Paris race takes place as the first official automobile race

1900 James Gordon Bennett (U.S.A.) inaugurates the first international auto racing event

1906 The first Grand Prix takes place, at Le Mans, France

1907 Brooklands opens in Surrey, England, as the world's first purpose-built motor-racing circuit. The first Isle of Man TT (Tourist Trophy) motorbike race takes place; won by Charlie Collier

1911 Carl Fisher (U.S.A.) organizes the first Indianapolis 500

1923 The first Le Mans 24-hour race takes place, won by A. Lagache and R. Leonard (both France) in a Chenard-Walker. Johnnie S. Hoskins (New Zealand) initiates the first organized motorcycle speedway race (at West Maitland, Australia)

1949 The National Association of Stock Car Auto Racing Inc. (NASCAR) in the United States inaugurates the Grand National series, later known as the Winston Cup

On July 22, 1894 the Concours des Voitures sans Chevaux (Exhibition of horseless carriages) was organized by French newspaper *Le Petit Journal* to demonstrate the reliability of a relatively new means of transport—the automobile. The Concours consisted of a journey from Paris to Rouen and back but, of course, the participants wanted to demonstrate not only the reliability but also the speed of their cars, turning the reliability test into the first automobile race, although the first *official* race did not take place until the following year, from Paris to Bordeaux and back.

James Gordon Bennett (U.S.A.), proprietor of the *New York Herald*, was enthralled by this and other early car races, and in 1899 he initiated the first international motor racing event, the Coupe Internationale, which first took place in 1900 and was soon renamed the Gordon Bennett Trophy. Fernand Charron (France) was the first winner. The Gordon Bennett Trophy pitched nation against nation but this system excluded some manufacturers

Above Poster for the 1930 Monaco Grand Prix
Right Giuseppe Farina wins the International Trophy Race at Silverstone, England, on his way to winning the first Formula One Drivers' Championship (August 26, 1950)
Opposite top British motorcycling legend Barry Sheene, twice winner of the 500 cc World Championship

1950 Nino Farina (Italy) wins the first Formula One Drivers' Championship

1958 Maria Teresa de Filippis (Italy) becomes the first ever woman F1 driver, with a 10th place at the Belgium Grand Prix

1959 The first Daytona 500 takes place

1964 John Surtees (England) wins the Formula One Drivers' Championship to become the first person to win world championships on two and four wheels, having already won the 350 cc and 500 cc world motorcycle championships several times between 1956 and 1960

1966 Jack Brabham (Australia) becomes the first driver to win the Formula One Drivers' Championship (his third) in a car he had designed and built himself, also winning the Constructors' Championship in the process

1975 Lella Lombardi (Italy) is the first woman to finish in a points' scoring position in a Grand Prix, coming sixth in the Spanish Grand Prix

1978 The first Paris–Dakar Rally is held

1984 The British Truck Racing Association organizes Europe's first international truck race, at Castle Donington, England

1997 Jacques Villeneuve (Canada) becomes the first North American to win the Formula One Drivers' Championship. By winning the championship, he becomes the first driver to win the three major auto racing crowns—Formula One, CART Indy and the Indianapolis 500

2003 The first racing Series devoted entirely to female drivers, the Mazda RX-8 Formula Woman Championship, is launched

from countries with a large number of car-makers—in 1906 it was replaced by the first Grand Prix, in which all manufacturers could enter three cars regardless of nationality. The first Grand Prix took place at the Circuit de la Sarthe in Le Mans, France, and was won by Ferenc Szisz (Hungary) in a Renault. The first Indianapolis 500 ("Indy") was organized in the United States in 1911 by Carl Fisher (U.S.A.) over 500 miles on a brick circuit known as the Brickyard. The first winner was Ray Harroun (U.S.A.). Apart from Harroun, the first driver to win the Indianapolis 500 on his debut was Graham Hill (England) in 1966, and the first man to win the Indycar championship in his debut season was Nigel Mansell (England) in 1993.

THE BEST OF THE REST...

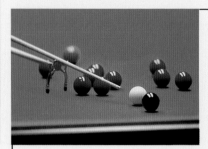

Snooker

Snooker was devised by Lt-Gen. Sir Neville Chamberlain while serving in the British army in India. The first recorded game took place between British army officers at Jubbulpore in 1875, when the game was named after the word for new cadets at the Royal Military Academy at Woolwich, England. The first official rules were posted in the billiard room of the Ootacumund Club in 1882 and the game was introduced to England by professional billiard-player John Roberts in 1885. The first World Professional Snooker Championship was held in 1927 (won by Joe Davis, England), the first World Amateur Championship in 1963 (won by Gary Owen, England), and the first World Cup in 1979 (Wales beat England 14–3 in the final). The first women's World Professional Snooker Championship was held in 1976 (won by Vera Selby, England)

Australian Football

Australian Rules Football, as it is known to the rest of the world, was devised by Australians Henry Harrison and Tom Wills (Wills had been captain of football at Rugby School in England). The sport was first played in 1858, when Melbourne Church of England Grammar School drew with Scotch College on the site of the present Melbourne Cricket Ground. The first club was Melbourne Football Club, founded in 1858. The rules were not officially formulated until 1866, by Wills, Harrison and two others at a meeting in the Freemasons' Tavern in Melbourne

Lawn Bowling

The first bowling green on record was laid out in Southampton, England, during the reign of Edward I (1272–1307). The game subsequently declined, but was revived in Scotland, where the modern rules were set out by Glasgow solicitor William W. Mitchell in 1848–49. The Scottish Bowling Association was formed in 1892, the English in 1903 (initiated by cricketer W.G. Grace), the Welsh in 1904 and the International Board in 1905. The first ladies' bowling organization was the Victorian Ladies' Bowling Association, founded in 1907 in Victoria, Australia. The first World Championships were held at the Kyeemagh Bowling Club, Sydney, in 1966

Tenpin Bowling

The first known game of bowling is a stone ball and nine pins that were found in a grave dating from c.5200 b.c. in Egypt. Ninepin bowling was introduced to North America in the 17th century by Dutch settlers, and became tenpin bowling in the early 19th century when the American states of New York and Connecticut banned ninepin bowling because of the associated gambling—the obvious way of circumventing this law was to add an extra pin. The first world championships took place in 1954

Boxing

The ancient Greeks and Romans held boxing competitions, but the sport died out after the fall of the Roman Empire and was not revived until the 17th century. The first rules of boxing, and the idea of rounds, were introduced by Jack Broughton (England) in 1743; these had developed into the London Prize Ring Rules by 1838 and were superseded in 1867 by the Queensberry Rules, which were drawn up by John Graham Chambers (England, founder of the Amateur Athletic association in 1866) for Sir John Sholto Douglas, 8th Marquis of Queensberry (Scotland). The first world heavyweight title fight under the Queensberry Rules took place on September 7, 1892, when "Gentleman Jim" Corbett (U.S.A., properly James John Corbett) defeated John Lawrence Sullivan in 21 rounds in New Orleans, LA

Four-minute mile

The first person to break the four-minute barrier for running the mile was Dr. Roger Gilbert Bannister (England), who recorded a time of 3 mins 59.4 secs at Iffley Road, Oxford, England, on May 6, 1954. Afterwards Bannister wrote that, "Records should be the servants, not the master of the athlete," but he must have realized that this particular record, sometimes referred to as "the Everest target," would always be remembered. While his time may have been beaten, his first can never be taken away

Roger Bannister breaks the tape for the first sub-four minute mile (1954)

Yachting

Yachts were first used for recreation in the Netherlands in the early 17th century. The idea was brought to England by Charles II, who initiated the world's first recorded yacht race in 1661 when he bet his brother James, Duke of York, that he could win a race from Greenwich to Gravesend and back along the Thames. In 1851 the New York Yacht Club's *America* visited Cowes, Isle of Wight, and won the Hundred Guinea Cup for a race around the island. The trophy has been known ever since as the *America*'s Cup, and survived 24 challenges (best of seven races) to wrest it from the New York club. Then, in 1983, Alan Bond's *Australia II* won the trophy for the first time since *America* in 1851. The first organized ocean race took place in 1866—a transatlantic race from Sandy Hook, USA, to Cowes, won by the U.S. yacht *Henrietta*

America's Cup, Defender Series (January 1992)

Rowing

The world's oldest sculling race, and Britain's oldest annually contested sporting event, is the Doggett's Coat and Badge Race from London Bridge to Chelsea on the Thames River, first contested in 1716. The first Oxford v. Cambridge University Boat Race took place at Henley in 1829, when Oxford won. It became an annual event in 1856. The first Henley Regatta took place in 1839. In 1851 the regatta was attended by Prince Albert (England, consort of Queen Victoria), which is when it gained its royal title

Disabled sport

The 2002 Commonwealth Games in England was the first multisport event at which medals won by disabled athletes were included in the medals table

Volleyball

Volleyball was invented in 1895 as Mintonette by William G. Morgan at the YMCA in Holyoke, Massachusetts. The Fédération Internationale de Volleyball (FIVB) was formed in Paris, in 1947. The World Championships were first contested in 1949 in Prague, Czechoslovakia. Beach volleyball was first played in California in the 1920s as a six-a-side game. The current two-a-side format evolved during the 1930s and the first official two-a-side competition took place at State Beach, California, in 1947

Basketball

Basketball was invented by James A. Naismith (Canada) at the YMCA College in Springfield, MA, in 1891, and the first game was played in January 1892, using peach baskets fixed to the gym wall; nets replaced baskets in 1893. Men's basketball became an Olympic sport in 1936 and women's in 1976. World Championships were first played in 1950 (men's), 1953 (women's), 1973 (men's wheelchair) and 1990 (women's wheelchair)

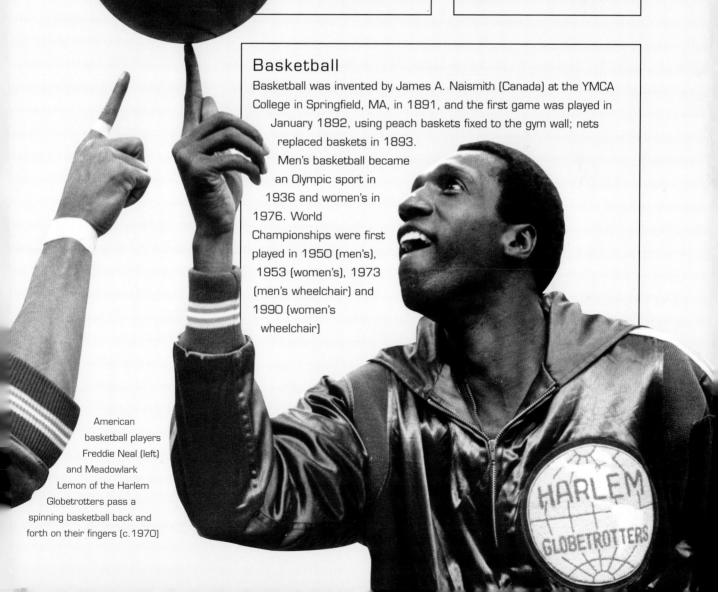

American basketball players Freddie Neal (left) and Meadowlark Lemon of the Harlem Globetrotters pass a spinning basketball back and forth on their fingers (c.1970)

Timeline Overview: b.c. to 1900

Human Endeavour	**1492–3** Christopher Columbus (Italy) becomes the first modern European to discover the New World	**1522** Juan Sebastian del Cano (Spain) captains the first ship to circumnavigate the globe			**1785** First aerial crossing the English Channel is made by Blanchard (France) & Jeffries (U.S.A.) in a hydrogen balloon
Food & Drink	**1494** First written record of Scotch whisky, as distilled by Friar John Cor of Dunfermline	**c.1640s** Ice creams are first recorded (England, French chef)		**1688** Dom Pierre Pérignon (France) makes the first champagne	**1819** First chocolate bar (Switzerland)
Trade & Technology	**1421** Filippo Brunelleschi (Italy) is granted the first known patent for invention	**1590** First microscope is built (Netherlands)	**1659** First known check issued (England)	**1661** First banknotes issued (Sweden)	**1829** First public elevator (England)
Lifestyle & Leisure	**16th century** First cigarettes (Spain)	**1589** First non-gravity-fed flushing toilet (England)		**1747** François Fresnau (France) makes first raincoat	**1827** First sale of friction matches (England)
Transportation	**1430** First recorded railway (Germany)			**1662** First bus service goes into operation (France)	**1804** First steam railway locomotive (invented England, demonstrated Wales)
Arts & Entertainment	**534 b.c.** Thespis (Greece) wins the first drama competition	**1520** First post-Roman public theatre in Europe opens (Spain)	**1597** First opera performed (Italy)	**1672** First public concert before a paying audience (England)	
Medical Achievement	**1280s** First eyeglasses (Italy)		**1592** Galileo (Italy) invents the first thermometer	**1699** First professional dental qualification (France)	**1818** First transfusion of human blood (England)
Government, Law & Order	**c.750 b.c.** The Romans produce the first locks	**1518** First recorded fire engine built (Germany)		**1667** First police force independent of the judiciary (Paris, France)	**1794** First air force is formed (France)
Communication		**1565** Gesner (Switzerland) provides first description of a pencil	**1653** First system of pre-paid postage (France)		**1826-7** Joseph Nicéphore Niepce (France) takes the first photograph
Sporting Milestones	**776 b.c.** First recorded Olympic contest (Greece)			**1744** First printed rules of cricket (England). World's first golf club founded (Scotland)	

1859 Charles Blondin (France) makes the first crossing of the Niagara River on a tightrope

1875 Matthew Webb (England) becomes the first person to swim the English Channel

1848 First commercial manufacture of chewing gum (U.S.A.)

1853 First potato chips (U.S.A.)

1875 First canned baked beans (U.S.A.)

1886 Coca-Cola is sold for the first time (U.S.A.)

1896 First patent for a tea bag (England)

1848 First department store opens (U.S.A.)

1879 Joseph Swan (England) demonstrates the first practicable light bulb

1885 Completion of the first skyscraper (Chicago, U.S.A.)

1899 First escalator (U.S.A.)

1830 First lawnmower patented (England)

1850 First jeans (U.S.A.)

1862 Thomas Cook (England) organizes the first package holiday

1886 First dinner jacket, worn at Tuxedo Park, U.S.A.

1897 First motor-hauled caravan (France)

1839 First national railway timetable published (England)

1861 First rotary pedal bicycle built (France)

1862 First motorcar with an internal combustion engine built (France)

1885 First motorcycle built (Germany)

1895 First pneumatic motorcar tires (France)

1857 First machine to record sound invented (France)

1875 A. P. Watt (Scotland) establishes first literary agency

1887 Emile Berliner (Germany–U.S.A.) patents the first gramophone

1895 The brothers Lumière (France) make the first commercial cinema screening

1842 First operation performed using ether as a general anaesthetic (U.S.A.)

1865 Joseph Lister (England) introduces antiseptics to surgery

1881 First birth control clinic opens (Netherlands)

1895 Wilhelm Konrad von Roentgen (Germany) discovers X-rays

1835 Samuel Colt (U.S.A.) patents the first commercially successful revolver

1869 First incinerator built for cremation (Italy)

1888 The Sultan of Turkey is first monarch to drive a car

1893 New Zealand becomes the first country to allow women the right to vote

1840 The General Post Office (Britain) issues the world's first official adhesive postage stamp, the Penny Black

1860 Philipp Reis (Germany) makes the first public demonstration of the telephone

1883 Lewis E. Waterman (U.S.A.) files a patent for the first successful fountain pen

1896 Guglielmo Marconi (Italy) is granted the first patent for radio

1845 First rules of organized baseball (U.S.A.)

1848 First published rules of what later becomes association football (England)

1863 Formation of the Football Association (England)

1874 First game of American Football

1891 Invention of basketball (U.S.A.)

1896 First modern Olympic Games (Greece)

1901 First Nobel prizes are awarded (Sweden)

1904 Louis Rigolly (France) becomes the first person to travel faster than 160km/h (100mph)

1911 Roald Amundsen (Norway) leads the first team to reach the South Pole

1933 Wiley Post (U.S.A.) makes the first solo round-the-world flight

1947 Chuck Yeager (U.S.A.) becomes the first person to break the sound barrier

1904 John J. McLaughlin (Canada) patents Ginger Ale

1913 First domestic refrigerator (U.S.A.)

1928 First wrapped, pre-sliced bread (U.S.A.)

1938 Nescafé is launched as the first instant coffee (Switzerland)

1946 First microwave oven (U.S.A.)

1948 Richard & Maurice McDonald (U.S.A.) open the world's first fast food restaurant

1901 Hubert Cecil Booth (England) patents the first vacuum cleaner

1907 First electric clothes-washing machine (U.S.A.)

1924 First domestic spin-dryer manufactured (U.S.A.)

1937 First supermarket trolley (U.S.A.)

1948 First computer (England)

1901 King Camp Gillette (U.S.A.) patents the first safety razor

1914 Gideon Sunbeck (Canada) patents the zipper

1932 First air charter holiday (England to Switzerland)

1942 First T-shirt (U.S.A.)

1946 First bikini (France)

1903 Orville Wright (U.S.A.) makes first manned, powered, sustained, controlled flight in a heavier-than-air machine

1927 First commercially manufactured car radio (U.S.A.)

1901 First Nobel Prize for Literature awarded

1906 First feature-length film (Australia) released

1913 *Billboard* (U.S.A.) publishes the first music charts

1926 John Logie Baird (Scotland) makes the first public demonstration of television

1935 First mass-market paperback books (England)

1901 First electric hearing aid (U.S.A.)

1903 First effective ECG (Netherlands)

1921 Insulin is synthesized for the first time (Canada)

1928 Alexander Fleming (Scotland) discovers penicillin, the first antibiotic

1943 First kidney dialysis machine is built (Netherlands)

1907 Finland becomes first country to elect female MPs

1923 Interpol is founded

1937 King George VI (Britain) is first monarch to be televised

1945 First atomic bomb is dropped (by U.S.A. on Japan)

1901 The Belgian Automobile Club publishes the first road map

1917 Superheterodyne circuit invented (U.S.A.)

1933 First speaking clock (France)

1943 Laszlo Biró (Hungary) patents the first practical ballpoint pen

1903 First World Series (baseball) (U.S.A.)

1906 First Grand Prix (motorcar racing) (France)

1911 First Indianapolis 500 (motorcar racing) (U.S.A.)

1930 First FIFA (Association Football) World Cup final (Uruguay)

1938 Don Budge (U.S.A.) first person to win tennis Grand Slam (4 titles)

Human Endeavour

1953 Hillary (NZ) & Norgay (Nepal) are first to reach summit of Mount Everest

1961 Yuri Gagarin (USSR) makes the first successful space flight and becomes the first human to orbit the earth

1968 Ralph Plaisted (U.S.A.) leads the first team confirmed to have reached the North Pole overland

1969 Neil Armstrong (U.S.A.) becomes the first person to walk on the moon

2002 Steve Fossett (U.S.A.) completes the first solo non-stop circumnavigation by balloon

Food & Drink

1953 First fish sticks (U.S.A.)

1965 First freeze-dried instant coffee (Switzerland)

1985 First beer can widget patented (Ireland)

Trade & Technology

1950 The Diners Club Card is inaugurated as the first charge card (U.S.A.)

1958 The BankAmericard (later Visa) is launched as the first credit card (U.S.A.)

1967 First cash dispenser installed, by Barclays Bank (England)

1970 First electronic pocket calculator (U.S.A.)

1999 The Euro is launched as pan-European currency in several countries

Lifestyle & Leisure

1952 Velcro manufactured (patented 1941) (Switzerland)

1963 First hover-mower, the Flymo, invented by Karl Dahlman (Sweden)

1971 First ban on cigarette advertising on radio and television (U.S.A.)

Transportation

1950 Alex Moulton (England) develops first folding bicycle

1959 Launch of first hovercraft (England)

1965 First regular railway service to average over 100mph (160km/h) (Japan)

1974 Airbags are fitted to cars for the first time (U.S.A.)

1994 First tunnel under English Channel between England and France opens

Arts & Entertainment

1953 First feature film to be shot in CinemaScope premières (U.S.A.)

1964 Robert Moog (U.S.A.) produces the first Moog synthesizer

1972 Atari (U.S.A.) launches Pong, the first commercially successful arcade computer video game

1982 First CD player goes on sale (Japan)

Medical Achievement

1954 First successful human kidney transplant (U.S.A.)

1960 The contraceptive pill becomes commercially available for the first time (U.S.A.)

1967 Christian N. Barnard (South Africa) performs the first successful human heart transplant

1978 Louise Brown (England) is born as the first test-tube baby

Government, Law & Order

1952 First hydrogen bomb is tested (U.S.A.)

1960 Sirimavo Bandaranaike (Ceylon, now Sri Lanka) becomes the world's first female prime minister

1987 Robert Melias (England) becomes the first criminal to be convicted using DNA evidence

Communication

1959 Haloid Corp. (U.S.A.) produces first successful photocopier

1969 Seiko (Japan) launches the first quartz wristwatch

1978 First GPS satellite is launched

1989 Tim Berners-Lee (England) initiates the World Wide Web

Sporting Milestones

1954 Roger Bannister (England) runs the first sub-four minute mile

1967 First Super Bowl (American Football) (U.S.A.)

1973 First all-women's marathon is held, in Germany

2000 S. Redgrave (England) is first to win 5 consecutive gold medals in modern Olympics

These fantastical firsts are all ideas that were ahead of their time. Some of them have never been realized, while others have been created hundreds of years after they were first suggested. Some of them may yet become firsts of the future.

FANTASTICAL FIRSTS

Top Experimental Flying Machine incorporating a corkscrew-shaped sail invented by Leonardo da Vinci
Left Da Vinci's glider, flown by British hang-gliding champion Judy Leden
Opposite Jean-Philippe Zoppini's 'AZ Island'

Frank Lloyd Wright's mile-high building

US architect Frank Lloyd Wright is perhaps best known for Fallingwater (1936–39), his house at Bear Run, Pennsylvania, and the Guggenheim Museum in New York City (1960), but he also designed a building that was never built—the would-be first mile-high skyscraper. In 1956 he designed the mile-high Illinois Tower for the city of Chicago, inspired by the first successes in the production of atomic energy. This slender, tapering skyscraper was intended to house 130,000 people on 528 floors with 56 atomic-powered elevators. In 2002 one American suggested building a half-scale version of Wright's tower on the site of the World Trade Center.

Jules Verne's floating city

There have been numerous studies into the feasibility of building artificial islands since novelist Jules Verne (France) described an *île à hélice* ("flying island") in 1895, including one by underwater explorer Jacques Cousteau and architect Edouard Albert (both France). It seems that the French will be the first to achieve this fantastical first if architect Jean-Philippe Zoppini's plans come to fruition for the "AZ Island," a floating city 300m by 400m (980 x 1300 ft), complete with its own harbor and 4,000 cabins on 15 storeys. Zoppini is president of the *Association Cités Marines* (Association of Marine Cities).

Leonardo da Vinci

The Italian painter, sculptor, architect and engineer Leonardo da Vinci designed a number of would-be firsts that were never built, including a helicopter, an armoured car, several diving suits, a machine gun and a robot.

He also designed a parachute (1485) and a glider (1490 and 1505) that have since been created more than 500 years after they were illustrated. Katarina Ollikainen (Sweden) built the rigid pyramidal parachute according to da Vinci's 1485 drawings and, in South Africa on 26 June 2000, skydiver Adrian Nicholas (England) made a safe descent after being strapped to the parachute and lifted to 3,000m by a hot-air balloon. Afterwards, Nicholas said: "It took one of the greatest minds who ever lived to design it, but it took 500 years to find a man with a brain small enough to actually go and fly it."

Two years later Leonardo's fixed-wing glider was built by Steve Roberts (England) for a British television documentary about da Vinci's inventions, and it was first flown in October 2002 by British hang-gliding champion Judy Leden. Like the parachute, the glider was built only from materials that were available in da Vinci's time and, like the parachute, it proved perfectly airworthy. Leden flew the glider from the appropriately named High and Over Hill in Sussex, saying, "It was the most dangerous flight of my life. It was very, very thrilling. It really shouldn't have worked but it did!"

Channel Tunnel
The idea of a Channel Tunnel was first envisioned 200 years ago after the Treaty of Amiens in 1802. Plans were drawn up for two tunnels meeting at an artificial island built mid-Channel, with stabling facilities for the horses that drew the coaches, but the project was scrapped when war broke out again a year later and Napoleon began planning an invasion of England. After two false starts during the 19th century, the tunnel was finally sanctioned in 1986 and officially opened in May 1994.

Transatlantic Hovercraft
At the Browndown Hovershow (England) in 1965, plans were announced for a 5,000-ton transatlantic hovercraft powered by jet engines from the then-embryonic Concorde. At the time it probably seemed no more unlikely than the first supersonic airliner, but, while Concorde became a reality, the transatlantic hovercraft did not.

NAME INDEX

Indexer's Note: This index is arranged alphabetically. Illustrations are indicated by page numbers in italic.

SUBJECT INDEX

Indexer's Note: This index is arranged alphabetically. Illustrations are indicated by page numbers in italic.

SELECTED BIBLIOGRAPHY

General Firsts, Inventions and Inventors

Brown, Travis. *Popular Patents*. Scarecrow Press Inc., 2000.

Cunningham, Antonia (managing ed.). *Guinness World Records 2002*. Guinness World Records Ltd, 2002.

Giscard d'Estaing, Valérie-Anne. *The Second World Almanac of Inventions*. World Almanac, 1992.

Harris, Melvin. *ITN Book of Firsts*. Michael O'Mara Books, 1994.

Hillman, David & David Gibbs. *Century Makers*. Weidenfeld & Nicholson, 1998.

Parry, Melanie (ed.). *Chambers Biographical Dictionary*. Chambers, 1999.

Robertson, Patrick. *The Shell Book of Firsts*. Ebury Press & Michael Joseph, 1994.

Robertson, Patrick. *The Guinness Book of Australian Firsts*. Collins Australia & Guinness Superlatives, 1987.

Tibballs, Geoff. *The Guinness Book of Innovations*. Guinness Publishing, 1994.

Uhlig, Robert (ed.). *James Dyson's History of Great Inventions*. The Telegraph Group, 2000.

van Dulken, Stephen. *Inventing the 19th Century*. The British Library, 2001.

van Dulken, Stephen. *Inventing the 20th Century*. The British Library, 2000.

Zilboorg, Caroline (ed.). *Women's Firsts*. Eastword Publications, 1997.

Specific Subjects

Arlott, John (ed.). *The Oxford Companion to Sports & Games*. OUP, 1975.

Baker, W.J. *A History of the Marconi Company*. Routledge, 1970.

Baren, Maurice. *How It All Began*. Smith Settle Ltd, 1992.

Bennett, David. *The Creation of Bridges*. Chartwell Books Inc, 1999.

Berton, Pierre. *Niagara*. McClelland & Stewart, 1992.

Billington, Michael. *The Guinness Book of Theatre Facts & Feats*. Guinness Superlatives Ltd, 1982.

Brown, David J. *Bridges: 3000 Years of Defying Nature*. Mitchell Beazley, 1993.

Byers, Anthony. *The Willing Servants*. The Electricity Council, 1988.

Cannon, John (ed.). *The Oxford Companion to British History*. OUP, 1997.

Chant, Christopher & Michael J.H. Taylor. *The World's Greatest Aircraft*. Regency House Publishing Ltd, 1999.

Clew, Jeff. *Veteran Motorcycles*. Shire Publications Ltd, 1995.

Davidson, Alan. *The Oxford Companion to Food*. OUP, 1999.

Emmins, Colin. *Soft Drinks*. Shire Publications Ltd, 1991.

Geddes, Keith & Gordon Bussey. *Television: The First 50 Years*. Philips Electronics, 1986.

Gross, N., Peacock, A., Raymond, K., Scott, T., Sutherland, J. & von Wegner, A. *Speed and Power*. Parragon, 1998.

Hobhouse, Henry. *Seeds of Change*. Papermac, 1999.

Hogg, Ian V. *The Illustrated Encyclopedia of Firearms*. Hamlyn, 1978.

Kemp, Peter (ed.). *The Oxford Companion to Ships & The Sea*. OUP, 1979.

Kim, Irene. "Handheld Calculators," *Mechanical Engineering*. ASME, 1990.

King, Constance Eileen. *The Encyclopedia of Toys*. Quarto, 1978.

Laidlaw, Renton (ed.). *Royal & Ancient Golfer's Handbook*. Macmillan, 2000.

Little, Alan. *This is Wimbledon*. The All England Lawn Tennis and Croquet Club, 1999.

O'Hara, Georgina. *The Encyclopaedia of Fashion*. Thames & Hudson, 1986.

Opie, Robert. *The Packaging Source Book*. MacDonald Orbis, 1989.

Porter, Roy. *The Greatest Benefit to Mankind: A Medical History of Humanity*. HarperCollins, 1997.

Reader's Digest Association. *Reader's Digest Book of Facts*. Reader's Digest Association Ltd, 1985.

Schlosser, Eric. *Fast Food Nation*. Penguin Books, 2002.

Simmons, Jack & Gordon Biddle (eds). *The Oxford Companion to British Railway History*. OUP, 1997.

Walton, John, Paul B. Beeson & Ronald Bodley Scott (eds). *The Oxford Companion to Medicine*. OUP, 1986.

Dedicated to my daughter Megan

ACKNOWLEDGMENTS

I would like to thank Polly Powell for involving me with this project, Caroline Allen for getting me started, and Phil and Mary Harrison for providing such a large proportion of the bibliography. Thanks also to Myriam Raynier Neil for translating so many words, phrases and titles, and to the following people and organizations for their help in researching *The Book of Firsts*:

Gordon Bussey (Historical adviser to Philips Electronics UK Ltd.); Hanne Drewsen; Liz Elliot (Philips Electronics); Robert Gate; John Goodchild; Ben Grindley; Pat Hammond; Alison Henesy (National Coalmining Museum); John Jenkins; Amy Johnson (Diners Club International); Fritz Neil; John O'Maoileoin (British Dental Association); Richard Penfold (IP Partner, Harbottle & Lewis Solicitors); Liz Price (HJ Heinz Co Ltd.); Paul Smith (Thomas Cook Archives); Martin Wattam (International Coffee Organization); Alan Widdowson; Adam Woolfitt (Association of Photographers); British Library Patents Information; British Soft Drinks Association; Cadbury-Schweppes; Chocolate Information Line; Lyle & Scott; Microsoft; Nestlé UK; Procter & Gamble; The Royal Society; Sony United Kingdom Ltd.; The Tea Council; Wimbledon Lawn Tennis Museum.

Picture credits